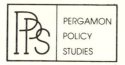

PERGAMON
POLICY
STUDIES

ON U.S. AND
INTERNATIONAL BUSINESS

Transnationalism in World Politics and Business

Edited by
Forest L. Grieves

Pergamon Press

NEW YORK • OXFORD • TORONTO • SYDNEY • FRANKFURT • PARIS

Pergamon Press Offices:

U.S.A.　　　　　Pergamon Press Inc., Maxwell House, Fairview Park,
　　　　　　　　　Elmsford, New York 10523, U.S.A.

U.K.　　　　　　Pergamon Press Ltd., Headington Hill Hall,
　　　　　　　　　Oxford OX3 0BW, England

CANADA　　　　Pergamon of Canada Ltd., 150 Consumers Road,
　　　　　　　　　Willowdale, Ontario M2J 1P9, Canada

AUSTRALIA　　 Pergamon Press (Aust) Pty. Ltd., P O Box 544,
　　　　　　　　　Potts Point, NSW 2011, Australia

FRANCE　　　　Pergamon Press SARL, 24 rue des Ecoles,
　　　　　　　　　75240 Paris, Cedex 05, France

FEDERAL REPUBLIC　Pergamon Press GmbH, 6242 Kronberg/Taunus,
OF GERMANY　　　　Pferdstrasse 1, Federal Republic of Germany

Library of Congress Cataloging in Publication Data

Main entry under title:

Transnationalism in world politics and business.

　　　(Pergamon policy studies)
　　　Includes bibliographical references and index.
　　　1.　　International economic relations—Addresses,
essays, lectures.　　2.　　International business
enterprises—Addresses, essays, lectures.
3.　　Investments, Foreign—Addresses, essays, lectures.
4.　　International relations—Addresses, essays,
lectures.　　I.　　Grieves, Forest L.,　1938-
HF1411.T72　　1979　　　　382.1　　　　79-1397
ISBN 0-08-023892-0

Printed in the United States of America

Transnationalism in
World Politics
and Business

(Pergamon Policy Studies—35)

Pergamon Policy Studies on U.S. and International Business

Joyner JOYNER'S GUIDE TO OFFICIAL WASHINGTON FOR DOING BUSINESS OVERSEAS

Tasca U.S.-JAPANESE ECONOMIC RELATIONS

United Nations Centre for Natural, Resources, Energy and Transport STATE PETROLEUM ENTERPRISES IN DEVELOPING COUNTRIES

Neghandi FUNCTIONING OF THE MULTINATIONAL CORPORATIONS

Thorelli & Becker INTERNATIONAL MARKETING STRATEGY

Davis MANAGING AND ORGANIZING MULTINATIONAL CORPORATIONS

Feld MULTINATIONAL CORPORATIONS AND U.N. POLITICS

Kerr & Kornhauser PRODUCTIVITY IN U.S. RAILROADS

Liebling U.S CORPORATE PROFITABILITY AND CAPITAL FORMATION

Taylor & Yokell YELLOWCAKE

Ways THE FUTURE OF BUSINESS

Related Titles

Owen THE MANAGER AND INDUSTRIAL RELATIONS

Tavel THE THIRD INDUSTRIAL AGE

Hill & Utterback TECHNOLOGICAL INNOVATION FOR A DYNAMIC ECONOMY

Contents

Introduction

The following collection of studies on selected aspects of transnational relations had its genesis in a panel entitled "Transnationalism" that was part of the program of the thirty-second Annual Meeting of the Western Political Science Association held in Los Angeles (March 1978). The panel, organized by Professor Thomas Hovet (University of Oregon), stimulated a discussion that rapidly expanded beyond the original participants.

With the encouragement of Mr. Richard Rowson, president of Pergamon Press, I undertook (as chairman of the original panel) the task of gathering a selection of current and provocative professional examinations of transnational issues – a process that was greatly aided by the panel participants themselves. Additional contributions represent papers presented at the International Studies Association Annual Meeting held in Washington, D.C. (February 1978) or studies that were solicited directly for the present collection.

TRANSNATIONAL ACTIVITIES

As various authors have noted in recent years, the study of international relations from a transnational perspective is hardly new. What is rather new is the widespread and systematic scholarly interest in transnational studies. Scholars have sought newer and more satisfactory explanations for modern world politics, looking for alternatives to the traditional explanations based upon the legal-political structures recognized in 1648 by the Peace of Westphalia. The Westphalian nation-state system has dominated our understanding of world politics for over 300 years, and it is likely to continue to do so in the indefinite future. There is a growing awareness, however, that the traditional "state-centric model" does not adequately treat either the growing number of nonstate participants in international activities or the tremendously complex transnational ties that bind societies together in today's interdependent and "shrinking" world.

The studies gathered together in the pages that follow represent a sampling of current theoretical and substantive work in various areas of transnational activity. The studies are linked by their common transnational perspective, but the authors are by no means necessarily in agreement on the role, scope, and substance of a common transnational approach.

The term "transnational" is currently in a state of flux, although it is often used to refer primarily to nongovernmental activities across national boundaries. The various contributors to the present volume have used the term and the concept "transnational" in slightly varying fashion, but there is a clear awareness that both governmental and nongovernmental activities are often closely intertwined. Transnational activities may involve governments or, although thoroughly nongovernmental, such activities may be manipulated and exploited by governments. "Transnational" is not used, however, in any of the following studies to refer to purely formal intergovernmental activity normally studied as part of traditional foreign policy and diplomacy.

While theory development and substantive knowledge regarding transnational activities are still in a relatively underdeveloped stage, the term "transnationalism" was chosen as the introductory theme for this collection of studies in order to call attention to the notion of systematic theory and practice, both as an academic endeavor and as a reality of modern world politics. The studies were gathered together, not as a cohesive attempt to articulate a new theory, but as an effort to bring together a useful sample of work in a new, rapidly developing field focusing on the often neglected transnational dimension of world politics. The authors have undertaken to integrate their work extensively with the body of professional literature already available, as is evident in the notes appearing throughout the volume. The studies themselves should be provocative, interesting, and informative, not only to scholars with a special interest in transnational activities, but to all serious observers of world affairs.

TRANSNATIONALISM AS A PERSPECTIVE

In Part I of this volume, the essay by J. Martin Rochester titled "The Paradigm Debate in International Relations: Data in Search of Theory" focuses attention on the matter of perspective in international relations. The author distinguishes between "traditionalists" and "modernists" in the international relations field and examines the dimensions of the paradigm debate in which they have been engaged during recent years. The outcome of the debate, he feels, hinges on more theory building and systematic empirical analysis.

The "traditionalists" generally perceive international relations in terms of the classic nation-state system, with nation-states as the only significant actors. The "modernist" challenge has argued that the realities of modern world politics demand a new perspective which takes into account the significant role of transnational and subnational actors. Neither side in the debate has been entirely cohesive or consistent, and there is much to suggest that intellectual cross-pollination and some resultant compromise have taken place.

Professor Rochester feels that the debate, which has involved the extensive marshaling of data by both sides, has nevertheless been devoid of sound theory-building tied to empirical research. He suggests a series of general hypotheses on state-nonstate actor interactions which he hopes will be of heuristic value in stimulating further interest in theory development.

TRANSNATIONAL TIES

The three studies in Part II examine different transnational situations, reviewing selected problems and developments as well as offering provocative and useful assessments.

John Esterline's study, "Multinational Corporations and the Political Process: Looking Ahead," suggests that new actors have emerged in modern world politics and are dominating the international economic system. He offers the term "supernational" to describe these new actors, who have risen to prominence and power on the basis of symbiotic relationships between major nation-states and multinational corporations. These new actors, more powerful than either a nation-state or a multinational corporation acting alone, combine not only the strengths of both but have also joined politics and economics at a new, grand level with important implications for the future course of world order.

Professor Esterline argues that the 1973 Middle East War and the subsequent oil crisis inspired by the Organization of Petroleum Exporting Countries (OPEC) dramatically changed the pattern of international economic relations. The utility of the commodity cartel as a political weapon helped to crack American domination of international economic relations, which was crumbling anyway under pressure from Japan and Western Europe, but it also enhanced the political role of economic policies. Professor Esterline believes that five supernational actors (the United States, the European Community, Japan, the socialist bloc countries led by the Soviet Union, and the OPEC group — with the People's Republic of China as a potential sixth actor — all acting in concert with multinational corporations) are engaged in an essentially mercantilist struggle for world economic (political!) domination. The United States holds a weak position in this struggle because it has the lowest level of interdependence and cooperation between state and corporation.

P.G. Bock examines a related theme in "Controlling the Transnational Corporation: The Issue of Codes of Conduct." He notes the burgeoning interest in transnational (multinational) corporations in recent years and the efforts to define and describe their activities.

There appears to be an acceptance of transnational corporations as an established fact and as an ongoing feature of modern international relations. Attention has now turned to regulation of these corporations, by themselves, nation-states, or the United Nations. Professor Bock feels, due to our lack of knowledge about the corporations and given the intense conflict of interest among the parties involved, that efforts at regulating transnational corporations are doomed to failure.

Richard Siegel calls attention to an entirely different aspect of transnational ties in his study, "The Transnationalization of Domestic Policy: Social Security in Western Europe and the United States." He focuses on the transnational flow of ideas and experiences in the development of social security policy. The evolution of domestic social policies provides a good example of an issue area, traditionally regarded as the preserve of nation-states and national sovereignty, that is becoming internationalized through transnational pressures.

Professor Siegel reviews the development of transnational relations, interdependence, and regimes before probing the transnational influences on social security in particular. Those influences include transnational social science, the flow of foreign workers and immigrants, multinational enterprises, and international trade unionism. These influences have been played out in the context of traditional intergovernmental contacts, ranging from bilateral international agreements to the politics of intergovernmental organizations.

His conclusion notes the significance of standardization for domestic social security policies, although the need for full standardization and rigid enforcement is not advocated. While the transnationalization of social security policies could serve as a functional model for the evolution of policy regimes in other areas, the author concludes with several reservations concerning such a likelihood (e.g., the importance of national variations and the interdependence of functional areas).

OPEC: FOCUSED TRANSNATIONAL POLITICS

The 1973 oil crisis dramatically changed the context of modern international relations. The events surrounding the crisis represented the joining of politics and economics, of private enterprise and government policy, the result of which was the focusing of transnational politics to gain world political and economic leverage. The two studies in Part III probe in depth the political emergence of the Organization of Petroleum Exporting Countries (OPEC) as a new transnational force and the effects of its activities.

In "OPEC: The Basis of the Arab Developmental World; A Transnational Model," Tim Luke examines the emergence of OPEC and its implications. He reviews the traditional "Three Worlds" schema and the dramatic developmental events, which he suggests are part of a "catastrophic rite of passage" that propelled the OPEC (particularly Arab) countries into a new Third World status. As these new Third World countries approached the level of the First (North America, Western Europe, Japan, and client states) and Second (socialist bloc) World, they left behind the poor and less developed countries, which now constitute a Fourth World.

The stage was set for an OPEC developmental advance by the commodity (oil) dependency of particularly the First World, the practices of the major transnational oil corporations, and the circumstances of Middle East conflicts. Tim Luke compares the OPEC (Arab) developmental situation with several historically similar situations and concludes that new developmental worlds seem to emerge through cataclysmic changes in global relations. There will be forced capital redistribution toward the new Third World as long as oil holds its strategic value, while the Fourth World becomes dependent on both the First and new Third Worlds.

Frederic Pearson offers an analysis of one result of OPEC's rise to power in a case study entitled "Netherlands Foreign Policy and the 1973-74 Oil Embargo — The Effects of Transnationalism." While much past thinking regarding international crises has concerned military situations, the author believes that economic crises may be much more prominent in the future given the importance of scarce resource supplies. He also believes that transnationalism is one of the factors in modern international relations likely to condition responses to economic crisis.

With the new patterns of dependence and interdependence in world affairs, Professor Pearson argues that even weak countries will have some influence. In the case of the Netherlands, the oil crisis provides an opportunity to analyze the tactics of a small- to medium-sized advanced industrial state, particularly how its connections to the international community affect perception of the crisis and afford opportunities for relief. Transnational linkages appear as both strengths and weaknesses. Professor Pearson offers a penetrating and valuable case study of both Dutch foreign policy and transnationalism.

TRANSNATIONAL STRAINS: DEVELOPMENT, IMPERIALISM, AND PENETRATION

Part IV includes four studies that touch upon both the hopes and exploitations of transnational activities, each of which has involved strained international relations. One notes particularly in these studies the extensive intertwining (unintentional and intentional) of state foreign policies and transnational activities.

Charles Merrifield, in his essay titled "The Development Ethic: Experiences of the World Bank Group," looks at what he terms "an exercise in applied ethics," namely the "development" undertakings of the World Bank Group. He praises the group's functional approach to a peaceful world society and challenges us all to undertake a closer examination of "its learnings, disillusionments and its undoubted achievements." He sees the <u>voluntary</u> nature of support for the group's undertakings as a special strength and a demonstration of the useful role of transnational organizations.

Mansour Farhang examines a different aspect of transnational activity in "Imperialism: A Transnational System of Privilege." He is concerned with developing a new conceptual framework for analyzing the nature of contemporary imperialism. Neither Marxist nor non-Marxist models offer, he feels, adequate descriptions of the "transnational realities of the present day imperialist relations."

Traditional explanations of imperialism are seen as focusing primarily on the structural aspects of exploitation, dependence, and inequality. Professor Farhang argues that an imperialist relationship does not have to be formally constituted in order to exist. Modern imperialism does not require formal subjugations of national sovereignty, and governments may be willing participants in the subordination of their country as a means of insuring their own elite privileges. The "interdependence" of the modern world appears as the new rhetoric for a transnational system of privilege which constitutes imperialistic relationships. The interests of the state, representing the privileged few, are seen as often antagonistic to the interests of the populace in many of today's class-ridden nations.

Professor Farhang points out that national policymakers may not have intentionally created imperialistic relationships, but it is the reality that must be addressed. In the name of national security and Cold War strategies, or through the export of repressive technology and the creation of economic dependency, transnational systems of privilege are created and maintained.

"Nationalizing British Firms in Shanghai: The Politics of Hostage Capitalism in People's China, 1949-1957," by Thomas Thompson, is an interesting study of the loss of British privilege in China when the Chinese Communists came to power in 1949.

As part of the new Chinese government's policy of stabilization following the revolution, British firms operating in China were not confiscated outright but were forced to stay in the country and continue operations. This policy, which Professor Thompson calls "hostage capitalism," worked because of Britain's weakened position following World War II, because of a general Western wariness of getting entangled in China, and because China also held capitalists hostage. The Chinese Communist government required the continuing presence of a senior European firm executive in China. Hostage capitalism was not just a simple policy of revenge for past humiliations suffered by China at the hands of the West. It was also a pragmatic vehicle for stabilizing the Chinese economy and gaining transnational access to sterling deposits and external markets.

Following the end of hostage capitalism in the 1950s, many British firms relocated to Hong Kong where they now trade with China instead of in China. Professor Thompson feels that these firms play an important role in Sino-Western trade.

The final study in Part IV reminds us of the purposeful uses to which transnational ideologies and movements can be put in the implementation of a nation-state's foreign policy. Robert Bigler's "The Role of the German Democratic Republic in the Communist Penetration of Africa" offers not only a timely case study of contemporary events in Africa but also a sample of the recurring urge of some nation-states to export their national model, establish client states abroad, and establish spheres of influence.

Professor Bigler documents East Germany's efforts in Africa, which have been carried out with the support of the Soviet Union, and offers an analysis of the significance of those efforts.

The collected articles have called attention to various forms of national attempts to gain and exercise influence – economic, political, military, ideological. Clearly those attempts are enhanced when nations can tap transnational ties. An intriguing prospect presents itself, however, in the emergence of new and varied transnational actors and forces. As these actors and forces develop and become stronger, the potential exists for them to cease being agents of national foreign policy and to manipulate world politics themselves. To a surprising degree, such a process is already underway.

I
Transnationalism as a Perspective

1 The Paradigm Debate in International Relations: Data in Search of Theory

J. Martin Rochester

At the start a new candidate for paradigm may have few supporters, and on occasions the supporters' motives may be suspect. Nevertheless, if they are competent, they will improve it, explore its possibilities, and show what it would be like to belong to the community guided by it. And as that goes on, if the paradigm is one destined to win its fight, the number and strength of the persuasive arguments in its favor will increase. More scientists will then be converted, and the exploration of the new paradigm will go on. Gradually the number of experiments, instruments, articles, and books based upon the paradigm will multiply. Still more men, convinced of the new view's fruitfulness, will adopt the new mode of practicing normal science, until at last only a few elderly hold-outs remain.

> Thomas S. Kuhn,
> The Structure of Scientific
> Revolutions

It is too early to ascertain the outcome of the paradigm debate which has been occurring in recent years between "traditionalists" and "modernists" in the international relations field. The purpose of this paper is to point up some basic problems that have characterized this debate and that have resulted in more heat than light being generated on the subject. In particular, the author will argue that more theory-building tied to systematic empirical analysis is needed before one can properly evaluate the merits of the two sides.(1) The paper will first articulate the case for more theory and then suggest some lines that theory development might follow.

THE NATURE OF THE DEBATE

The positions of the two schools can be stated fairly simply, notwithstanding the fact that there are several variations to be found. The traditional paradigm in which phenomena in the field have been conceptualized in the past (variously labeled "international politics," "state-centric," or "billiard ball") has its roots in the realist thought of E.H. Carr and Hans Morgenthau.(2) It assumes that nation-states, acting through official representatives (decisionmakers, diplomats, soldiers, etc.) are the only significant actors in world affairs. Neither subnational actors (bureaucratic and societal interest groups) nor transnational(3) actors (intergovernmental and nongovernmental organizations, including multinational corporations) are treated as distinct and autonomous actors, with the former subsumed by the nation-state and the latter considered as extensions of the nation-state or, at best, marginal factors influencing nation-state interactions. The paradigm assumes a hierarchically ordered set of relationships with demands flowing from bureaucratic and societal groups to national leaders located at the apex of the authoritative decision-making apparatus who resolve whatever internal conflicts exist and whose actions then become the nation's actions and the source of interactions between the national unit and other national units.

The traditional paradigm has come under attack by the "modernists,"(4) represented by Keohane and Nye, Modelski, Coplin et al., Brown, Burton et al., Mansbach et al., and Morse, who have argued that the paradigm never has entirely corresponded with reality and is especially inadequate to comprehend contemporary events.(5) In its place (or at least beside it) another paradigm is suggested (variously labeled "world politics," "world policy process," "cobweb," "complex interdependence," or "complex conglomerate") which takes into account relatively new, more complex phenomena.(6) The key assumption of this paradigm, in contrast to the former, is that subnational and transnational actors can be treated as distinct and autonomous actors apart from national actors and that there are no hierarchically organized patterns of influence and authority among these three categories of actors. The world is conceived of as a set of interacting systems rather than a set of geographically and legally defined interacting entities. In other words, not all stimuli which provide the inputs for world politics travel through and are emitted from Washington or Paris or Cairo; instead some bypass national capitals and travel by way of places like Poughkeepsie and Peoria. The paradigm suggests that subnational actors can affect world politics directly — and not just indirectly through domestic political processes — by initiating or serving as targets of interactions with either foreign governments or subnational groups located in other countries. It tends to accentuate conflict within national units and cooperation across national units — allowing for the possibility that coalitions of interests among bureaucrats or private interest groups in different countries may be found that are stronger than intranational coalitions — although there is nothing in the paradigm which precludes the kinds of cooperation and conflict patterns assumed by the traditional paradigm.

There have been signs lately suggesting some rapprochement between proponents of these different views. Even such orthodox realists as Morgenthau and Kissinger have felt the need to modify their thinking somewhat. Morgenthau has gone so far as to confess that

> the technological revolutions of our age have rendered the Nation-State's principle of political organization as obsolete as the first modern industrial revolution of the steam engine did feudalism. The governments of Nation-States are no longer able to perform the functions for the sake of which civilised governments have been instituted in the first place: to defend and promote the life, liberty, and pursuit of happiness of its citizenry. Unable to perform these functions with regard to their own citizens, these governments are incapable of performing them in their relations with each other.(7)

Kissinger has made similar pronouncements (which, even if calculated to appeal to world public opinion, still represent remarkable concessions on his part) such as his statement before the World Food Conference in November 1974 that "we are stranded between old conceptions of political conduct and a wholly new environment, between the inadequacy of the Nation-State and the emerging imperative of global community."(8) A number of modernists, for their part, have adopted a more conciliatory attitude toward the traditionalists, as reflected in the latest work of Keohane and Nye:

> We do not argue . . . that complex interdependence (their label for their alternative paradigm) faithfully reflects world political reality. Quite the contrary: both it and the realist portrait are ideal types. . . . Sometimes, realist assumptions will be accurate, or largely accurate, but frequently complex interdependence will provide a better portrayal of reality.(9)

Still, notwithstanding the mollification of views, fundamental differences between the two schools remain and the debate goes on.(10) It is safe to say that the "revolution" has not yet been won by the modernists. Not only are there more than "a few elderly hold-outs" remaining but the traditional paradigm still dominates the field despite gains made by the modernists.(11) Those who have gravitated toward the modern paradigm do not appear to represent any distinct normative or methodological persuasion, although the traditionalist critic might characterize them as normatively oriented "idealists" who have become restless looking for the growth of world order in legal-institutional terms and have sought to broaden the concept of "international organization" to uncover it in more informal terms; and methodologically oriented "behavioralists" who have tired of collecting data on nation-states and having failed to achieve high correlations have discovered a whole new area for data collection and analysis that is in some respects easier to deal with — both coming together under the banner of what could be called "neo-neofunctionalism." However, this would be an unfair characterization of the modernists insofar as the latter on the whole have been careful to point out the potentially negative effects of interdependence and transnationalism, and most have contended that the new paradigm should supplement rather than supplant the old one since neither by itself can account for all international relations phenomena.

There is one criticism, however, that the author would argue that the modernists are especially vulnerable to. For the most part, all that the modernists have offered to support their claims for the new paradigm are isolated case studies focusing on particular issue-areas along with isolated statistics that purport to demonstrate the increased importance of nonstate actors in world politics.(12) To cite just a few examples, one writer notes that "in the first 100 (economic units in the world), countries outnumber corporations, but only by 59 to 41."(13) Another writer notes that "the Town Affiliation Association lists over 400 U.S. cities with over 500 affiliations with cities in nearly 70 countries."(14) Still another points out that "there were at least 2,190 (nongovernmental organizations) in 1972 as compared to under 1,000 in 1958."(15) And another writes that "beginning with 1815 . . . the number of intergovernmental organizations has been rising exponentionally at a doubling rate of about twenty years."(16) Pointing up the fragmentation of the "foreign policy establishment" into several bureaucratic actors, one author comments that "in 1973, of 19,000 Americans abroad on diplomatic missions, only 3400 were from the State Department and less than half of the governmental delegates accredited to international conferences came from the State Department."(17) In the same vein, another observer states that "from 1960 to 1970 the Labor Department's international expenditures increased eightfold, Agriculture's went up about ten times, and Commerce five and one-half, while the State Department's budget doubled" and that "overseas travel (in 1972) by State was only about half (53%) of the total travel by the seven largest departments excluding Defense."(18)

In short, the debate has largely consisted of volleying bits of data back and forth and has been remarkably devoid of theorizing on the part of the modernists. The problem with this is that for every analyst whose data confirm that the nation-state as traditionally conceived is no longer the sole or primary actor in the international system, there is another whose data indicate otherwise. With little good theory to go on, we are left essentially with random facts that offer an inadequate basis for reaching conclusions about the relative strength of the two paradigms. While case studies in some instances have generated hypotheses, they have primarily been employed by modernists to illustrate the significance of nonstate actors rather than as theory-building vehicles attempting to specify how the latter relate to each other and to nation-state actors and how they influence world politics.

This preoccupation with seeking out "evidence" has perhaps been the result of a defensive overreaction by the modernists to traditionalist demands for proof of the validity of the new paradigm. Only very recently have there been some explicit attempts at theory construction, such as the latest work of Keohane and Nye.(19) But these mark only a beginning. What is needed at this stage in the debate is more theorizing tied to empirical research, and not "data-making" alone, if the new paradigm is to justify its existence by yielding useful insights into the dynamics of foreign policy-making and international politics. There is no need here to recite the role of theory in the pursuit of knowledge. Abraham Kaplan's remarks should suffice: "Every theory serves . . . as a research directive; theory guides the collection of data and their subsequent analysis, by showing us beforehand where the data are to be fitted and what we are to make of them when we get them . . . .Without a theory . . . there is only a miscellany of observations. . . ."(20)

Edward Morse acknowledges the atheoretical nature of the paradigm debate and the limitations of his own recent theoretical effort when he states:

> The relationship between the processes (of modernization) and the transformations in international society are supported only by streams of indirect and often conflicting evidence. Although no one . . . has yet made a strong . . . theoretical link between the two, I feel strongly that efforts will be made in this direction in research during the coming years.(21)

Morse goes on to state that "this theoretical task is an urgent one" since "policy, more than ever, must be based on sound theory. It must be predicated upon an understanding of the costs of manipulating different variables and of the relationships among these variables in the process of change."(22) At the same time, one must keep in mind Charles McClelland's admonition that a single theory will not suffice when one is dealing with such a large-scale phenomenon as the transformation of the international system:

> It might be a momentous event if someone should publish just the right theory of the transformation of the international system.
>
> (However) . . . we shall be poorly advised to look for a creative formulation that would take into account all the various . . . trends, indications, and forewarnings. . . . We are aware already of too much happening in too many places and in too many ways to develop readily a   profitable and comprehensive viewpoint. (Also) . . . effective theory distorts, simplifies, and ignores wide ranges of observed experiences in order to get at crucial variables. . . . The very wide span of relevant changes and the large size of the international system may not allow the development of any unitary theory but may encourage, instead, the formulation of clusters of theoretical questions and state-ments.(23)

In the following section, the author suggests one avenue of theoretical development that might be pursued which supplements the "partial theories of inter-nation relations"(24) and "inter-nation in-fluence models"(25) of the past with generalizations about state-nonstate actor interactions.(26)

HYPOTHESES ON STATE-NONSTATE
ACTOR INTERACTIONS

Given the need for theory which can specify relationships between state and nonstate actors, how does one go about theory-building in the first place? Essentially, one can either start "from scratch" or one can rely on analogy, i.e. borrowing and adapting a relatively developed body of theory relating to some other system or process that is deemed to resemble the one in question. The use of analogy can be very economical and enlightening, assuming of course that an appropriate analogue can be found. The role of analogy is discussed by Nagel:

> The widespread use of metaphors . . . testifies to a pervasive human talent for finding resemblances between new experiences and familiar facts, so that what is novel is in consequence mastered by subsuming it under established distinctions. In any event, men do tend to employ familiar systems of relations as models in terms of which initially strange domains of experience are intellectually assimilated. (Accordingly) . . . when familiar notions are extended to novel subject matters on the basis of unanalyzed similarities, serious error can easily be committed. . . Nonetheless, apprehensions of even vague similarities . . . are often starting points for important advances in knowledge. When reflection becomes critically self-conscious, such apprehensions may come to be developed into carefully formulated analogies and hypotheses that can serve as fruitful instruments of research.(27)

The author proposes to derive some hypotheses on state-nonstate actor interactions from existing theories that have been employed in connection with internation interactions. Admittedly, there may be a certain irony here in utilizing theories that have been associated with the traditional paradigm to sharpen one's thinking about the modern paradigm. However, the theories that will be relied on have been applied at a variety of levels of analysis – including the individual (interpersonal relations) and societal (political party competition) in addition to the internation level alliances – and there is no reason in principle that they cannot also be applied in the context of state-nonstate actor phenomena. While there are obvious differences between these levels and units of analysis, there are also more than "vague similarities." The theories referred to here are collective goods theory, coalition theory, and learning theory. What all of these theories have in common is that they deal with the dynamics of cooperation and conflict among actors, which is after all the central concern of the paradigm debate.

Hypothesis I: Subnational, National, and Supranational
Elites Compete in Seeking to Produce a Maximum
Supply of Goods for Different Collectivities.

The Frolich-Oppenheimer "entrepreneurial" theory of politics, which is
a refinement of collective goods theory as originally developed by
Mancur Olson,(28) posits that "the leaders of nations may be conceptualized as political entrepreneurs who supply goods to their populace
for their own gain."(29) In other words, national leaders will pursue
policies which are calculated to maximize their own interests (i.e.
maintaining their leadership position, increasing their resource base,
and enhancing their prestige) and not the "national interest" (i.e.
physical survival, economic well-being and political self-determination
of the society), although these elites will tend to identify their own fate
with the fate of the nation. By national elites, then, we simply mean
central governmental decision makers who define their primary constituency as the nation-state and who seek to maximize goods in the form
of a strong defense and high gross national product in return for payoffs
they derive from their leadership position.

We can also identify two other categories of elites in the
international system – subnational and supranational elites – who may
be considered political entrepreneurs oriented toward different collectivities or clienteles than national elites. Subnational elites may be
leaders of either societal interest groups or governmental bureaucracies, who view their own interests as being served by maximizing the
supply of goods received by the members of their particular constituen-
cies and not necessarily by the wider collectivity represented by the
nation.   Supranational elites are the heads of intergovernmental
organizations, who tend to be guided more by their special organizational interests than by any larger concern for "mankind," although the
former and latter may often converge.

Subnational elites tend to deal in goods that are produceable for the
most part within the framework of the nation-state. In attempting to
maximize the supply of these goods for their members, a given
subnational elite tends to come into conflict with other subnational
elites over various issues that relate to the production of the goods in
question. If one views the world as a political system, an overwhelming
number of issues in the system involve conflicts over the distribution of
goods between subnational elites that do not surface above the level of
the nation-state – the imposition of stricter auto emission standards,
no-fault insurance, right-to-work laws, and so forth. National elites
assume a mediating role in these conflicts but tend ultimately to
support those subnational elites who can most help them maintain their
national leadership position.

In addition to these intranational conflicts between subnational
elites, there is, of course, another axis of conflict existing between
national elites representing different countries. International conflict
has been the focal point for the study of world politics. Clearly there
are many issues (e.g. arms control) that do not occupy the attention of
subnational elites but are highly salient to national elites insofar as they

involve the production of goods that national elites in particular feel they will be held accountable for. Supranational elites may play a mediating role in these international conflicts although, as in the case of national elites managing intranational conflicts, they will tend to support those parties (national elites) whose support can most benefit them. National elites have a much larger role to play in managing intranational conflicts than supranational elites in international conflicts since the former are far more institutionalized. A third axis of conflict in the system that is relatively insignificant but can have some strategic importance is the competition between supranational elites themselves over the distribution of goods among their individual intergovernmental organizations.

Comparativists have been traditionally concerned with the first axis of conflict, international relationists with the second, and marginally with the third. However, these various lines of conflict are less clearly drawn and more intersecting when issues (deep-sea mining, skyjacking, etc.) arise which do not fall neatly into the domains of subnational, national, or supranational elites; which open up possibilities for bargaining among all three types of elites; and which tend to disrupt the normal mode of goods production. In these instances subnational elites, in particular, may expand the conflict beyond national boundaries against the will of national elites by entering into coalitions with counterpart subnational elites in other countries. These coalitions may be transnational in nature (involving leaders of societal interest groups) or transgovernmental (involving leaders of governmental bureaucracies).

Hypothesis 2: Transnational and Transgovernmental
Coalitions Will Occur Only as a Last Resort After
Subnational Elites Have Failed to Produce Desired
Results through National Political Processes.

Whether or not subnational elites in a particular country will seek coalition partners in other countries on a given issue will depend on whatever success they have had in enlisting the support of other subnational elites and the national elites within their own country. Since aside from their immediate clientele their primary reference point remains the nation-state, the first impulse of subnational elites will be to try to achieve their goals through intranational coalitions. Only at the point where subnational elites have been frustrated will they feel compelled to pursue coalition-building outside the nation. The reasoning behind subnational elites pursuing crossnational coalition-building only as a last resort is that there are two kinds of costs entailed in such a strategy. First, subnational elites may alienate national elites in their country whose support might be needed in the future and who view the search for allies across national boundaries by subnational elites as challenging and undermining their national leadership position. Secondly, subnational elites may alienate their own followers who remain largely attached to national symbols and whose nationalistic sensibilities might be offended by such internally divisive tactics. The "nation" has a more powerful hold on followers than elites, a fact that is not lost sight of by the latter. Both types of costs will be felt more by bureaucratic elites than societal elites, so that there will be greater constraints on transgovernmental than transnational coalition-building.

Transnational and transgovernmental coalition-building processes will follow essentially the same pattern. They have the same starting point – the frustration experienced by certain subnational elites with national political processes on a given issue, and the same end point – the final disposition of the issue, successfully or unsuccessfully for the subnational elites, and its removal from the agenda of the national elites. In the case of both transnational and transgovernmental coalition-building, the frustrated subnational elites in country A will attempt to find counterpart elites elsewhere who are willing and able to apply pressure on their respective national elites so that the latter might then persuade the national elites in country A to reconsider the policy in question. The subnational elites in country A are interested solely in the effects on their immediate constituency in country A; whatever benefits might accrue to their counterparts in other countries are of merely incidental concern to them. By the same token, their counterparts in other countries are likely to enter into a coalition with the subnational elites of country A only if the former share a similar frustration or if their demands have been accepted by their national elites but require similar acceptance by the national elites of country A to be fully realized (i.e. internation cooperation is required).

Transnational coalition-building may be facilitated by the existence of a nongovernmental organization (NGO) in the issue-area in question which can be mobilized by subnational societal elites. Transgovernmental coalition-building will tend to be more ad hoc, although it may likewise be facilitated by the existence of an intergovernmental organization (IGO) that can serve as a locus for consultation among subnational bureaucratic elites with shared interests. Transnational and transgovernmental coalitions may join forces when their mutual interests are at stake. Supranational elites are potential partners in both transnational and transgovernmental coalitions, although they will be more inclined toward the latter insofar as they have more formal links with governmental actors than with societal actors. In considering coalition participation, supranational elites will weigh the relative benefits that might be gained by their organizations against the possible costs entailed in alienating national elites who might resent the latter's intrusion into national political processes.

Once subnational elites in country A decide that coalition-building across national boundaries is called for, the problem becomes one of with whom exactly to ally. As suggested above, subnational elites will seek to identify counterpart elites elsewhere who are willing and able to exert influence on national elites in the desired direction. In other words, the potential partner(s) must have at least two basic attributes: a willingness to participate based on a shared interest in the outcome preferred by the subnational elites in country A; and an ability to contribute to victory. While Riker's "size principle" that "coalitions will increase in size only to the minimum point of subjective certainty of winning"(30) is not applicable here since it is irrelevant to nonzero sum situations of the type treated in this analysis, it can still be expected that coalition partners will not be courted and added frivolously. Because subnational elites tend to undertake crossnational coalition-building either to avert a policy decision that is otherwise imminent or to reverse one already taken, there is likely to be a felt need on their part to act quickly and, hence, to focus attention on those parties whose collaboration is deemed most crucial.

However, aside from these pragmatic considerations, there may be some other intervening factors that will affect the nature of trans-national and transgovernmental coalitions that are formed. Some coalitions are more probable than others, given the characteristics of the subnational elites who are initiating coalition-building. In studies of alliance formation and other types of collaboration among nations, several observers have noted the importance of political and cultural homogeneity in accounting for membership patterns;(31) as Guetzkow hypothesizes, "the greater the similarity of language, customs, and ideology among nations, the more easily will their members collaborate with one another."(32) Applying this same sort of reasoning to relationships between nonstate actors, we can generate a more elaborate set of hypotheses.

Hypothesis 3: Societal Elites from a Developed Democratic State Will Be More Likely to Participate in Transnational Coalitions with Societal Elites from Other Developed Democratic States Than with Societal Elites from Developed Nondemocratic States.

Hypothesis 4: Bureaucratic Elites from a Developed Democratic State Will Be More Likely to Participate in Transgovernmental Coalitions with Bureaucratic Elites from Developed Democratic States Than with Bureaucratic Elites from Developed Nondemocratic States.

Hypothesis 5: Transgovernmental Coalitions between Bureaucratic Elites from Developed Democratic States and from Developed Non-democratic States Are More Likely to Occur Than Transnational Coalitions between Societal Elites from Developed Democratic States and from Developed Nondemocratic States.

Hypothesis 6: Both Transnational and Transgovernmental Coalitions Are More Likely to Occur between Elites from Developed Democratic States and Elites from Developed Nondemocratic States Than between Either of the Latter and Elites from Underdeveloped States.

It must be noted that the theoretical formulation that has been presented thus far in this section is relevant primarily to relations between developed pluralist democracies, relevant only secondarily to developed nondemocratic states, and even more marginally to under-developed states. The reason is simply that transnational and trans-governmental coalition activity assumes both a relatively high degree of specialization of interests and a high level of autonomy on the part of the subnational elites of a society vis-à-vis national elites – conditions that are found predominantly in developed democratic states.(33) One would expect, then, to find transnational and transgovernmental coalition activity occurring mostly between members of the latter societies. This is not to say that subnational elites in developed nondemocratic systems do not engage in transnational and trans-governmental activity. Coalitions that do occur will be relatively infrequent, and will tend to be with counterpart elites in other developed nondemocratic states (Hypotheses 3 and 4). The rationale here is not merely the natural affinity that might be expected to exist between subnational elites from similar political systems but also the logic of the coalition-building process described earlier, i.e. the proclivity of subnational elites to search for counterpart elites in other countries whose national elites are on good terms with their national elites and can thereby exercise influence. These allies are more likely to be found in similar than dissimilar political systems.

In the relatively few instances where coalition-building occurs between subnational elites in developed democratic states and devel-oped nondemocratic states, it will tend to take the transgovernmental form more than transnational collaboration (Hypothesis 5). While it was stated earlier that as a general rule there are more constraints on transgovernmental than transnational coalition activity, this is much less true in the case of relations between democratic and nondemo-cratic systems than between democratic systems. Developed nondemo-cratic states generally permit somewhat more transgovernmental than transnational activity since bureaucratic elites in these societies tend to have greater autonomy than societal elites; even though the latter may be more interested in coalition-building, the former are more able to do it. Transnational coalition-building with societal elites in democratic systems tends to be especially threatening to the national elites in nondemocratic systems and will be monitored more closely than transgovernmental activity. In addition, developed nondemocratic states are far better represented in IGOs than NGOs, so that transgovernmental contacts and coalitions are facilitated more readily than transnational ones. Subnational elites in underdeveloped countries – with the exception of a few larger ones – will be particularly poor candidates for transnational and transgovernmental coalitions with anyone (Hypotheses 6), given the relatively low level of interest group differentiation (which will limit the number of societal elites who are potential coalition partners) and the relative smallness of their bureaucracies (which is likely to inhibit attempts at autonomous action by bureaucratic elites).

We have posited thus far that the instrumental needs of subnational elites will be the primary determinant of the composition of a given coalition, but that homogeneity factors operate as intervening vari-ables. We need to add one other set of factors – past experiences – that may also affect the nature of the coalitions that are formed, whether these are between elites in democratic or nondemocratic states. These factors will introduce a dynamic element into the coalition-building process.

Hypothesis 7: The More Successful a Transnational or
Transgovernmental Coalition Is on an Issue, the More
Likely the Same Coalition Will Materialize on Another
Issue in the Future; and, Conversely, the Less Successful
the Less Likely the Same Coalition Will Form.

It was stated earlier that the "end point" of a particular transnational or transgovernmental coalition effort coincides with the final
disposition of the issue, successfully or unsuccessfully, for the subnational elites who entered into the coalition. Having won or lost, the
coalition loses its raison d'être. However, whether the outcome was a
successful one or not in terms of averting or reversing an adverse
decision taken by national elites, can have important implications for
participation by the subnational elites in such coalitions again in the
future on some other issue. As learning theorists such as Raser and
Rapoport have commonly pointed out in connection with interpersonal
and internation relations, positive or negative past experiences that one
party has with another conditions their future behavior toward each
other.(34) In the case of transnational and transgovernmental coalitions,
if good experiences (i.e. successful results) are repeated often enough
by coalition partners, the latter may even develop "habits . . . of mutual
attention, communication, and responsiveness,"(35) although such coalitions will still tend to be activated only as a "last resort."

Even if the same exact coalitions are not reconstituted intact, at
the very least one would expect that those subnational elites who have
participated in winning transnational or transgovernmental alliances
will be more likely to undertake similar efforts across national
boundaries again than those who have been on the losing side. There will
be a tendency, in other words, to generalize from past positive or
negative experiences about the virtues of transnational and transgovernmental coalition formation. The cumulative effect of successful
transnational and transgovernmental activity may ultimately produce a
dramatic transformation of the international system whereby the latter
becomes the normal mode of goods production among subnational elites
rather than the exception. The "vanguard" of this new international
system, though, are more likely to come from the ranks of societal
elites than bureaucratic elites since the latter can only go so far in
dismantling the nation-state before they begin to jeopardize their own
existence.

This sort of transformation, of course, is not likely to occur in the
near future. There are too many obstacles to contend with, not the least
of which are recalcitrant national elites in some 150 nation-states. In
addition, there are limits to the extent to which the international
system can be transformed along the lines suggested above as long as
certain key "discontinuities" remain in the system. In particular, the
existence of many nation-states – politically nondemocratic and
economically underdeveloped societies – whose structures allow only
low levels of participation in transnational and transgovernmental
networks means that these societies are unable to relate to other
societies except through national elites, so that traditional internation
issues will persist along with the central role of national elites in

presiding over conflicts surrounding these issues. As for the supranational elites, there is relatively little they can do to expedite the transformation of the system beyond providing modest but strategic support to subnational elites in the form of making their organizations available as vehicles for coalition-building. Should the transformation of the international system ever come to pass, the supranational elites figure to be among the chief beneficiaries insofar as they replace the national elites as the chief mediators of conflict in the system.

CONCLUSION

The hypotheses that have been formulated in this paper admittedly are couched at a relatively high level of abstraction. However, they have been offered primarily for heuristic purposes and are not meant to represent a completely testable theory or model of state-nonstate actor interactions. The author has simply attempted to point out the need for more theory development in the paradigm debate and to indicate what form this might take. There remains the task of developing testable propositions about state-nonstate actor relations and submitting them to systematic empirical analysis for verification. If the paradigm debate has proceeded thus far with an excess of data and a dearth of theory, it would be equally unfortunate if in the future an imbalance of the opposite kind were to occur. The author is not suggesting that the search for evidence should be suspended or abandoned, only that it should be conducted in conjunction with more explicit theorizing so that we can make more sense out of the welter of facts and trends that are to be found. A particularly fruitful line of research, for example, might be to articulate more precisely the theoretical links between various elites and their followers and to gather attitudinal data to test out these ideas. While the congruence/conflict of elite-mass attitudes has been a frequent subject of investigation in political science and international relations, it has hardly been studied in the context of the kinds of nonstate actor phenomena discussed in this paper. Only with the proper mix of theory and data can the paradigm debate be intelligently conducted and the new paradigm reasonably accepted or dismissed.

NOTES

(1) The lack of recent theory-building in the international relations field has received considerable attention in such writings as Oran R. Young, "Professor Russett: Industrious Tailor to a Naked Emperor," World Politics XXI (1969): 486-511; Marion J. Levy, "Does It Matter If He's Naked?' Bawled the Child," in Klaus Knorr and James N. Rosenau, eds., Contending Approaches to International Politics (Princeton: Princeton University Press, 1969), pp. 87-109; and Warren R. Phillips, "Where Have All the Theories Gone?" World Politics, XXVI (1974): 155-88. However, the dearth of theory has hardly been discussed at all in the context of the paradigm debate.

(2) E.H. Carr, The Twenty Years' Crisis (London: MacMillan, 1939) and Hans J. Morgenthau, Politics Among Nations (New York: Knopf, 1949).

(3) The term "transnational" has been used in various ways by various writers. The author is using it here as a label for any actors, such as IGOs and NGOs, that share the characteristic of having organized relations across national boundaries that are not explicitly directed by central governmental decisionmakers. Another actor of this type that has attracted attention recently is the "transgovernmental" actor, i.e., coalitions between members of one national bureaucracy and their counterparts in other national bureaucracies that are not sanctioned "from above." Although there may be a conceptual difference between "transgovernmental" and "transnational" – insofar as "transgovernmental" applies when we relax the realist assumption that states act coherently as units" while "transnational" applies when we relax the assumption that states are the only units" – both present equal challenges to the traditional paradigm. See Robert O. Keohane and Joseph S. Nye, Jr., Power and Interdependence: World Politics in Transition (Boston: Little, Brown & Co., 1977), p. 25.

(4) The "modernists," of course, could be said to have at least as long a tradition as the "traditionalists," if one considers the current school the intellectual descendants of such early "cosmopolitans" as Dante, Kant, and Diderot, and later ones like David Mitrany. However, the differences between current and past "modernists" are greater than the similarities.

(5) See Robert O. Keohane and Joseph S. Nye, Jr., eds., Transnational Relations and World Politics (Cambridge: Harvard University Press, 1971) and Power and Interdependence; George Modelski, Principles of World Politics (New York: The Free Press, 1972); William D. Coplin et al., "Color It Morgenthau: A Data-Based Assessment of Quantitative International Relations Research" (paper presented at the International Studies Association Annual Meeting, New York, March 14-17, 1973), Seyom Brown, New Forces in World Politics (Washington: Brookings Institution, 1974); J.W. Burton et al., The Study of World Society: A London Perspective (Pittsburgh: International Studies Association, 1974); Richard W. Mansbach, Yale H. Ferguson, and Donald E. Lampert, The Web of World Politics: Nonstate Actors in the Global System (Englewood Cliffs: Prentice-Hall, 1976); and Edward L. Morse, Modernization and the Transformation of International Relations (New York: The Free Press, 1976).

(6) Although the above writers do not all share exactly the same viewpoint – Keohane and Nye along with Brown and Morse have been more restrained than the others in attacking the traditional paradigm – all do see the need to consider an alternative framework. The author cannot help noting that the structure of scientific revolutions bears some resemblance to the "anatomy" of political revolutions as discussed in Crane Brinton's well-known work The Anatomy of Revolution (New

York: Random House, 1952). In the context of the paradigm debate in international relations, scholars like Graham Allison who introduced the "bureaucratic politics" approach in the late sixties and early seventies could be considered the "moderate reformers" initially tinkering with but not dismantling the traditional paradigm; scholars such as Coplin and Burton who urged total repudiation of the traditional paradigm in the mid-seventies could be considered the "radicals" taking over the banner of revolution; and Keohane and Nye, especially with their most recent work, could be viewed as the pragmatic "consolidators" of the revolution insofar as they have qualified some of their earlier criticism of the traditional paradigm while continuing to develop the new paradigm.

(7) Hans J. Morgenthau, "The New Diplomacy of Movement," Encounter XLIII (August 1974): 57.

(8) Henry A. Kissinger, "The Global Community and the Struggle Against Famine" (Address to the World Food Conference on November 5, 1974, Department of State Press Release).

(9) Keohane and Nye, Power and Interdependence, p. 24.

(10) The problems involved in trying to reconcile the different perspectives are discussed very clearly in R. Harrison Wagner's excellent essay on "Dissolving the State: Three Recent Perspectives in International Relations," International Organization XXVIII (1974): 435-66.

(11) If one takes as an indicator of trends in the field the amount of space allocated in professional meeting programs to "traditional" concerns as opposed to "nonstate" phenomena, then it would appear that the modernists have indeed made significant strides. For example, roughly 30 percent of the panels at the 1977 International Studies Association Annual Meeting were devoted to what could be considered "nonstate" phenomena, while the theme of the 1978 convention was "The Emerging Transnational World – The Place of Individuals, Groups, and States." However, if one looks at the scholarly journals, which tend to be not quite so "faddy" as convention programs, one can detect the continued predominance of the traditional paradigm with the exception of a few specialized journals such as International Organization.

(12) For example, see Young W. Kihl, Conflict Issues and International Civil Aviation Decisions: Three Cases (Denver: University of Denver Press, 1971); Ann L. Hollick, "Seabeds Make Strange Politics," Foreign Policy IX (1972): 148-70; Robert W. Russell, "Transgovernmental Interaction in the International Monetary System, 1960-1972," International Organization 27 (1973): 431-64; Anne T. Feraru, "Transnational Political Interests and the Global Environment," International Organization 28 (1974): 1-30; Lawrence Juda, Ocean Space Rights: Developing U.S. Policy (New York: Praeger, 1975); Jonathan Aronson, "Multiple

Actors in the Transformation of the International Monetary System" (Paper presented at Annual Meeting of the International Studies Association, Toronto, February 25, 1976); David P. Forsythe, "The Red Cross As Transnational Movement: Conserving and Changing the Nation-State System," International Organization 30 (1976): 608-30; C. Robert Dickerman, "Transgovernmental Challenge and Response in Scandinavia and North America," International Organization 30 (1976): 213-40; and Mansbach et al., The Web of World Politics.

(13) Lester R. Brown, World Without Borders (New York: Random House, 1972), p. 213.

(14) Chadwick F. Alger, "'Foreign' Policies of U.S. Publics," International Studies Quarterly 21 (1977): 308.

(15) Mansbach et al., The Web of World Politics, p. 40.

(16) Modelski, Principles of World Politics, p. 194.

(17) Joseph S. Nye, Jr., "Independence and Interdependence," Foreign Policy 22 (1976): 138.

(18) Raymond F. Hopkins, "The International Role of 'Domestic' Bureaucracy," International Organization 30 (1976): 405-32.

(19) Keohane and Nye, Power and Interdependence. See also Donald E. Lampert, and Richard W. Mansbach, "A Model of Multiple Systems in World Politics" (Paper delivered at the Annual Meeting of the International Studies Association, Toronto, February 25-29, 1976); and Richard W. Mansbach, John A. Vasquez, and Lawrence S. Falkowski, "From Unity to Fragmentation: Actors as a Conceptual Variable in World Politics" (Paper delivered at Annual Meeting of the American Political Science Association, Washington, D.C., September 1-4, 1977).

(20) Abraham Kaplan, The Conduct of Inquiry (San Francisco: Chandler, 1964), p. 268.

(21) Morse, Modernization, xvii-xviii.

(22) Ibid., xviii.

(23) Charles A. McClelland, Theory and the International System (New York: Macmillan, 1966), pp. 54-5.

(24) Harold Guetzkow, "Isolation and Collaboration: A Partial Theory of Internation Relations," Journal of Conflict Resolution I (1957): 48-68.

(25) J. David Singer, "Inter-Nation Influence: A Formal Model," American Political Science Review LVII (1963): 420-30.

(26) The difficulty of breaking away from internation interaction analysis and examining state-nonstate actor interactions is exemplified by a recent modernist writing in which the authors attempt to reformulate the concepts of bipolarity and multipolarity "in light of a new paradigm" but essentially end up confining their analysis to cooperation and conflict processes between nations. See P. Dale Dean and John A. Vasquez, "From Power Politics to Issue Politics: Bipolarity and Multipolarity in Light of A New Paradigm," Western Political Quarterly XXIX (1976): 7-28.

(27) Ernest Nagel, The Structure of Science (New York: Harcourt, Brace and World, 1961), p. 108.

(28) Mancur Olson, The Logic of Collective Action (Cambridge: Harvard University Press, 1965).

(29) Norman Frolich and Joe A. Oppenheimer, "Entrepreneurial Politics and Foreign Policy," in Raymond Tanter and Richard H. Ullman, eds., Theory and Policy in International Relations (Princeton: Princeton University Press, 1972), p. 165. A more expanded discussion of the concept of "entrepreneurial politics" can be found in Norman Frolich, Joe A. Oppenheimer, and Oran R. Young, Political Leadership and Collective Goods (Princeton: Princeton University Press, 1971).

(30) William H. Riker, The Theory of Political Coalitions (New Haven: Yale University Press, 1962), Ch. 2-4.

(31) See Ole Holsti, P. Terrence Hopmann, and John D. Sullivan, Unity and Disintegration in International Alliances (New York: John Wiley, 1973), pp. 11-12 and pp. 23-4.

(32) Guetzkow, "Isolation and Collaboration," p. 57.

(33) As Katzenstein reminds us, however, one must be careful in generalizing about even the degree of transnational and transgovernmental coalition activity among developed pluralist democracies since some of these systems will tend to be more promotive of such activity than others depending on the specific structure of the society and government. He cites France as an example of a democratic political system which tends to inhibit transgovernmental coalition activity in particular. Peter J. Katzenstein, "International Relations and Domestic Structures: Foreign Economic Policies of Advanced Industrial States," International Organization 30 (1976): 1-45.

(34) See John Raser, "Learning and Affect in International Politics," Journal of Peace Research II (1965): 216-26; and Anatol Rapoport and Albert M. Chammah, Prisoner's Dilemma (Ann Arbor: University of Michigan Press, 1965).

(35) Karl W. Deutsch, The Analysis of International Relations (Englewood Cliffs: Prentice-Hall, 1968), p. 201.

II
Transnational Ties

2 Multinational Corporations and the Political Process: Looking Ahead

John H. Esterline

INTRODUCTION

This paper hypothesizes that the international economic system is dominated by five supernational(1) actors whose economic policies are moving toward a basically mercantilist(2) orientation with the perspectives that posture implies – namely that international economic relations comprise essentially a zero-sum game (i.e., what one competitor accrues is at the expense of another) and are an expression of political struggle among the actors. The paper suggests further that the ability of the supernational actors to penetrate each other's markets will depend upon the comparative capability of each of the five competing political systems to manage its economic sector to achieve political ends.

SETTING

It is increasingly clear that the spectacular era (1945 to 1973) of American multinational corporations (MNCs) – characterized by direct investment and operations abroad rather than portfolio investment or simple export trade – is drawing to a close. In the words of Robert Gilpin, "the diminution of what has been a Pax Americana and the rise of powers hostile to the global activities of American multinational corporations threaten these MNCs' reign over international economic relations."(3) Not only have hostile powers (the Soviet Union and the People's Republic of China (PRC)) risen to "challenge the political and economic framework which has benefited the American multinationals," as Gilpin asserts, but new strong foreign economic competitors have emerged as exemplified by Japan and Western Europe and the very recent and rapidly growing new economic power centers in the less developed world such as the Organization of Petroleum Exporting Countries (OPEC) and cartel-oriented states rich in raw materials.(4)

It is my thesis that the MNC era, characterized by dominant nonstate actors who directly invested abroad with the objective of control of foreign production units, is being superseded by a new international economic order of five supernational entities within which government and economic enterprise enjoy, or are evolving toward, symbiotic relationships.   These actors are the United States as a political entity;   the EC in partnership with European-based MNCs, especially German, Dutch and Scandinavian; Japan, where a traditional government-business partnership facilitates penetration of the international market by Japanese MNCs; the two blocks of socialist countries characterized by state owned economic organization (one block coordinated by the Council for Mutual Economic Assistance (COMECON) and made up of the Soviet Union and its follower nations of Eastern Europe, the other comprising the PRC with a few client states in Asia (Cambodia and, to some extent, Thailand)); and that group of developing countries whose common feature is state control of raw materials essential to the industrialized world, and whose common objective, of which OPEC is the prototype, is to form state controlled cartels for economic and political leverage.   Some Third and all Fourth World countries (such as Burundi, Upper Volta and Rwanda) are acted upon rather than being actors on the world economic scene.(5)

The actors in the above five categories sometimes compete internally as well as externally. Especially pronounced is the competition within the socialist bloc between the Soviet Union and the People's Republic of China. Within the less-developed country (LDC) bloc competition occurs among cartel groups, and within the EC competition is frequently intense among MNCs of various nation states. Within the United States, MNCs compete against other United States-based MNCs as well as against other bloc competition. This study, however, will consider the five supernational actors as bloc actors.

1973: A WATERSHED YEAR

Overnight tripling of oil prices by the OPEC nations in 1973 precipitated a twentieth century economic revolution comparable to the 1917 to 1918 Soviet political revolution and the cataclysmic military-technological revolution resulting from the explosion of the atom in 1945. Quite aside from massive immediate economic disruptions, fundamental and lasting effects were to follow. Already discernible overtones of mercantilistic competition among the five supernational economic actors became much more obvious as each actor sought to protect itself in the wake of economic confusion.

The OPEC nations, principal beneficiaries of the revolution, split from the other developing nations and advanced toward internal affluence and external political and economic influence, an influence so great that the semiannual OPEC meetings to set oil prices are literally awaited with bated breath by every country in the world. OPEC export share of total world trade climbed from 6 percent in 1970 to 15 percent in 1976.(6) During the same period, the nonoil exporting LDCs – except those rich in essential raw materials – fell into seemingly bottomless economic chaos. The economic malaise extended beyond hopeless Fourth World countries. External public debt of 84 developing countries grew from about $98 billion in 1972 to $174 billion by the end of 1975. Accumulated debt of nonoil-exporting LDCs rose by almost 50 percent from 1973 to 1975.(7) Peru, for instance, one LDC not shackled by a "monoculture economy," nevertheless enters 1978 with interest and principal payments on its public and private foreign debt exceeding $5.2 billion which will consume nearly 40 percent of the nation's export earnings.(8)

The 1973 economic disarray also shook the EC to its roots. Common economic policy so painstakingly developed during the preceding decades was fragmented as, one by one, individual EC nations were forced to come to terms with OPEC through bilateral agreements which OPEC dictated. Nevertheless, the European nations were able to regain control of their economic fortunes. They immediately cranked the oil price increase into their economic calculations. Not restricted as the United States is by the two-price oil problem (over 50 percent of United States oil consumption is domestically produced and its price is determined by government policy rather than market factors), EC dependence upon OPEC actually became advantageous vis-à-vis United States competition because the community accepted reality and thus escaped the vacillation exhibited until 1978 by the comparatively oil rich United States. The healthier among the EC nations, in particular Germany, Belgium and the Netherlands, were again showing fairly strong balance of payments within two years of the crisis, whereas the United States slid into the worst balance of payments deficit in its history. Startlingly, the two traditionally weakest EC members, Italy and the United Kingdom, had, by 1977, achieved a dramatic turnaround. Both countries moved from large deficits to surpluses.(9) Italy had adopted economic reforms; North Sea oil had assured petroleum self-sufficiency to the United Kingdom for some 20 years.

Japan also faced up to reality, exhibiting a similar psychology and entering into bilateral arrangements with its petroleum suppliers. The Japanese economic miracle thus continued apace. Industrial efficiency, sophisticated research as a prelude to overseas market penetration, and the traditional symbiotic relationship between government and business – often termed "Japan, Inc." – overcame the impact of the oil price increases. Japan, strongest of the supranational actors, continues as the country with the fastest export growth. Between 1970 and 1976 the dollar value of Japan's exports increased a total of 248 percent.(10)

Among the supranational actors, the socialist countries presented a mixed bag in the wake of the oil price revolution. On the one hand their western leader, the Soviet Union, emerged as the largest oil producer in the world, its 10.9 million barrels a day in 1977 exceeding Saudi Arabia's production.(11) On the other hand, Eastern European countries suffered further chronic and massive shortage of foreign exchange and mounting external debt. But the socialist world is less affected than other supranational actors because socialist international economics disregard the free market mechanism. The PRC, the other world center of socialist power, has set a 3 billion barrel annual oil production goal for 1990 in consequence of offshore discovery. Significantly, the new "Taiwan Basin" discovery, albeit subject to competing claims of the PRC and Taiwan, has raised estimates of oil deposits claimed by the PRC to 83.8 billion barrels.(12)

And what about the United States? The impact of the oil price increases is universally considered the central factor contributing to an increasing toal trade deficit which reached $26.7 billion for 1977. The deficit, in turn, is most often cited as the primary reason why the American dollar has plunged to historic lows despite two Nixon era devaluations. Since overseas production and sales are a distinguishing feature of the MNC phenomenon, United States-based MNCs such as Exxon, which operates in over 100 countries, are adversely affected. Exxon's earnings decreased 8.7 percent in 1977 because of foreign exchange translation losses, and Gulf Oil's 1977 earnings decline of 8 percent was partly a consequence, the company said, of its being "penalized" by a "significant swing" in foreign currency translations.(13) Also significant in 1976 was the United States direct private investment in LDCs – another hallmark of the MNC phenomenon. It began to decline.(14)

ACTORS

The 1973 oil crisis, a landmark in economic history, demonstrates uniquely how supernational actors can create economic dislocation by use of economic weapons to achieve political gains, in this case, originally the Arab political leverage in the aftermath of the Yom Kippur War. The responses of non-Arab states and supernational actors to the oil crisis suggest that skillful employment of a variety of political system-economic sector partnerships is effective in reestablishing international political balances. In the United States, where political-economic partnership is weak, the resources of the most potent economic instrument – the MNC – were not channeled by the state toward redress of political imbalance. Thus the current international system appears to reflect the essential validity of the mercantilist perspective of the relationship between economic and political activities. This perspective, according to Gilpin, considers "that economic relations are essentially conflictual," that "the distribution of wealth and power among nation states is most significant," that "the real actors in international economic relations are nation states," and that "the political struggle among nation states determines the economic organization of the world." Marxists and mercantilists, Gilpin points out, together disagree with economic liberalism's contention, from Adam Smith forward, "that international economic relations could be made a positive sum game. . . ."(15) The mercantilists differ fundamentally, however, from both Marxists and liberals by contending that politics is primary rather than economics.(16) In their view, political rewards are likely in proportion to the degree to which economic organization and enterprise are utilized by state actors to support political aims. The more centralized their control, the more supportive the economic structures will be, taking whatever forms necessary to compete economically against other state actors and to penetrate the latters' internal markets.

What happened in 1973 can be explained within the following framework. A long smoldering Middle East political conflict erupted with the outbreak of the Yom Kippur War, and the Arab oil states used oil as an economic weapon to achieve political ends. The remaining OPEC members fell in line. The cartel was, and is, phenomenally successful. With this example at hand, other LDCs, in the words of Secretary of State Cyrus R. Vance, sought achievement of political ends by threatening to attempt "new cartels, built around raw materials and commodities other than oil."(17)

Arab inspired use of economic weapons to obtain political rewards, and the spread of the device to other raw material rich LDCs, e.g., bauxite and coffee-producing states, is the most dramatic example of the use of economic power to achieve national will. It is paralleled, however, by the actions of other supernational actors.

Socialist Countries

In the socialist bloc of European countries where all economic enterprises are government owned, basic decisions about economic priorities are made by political leaders and carried out by managers. Since foreign trade is a state monopoly, COMECON directs it to whatever end, both within and without the socialist bloc, is desired. Economic penetration of LDCs by the Soviets is being achieved through large arms sales which create economic binds and ties; through export of Soviet engineering expertise; through export of industrial plants complete with Soviet managers, consultants, machinery and equipment; and through petroleum and mineral sales.

Egypt is a prime example. The Soviets, although banished from Egypt today, built the Aswan High Dam. Generators, machinery, and the engineering expertise to operate and maintain it must, perforce, come from the Soviet Union. Egypt is awash in Soviet-built airplanes and tanks; spare parts must come from the USSR.

Numerous other state recipients of massive Soviet arms are in similar situations. Somalia has problems in pursuing its armed conflict with Ethiopia, for example, because its benefactor and supplier has changed from the USSR to the United States. Meanwhile, the great volume of general Soviet economic aid in the form of loans to LDCs binds the latter financially and politically to the USSR.

Soviet state enterprise increasingly reflects an MNC-type format external to COMECON as the USSR seeks economic penetration outside the socialist bloc and the LDCs in the developing supernational actor competition. From 28 overseas Soviet affiliates in 1970, the number expanded to 84 in 1976, and a 1977 CIA study states that "we expect the number of Soviet-controlled firms in the West to continue to grow in the coming years."(18) Five Soviet subsidiaries already operate in the

United States. "Whenever possible," the Wall Street Journal notes, "the Soviet government agency concerned — which incorporates the business locally — retains more than half the equity. . . ."(19) The fundamentally political character of Soviet overseas economic enterprise is underscored by the Wall Street Journal in commenting on the above study:

> Being the sort of agency it is, the CIA discreetly avoids mentioning another possible advantage to Moscow — that of intelligence. Rightly or wrongly, it is widely assumed that Moscow uses at least some of its business operations abroad as places to assign spies as part of its world-wide information-gathering network.(20)

The PRC power center of the socialist group, largely lacking overseas state economic enterprise, pursues political goals through direct economic assistance, mainly in the form of military aid which will increase donor dependency. The PRC has penetrated Burma by assisting and equipping northern provinces rebels who pose an increasing threat to the Ne Win government. Ne Win, the Los Angeles Times reports, "has already journeyed to Peking twice this year (1977) in an effort to halt the flow of Chinese aid to the insurgents."(21)

Vietnam is a prime example of the political efficacy of economic assistance. United States government sources in 1977 estimated that economic aid to Vietnam during the preceding 10 years amounted to about $2 billion from China and $3 billion from the Soviet Union and the Eastern European bloc. Moreover, in 1973, the USSR cancelled all Hanoi's debts to it in order to gain political leverage.(22) The superior Soviet economic presence in Hanoi helped dislodge the PRC, and Vietnam and Laos are tightly tied to the Soviet economy. The influence of the PRC is currently limited to Cambodia.

The recent "Gang of Four" controversy following the death of Chairman Mao Tse-tung has had its roots primarily in the Chinese theory of economic development. In China refusal to accept foreign technological and financial aid was based in part on Maoist ideology and in part on China's past experience with foreign exploitation, including its disillusionment with Soviet aid in the 1950s. This has applied even to tempting offers by foreign interests for joint-venture arrangements to develop its oil resources, which, according to 1974 estimates, account for over 56 percent of Asia's oil reserves.(23) However, as Selig Harrison notes, "as a totalitarian state China can allocate its human and other resources without the same concern for an early payoff that must necessarily govern the deployment of resources by Exxon or Gulf." Moreover, Harrison continues, "political and strategic considerations can be invoked to justify higher allocations for petroleum than for other sectors, despite the necessarily speculative character of oil exploration."(24)

Indication that the PRC is taking a new economic stance, however, is the signing on February 16, 1978 of a long-range trade agreement with Japan "calling for an additional $20 billion worth of trade above normal transactions from now through 1985."(25) The agreement calls for the

Chinese to buy some "$10 billion worth of factory plants and related construction materials from Japan," such as an integrated steel mill, a copper refinery, and a complete factory to manufacture TV sets and tubes.(26) If the political leadership remains stable and this agreement is honored, 1978 may see China moving into a new era where she will have to be reckoned with as a sixth separate supernational actor.

The European Community

The EC's nine member states (Belgium, France, the Federal Republic of Germany, Italy, Luxembourg, and the Netherlands, the founding members, and the United Kingdom, Ireland, and Denmark which joined in 1973) are linked together through a series of EC institutions (a Commission, a Council of Ministers, a fledgling European Parliament and a Court of Justice) and comprise the world's largest trading bloc. Its principal economic tools are a custom union which enforces a common external tariff, and a common agricultural policy – both highly successful. The EC has moved toward monetary union. Moreover, a joint European float, or "Snake," was set up in 1972 by some European countries in order to create a zone of monetary stability in a world of floating exchange rates. Currencies of the joint float countries are allowed to move only within narrow limits relative to each other and against the dollar. Although full economic union and political union are far from complete, EC nations have combined forces on major economic projects, e.g., the French-British development of the supersonic Concorde airliner, and the French, German, Spanish combine to develop the Airbus.

The United States has consistently supported development of the EC although the customs union and "free trade areas" have resulted in discrimination against United States trade. The hihgly protectionist common agricultural policy limits the European market for United States agricultural products, the largest category of United States exports; and preferential trading arrangements between the EC and certain European, African, and Mediterranean countries erode the most-favored-nation principle.(27) The lengthy Dillon-Kennedy rounds of talks in the 1960s to establish tariff reductions largely failed to resolve United States complaints. The 1978 Tokyo round which seeks general liberalization of trade barriers will only, in the planned Geneva conference, face up to the divergent positions of the United States, the EC, and Japan.

Aside from formidable economic problems for the United States spawned by the political organization of the EC, even more serious ones result from the differing organizational, philosophical, and operating conditions of United States and EC multinational corporations. It was fashionable in the late 1960s to speak of the American challenge to Europe in the form of United States-based MNCs.(28) According to this thesis, United States-based MNCs are controlled from the United States; European MNCs, such as Philips, are largely independent of the parent company and do not reflect excessive concentration of economic power. United States-based MNCs, the argument continues, enjoy superiority over European MNCs for a variety of reasons: size, ability to take advantage of the economics of scale, access to economical financing, a high state of technological development, and advanced management. The argument concluded that United States-based MNCs have penetrated Europe and will come to dominate key industrial centers there.

A response to the American challenge soon emerged in the United States. In the "American Challenge Challenged," (1969) John B. Rhodes suggested that the "American Challenge" idea overstated the case respecting the superiority of American business and the dominant role of American subsidiaries in Europe.(29) Rhodes pointed out that United States-based companies experience growing competitive pressure from highly modernized and efficient European industry in Europe and throughout the world. The study argues that in only a few fields, such as computers, do United States firms dominate. Moreover, United States firms have been catalysts for encouraging the technological, managerial, and competitive efficiency of European industry.

A case in point is the rising European-based MNC penetration of the world commercial aircraft market, heretofore dominated by United States MNCs. In early 1978, Airbus Industrie, a French-German-Spanish combine, appeared to be on the verge of achieving the first significant breakthrough into world markets at the expense of McDonnell Douglas and Lockheed. Responding to the request of the EC which seeks to reduce its trade deficit with Japan, the Japanese transport minister reportedly told Parliament in January that "the government feels it advisable that Japan's privately operated TOA airline buy the European A-300B Airbus instead of the Lockheed Tristar and the McDonnell Douglas DC-10."(30) The EC Airbus threatens to penetrate the United States commercial aircraft market as well. Eastern Airlines, Pacific Southwest Airlines, and Allegheny Airlines were all reported to be negotiating with Airbus Industrie for purchase of A-300s.(31) EC trade acumen was also underscored when the People's Republic of China initialed a five-year agreement with the EC, in 1978, designed to increase trade, but also to restrict imports "if it (the EC) finds they are disturbing European markets."(32)

William A. Dymsza, discussing such reverse phenomena, added that compared to United States-based MNCs, whose substantial domestic American market still remains in many cases the major one for them, European MNCs have long found that their growth has depended on international markets.(33) Unilever, Royal Dutch Shell, Imperial Chemical, and Nestlé are old timers, Dymsza noted, and have evolved more fully into true MNCs than have United States-based MNCs.

Japan

The Japanese economic miracle is basically the consequence of consensus achieved through partnership of government and business. That partnership constitutes a "Japanese challenge" of enormous proportion. Japan's recent achievements are witness to its recovery from the oil price crisis of 1973: the dramatic rise of the yen against the dollar (on October 1, 1977, a dollar was worth 292 yen; on June 1, 1978, it was worth 223 yen – a drop in value of the dollar to the yen of 23 percent in eight months!); Japanese capture of the small car market in the United States, especially in California which is the largest segment of the United States market; Japanese rout of United States steel which has prodded the United States to emergency protective measures despite formal United States opposition to protectionism; an overwhelming balance of payments surplus, including a $7 billion surplus with the United States alone in 1977; and the increasing importance of Japanese MNCs, at least eight of which rank among the top in the world.

Japan and its MNCs have vastly increased direct foreign investment abroad; the figure reached $3.46 billion for 1976 alone. Nearly one-fourth of Japanese overseas investment is in the United States and an even greater flow of investment to the United States is anticipated in 1978 to Japanese-owned subsidiaries which produce automobiles, TV sets, stereos, and chemicals in the United States.(34) Attempts to redress the imbalance have occupied the energies of United States trade negotiators for years. Most recently (in January 1978) Robert Strauss, United States special trade representative, returned from Japan with the statement that "I think we have really redefined the economic relationship between our two great nations."(35) But the Wall Street Journal called the Strauss achievement a "truce . . . a temporary one and the field is open for further skirmishes."(36) Moreover, how much actual relief for American exports was attained is suggested by the following. The publicized Japanese agreement with Strauss to increase Japanese annual imports of high quality beef from 1,000 to 10,000 tons actually refers to beef imports on a global basis, not from the United States alone.

The Japanese themselves admit that the gulf between Japanese and Western thinking about politics and economics is not easily bridged. Michiya Matsukawa, Japanese minister for international finance, recently said that Americans and Europeans are not likely to understand and tolerate the unique Japanese economic system; that Japanese government practices confuse foreigners; but that Japan is not likely to adjust its economy to fit the American-European pattern.(37)

United States

Certainly from a mercantilist perspective the United States government will eventually be obliged to marshall and employ the resources of American MNCs as principal economic devices for achieving political ends. As suggested, a symbiotic relationship between government and business is characteristic of all four of the other supranational actors. Socialist state economic enterprises are an integral part of the socialist states. The EC protects the interests of European international economic enterprises; the raw material rich developing states marshall economic resources for political purposes through cartels and seek to limit the degree of foreign economic penetration of their economies. Japan, second to the United States as the largest single private enterprise country in the world, demonstrates a unique affinity between government and private enterprise. Only in the United States is a skewed relationship evident between the state and economic enterprise.

"Fundamental US policy on international investment . . . is neither to promote nor discourage inward or outward investment through government intervention," according to the Department of State in 1977.(38) Beyond this, the United States government supports a set of voluntary guidelines embodied in a Declaration on International Investment and Multinational Enterprises emanating from the Organization for Economic Cooperation and Development (OECD) in June 1977. The International Labor Organization (ILO) Tripartite Declaration of Principles concerning Multinational Enterprises and Social Policy, April 1977, is in limbo so far as the United States is concerned because it has since withdrawn from the ILO.

United States-based MNCs in the early 1970s accounted for approximately 60 percent of overseas direct investment in the entire world. In 1971, the United States-based MNCs comprised 14 of the 20 top firms each with over $1 billion in annual sales.(39) These, plus many other United States-based MNCs on the list of the world's 100 biggest MNCs, operate in the absence of an American political-economic policy. As a consequence, United States-based MNCs increasingly suffer disadvantages both abroad and at home. Besides the barriers posed by the other supernational actors, United States-based MNCs encounter official limitation imposed by the Latin American Free Trade Area, the Andean Pact, and similar emerging regional organizations – aimed especially at American MNCs – with little United States government assistance. LDCs limit or even force abandonment of MNC subsidiaries. They use a variety of tactics to achieve their goals. According to the United States Department of State, these include outright expropriation of MNC subsidiaries, abrogation of valid contracts, formation of raw materials cartels, mandatory phased disinvestment, failure to compensate for expropriation, limitations on earnings reinvestment and/or remittance of profits, imposition of quantitative goals on foreign investors such as jobs, exports, and use of local materials in production, and efforts in the UN to impose international control of MNCs.(40) Since United States-based MNCs comprise the majority of major world MNCs, they bear the brunt of the attack. For example, International Business Machines Corporation, the world's largest computer manufacturer, decided in 1977 to sell its manufacturing facilities in India rather than comply with an Indian government demand that it surrender 60 percent ownership of its business in India to Indians.(41) Similarly in 1977 India served a virtual closure notice on Coca Cola, prompting admonition from United States Ambassador Robert F. Goheen that the policy would "discourage other American businessmen from seeking investment in India."(42) At the 1976 Non-Aligned Summit in Colombo, Sri Lanka, "US imperialism and MNCs" got top billing among the Third World's "most dangerous enemies."(43)

In Canada during 1977 United States-based MNCs experienced reverse pressure. The Canadian trade minister threatened to abrogate the 12-year-old automobile pact between Canada and the United States unless United States car manufacturers in Canada increase capital spending in that country.(44)

At home the problems of United States-based MNCs are legion. They range from attempts such as the Burke-Hartke bill to limit foreign investment, to a shakedown by Indonesian restaurant ventures in the United States of American companies doing business in Indonesia, the pressure being exerted by Indonesia's national petroleum enterprise, P.N. Pertamina.(45) The well-publicized payoffs by ITT, Lockheed, Gulf Oil, and other United States firms and the resulting United States political reactions are too familiar to need elaboration.(46)

Although the Burke-Hartke bill failed to become law, the Carter administration has shaken United States-based MNCs anew with 1978 proposals to repeal two foreign tax breaks, namely, deferral of tax on the export income of domestic international sales corporations (DISCs), a provision placed in the tax code in 1961 to encourage export sales; and deferral of tax on the unrepatriated earnings of United States overseas subsidiaries.(47)

Meanwhile, knowing a good thing when they see it, non-American MNCs are investing heavily in the United States because, in the words of one Japanese official, "the United States economy is free — few limitations on foreign investment."(48) To bear out these words, foreign direct investment in the United States expanded 10 percent in 1975 and another 9.1 percent in 1976. According to the Conference Board, a surge in the acquisition of United States firms by foreign companies occurred in the 1975 to 1977 period. Foreign companies, the Conference Board said, announced 274 investments in the United States in 1977 — up from 254 in 1976 and 161 in 1975.(49) Iran's Bank Omran, with its 1976 investment of $250 million for a New Orleans commercial and residential complex, made the largest acquisition of that year. Western European, Japanese, and Canadian entrepreneurs are the largest investors. OPEC countries significantly accounted for only $309 million, including the Iranian purchase, out of a total of $21 billion in foreign investment that could be valued in 1976.(50) It is a reasonable deduction that much OPEC investment continues to be a portfolio of short term deposit.

A most significant aspect of international economic competition for political ends is the sale of arms and weapons systems. In this area, also, United States policy is ambivalent, although the United States and the Soviet Union are actually the world's leading arms merchants. Annual United States arms sales, estimated by Senator William Proxmire (D.-Wis.) to be almost $10 billion in 1977, are also a major instrument for improving the United States balance of payments position.(51) An anomaly arises because President Carter came into office pledged to reduce the commerce in weapons, but quickly found that politics demands huge arms sales. Regimes friendly to the United States, e.g., Iran before the deposition of the Shah, Saudi Arabia, Indonesia, and Brazil, expect arms provision, as do the NATO countries to whom Carter has promised to provide a 3 percent increase in defense capability. Other LDCs seek arms. Political competition for influence in these countries demands that their expectations be met and currently they annually "buy an astonishing $6 billion worth – a large chunk going to the poor countries of Latin America, Africa and Southeast Asia."(52) Thus Carter finds that the set of controls on arms sales which he announced May 19, 1977, would be limited to only some 35 percent of all arms sales.(53) Among arms transfers exempted from controls are those for Israel. Paradoxically, the more the United States is drawn into the Middle East political conflict in consequence of the Sadat peace offensive, the greater are demands for arms from Israel and Egypt.

Despite lack of a policy toward MNCs, the United States has traditionally favored free trade. This posture is now under attack by emerging protectionist demands.Beginning with successful industry pressure for reduced quotas for import of shoes, textiles, and electronic products, the new protectionist movement achieved further success in 1977. The severe plight of American steel companies in consequence of Japanese competition led in that year to legal curbs on steel imports which set "reference prices" on imported steel. The object is to attempt to keep foreign manufacturers (read Japanese steel companies) from dumping their products in the United States at prices below the cost of production by imposing tariffs to equalize foreign and domestic prices. A second argument on behalf of the protectionist movement became evident as the biggest trade deficit in United States history developed – some $26.7 billion for 1977 – even though most of the deficit was in consequence of higher prices for imported oil. To date, remedial steps are aimed principally at reducing oil imports by curtailing use. The deep trade deficits are widely blamed for the dramatic fall of the dollar against European and Japanese currencies in 1977 and 1978. Two obvious remedies are to expand exports and curtail imports.

American labor today, however, is not only concerned with loss of jobs due to foreign competition in the United States; it is anti United States-based MNCs. For years the AFL-CIO has preached that MNCs export jobs overseas, a questionable but enticing assumption. Labor generally was held at bay by studies which suggest the reverse. In 1973, for instance, the United States Tariff Commission found that nearly all the consequences of MNC investment abroad were favorable to the United States. Specifically, the commission found that such investment made a large positive contribution to the United States balance of trade and payments; that it produced a gain of a half-million United States manufacturing jobs; that it helped rather than hindered United States trade expansion in high technology groups such as aircraft and computers; and that MNC technology transfers, for example, accounted for nearly all of the inflow of $2.3 billion during 1971 for fees and royalties paid for United States technology.(54)

On the heels of the malaise of certain United States industries, the huge and increasing balance of payment deficits, and the position of American labor, it comes as no surprise that Secretary of State Vance in January 1978, while paying tribute to the free trade ideal, nevertheless recognized the crux of the problem:

I know that this (economic recovery) is not an abstract, theoretical matter for the American worker or businessman or farmer who depends for his family's living on production of steel, CB radios, color television sets, microwave ovens, textiles, footwear, automobiles, computers, sugar and many other items. The changing world economy has made other nations competitive in production of these products and we are feeling the result of it.(55)

CONCLUSIONS

This paper suggests that the rise of the United States-based multinational corporation was the result of a favorable economic climate for United States MNC expansion as an adjunct of United States political power. Competition among regional and global political interests was increasing but the 1973 war in the Middle East and the subsequent OPEC-inspired oil price crisis dramatically altered the pattern of international economic relations. The success of the OPEC cartel demonstrated the vulnerability of the United States-based MNC. Other cartels were attempted. United States-based MNCs have also become increasingly vulnerable to the exercise of attributes of national sovereignty to limit foreign economic penetration. Utilization of state owned and controlled MNCs by the socialist countries and the phenomenon of "Japan, Inc." continue to challenge United States economic power. While the United States-based MNC continues to be enormously important, it competes with other actor MNCs and other forms of economic devices used by the four other supranational actors to assist them in reaching both their economic and political goals.

This paper also suggests that a mercantilist world-perspective prevails. Politics determines economic organization and economic competition is part of the political struggle among nations to determine the world order. The five supranational actors are engaged in a zero-sum game; a gain by one is a loss for the others. The differing natures of the five actors' political systems will dictate the approach each will adopt to the organization and regulation of the economic sector under its control. Looking to a future world of five supranational actors (or six with the PRC) in mercantilistic competition with each other, the conclusion is inescapable that the United States is presently the least equipped to deal with the competition. The closed political systems which characterize the socialist countries will result in a straight line authority relationship to the state-owned economic enterprises. The OPEC and other raw material rich countries, which have political systems closest to the authoritarian model among the remaining actors, will, through the traditionalist but modernizing elite, tailor economic organizations to political ends of the nation-states involved. The Japanese political system of an open society which reflects a unique and mutually reinforcing relationship between the state and economic enterprise, will exercise dominant influence over the course of economic activity. The European Community, a union of open political systems, banded together to increase their political and economic bargaining strength, will direct and utilize the combined power of the interacting economies. The United States, most open of the several political systems and the one most committed to the ethos of free trade and private enterprise, will experience more difficulty than the other four actors in directing its economy for political ends.

NOTES

(1) Super, meaning "surpassing all or most others of its kind" (Webster's New Collegiate Dictionary, 1974) is suggested as an appropriate prefix for a major actor in the international system. A supernational actor is superior to a transnational actor, but is not necessarily a superpower, which usually alludes only to the United States and the Soviet Union.

(2) Mercantile system: "a political and economic system or policy, evolving with the modern national state, seeking to secure a nation's supremacy over other states by the accumulation of precious metals and by exporting the largest possible quantity of products while importing as little as possible" (The Random House Dictionary of the English Language, College Edition, 1969).

(3) Robert Gilpin, "The Political Economy of the Multinational Corporation: Three Contrasting Perspectives," American Political Science Review, March 1976, p. 190.

(4) In a similar vein, Daniel Yergin, "Order and Survival," Daedalus, Winter 1978, addresses himself to "four severe challanges" to the "'order'" of political and economic rules which the United States shaped and managed. These are: "attainment of 'near economic parity' by Western Europe and Japan; the rapid rise of the OPEC; the call of the Third World for a radical transformation of the entire order; and the prospect of nuclear proliferation," p. 263.

(5) See K.J. Holsti, International Politics (Englewood Cliffs, N.J.: Prentice-Hall, Inc., 1977), p. 75.

(6) "International Trade," Road Maps of Industry, No. 1819, November 1977 (New York: The Conference Board, 1977).

(7) "Borrowing in International Markets," Road Maps in Industry, No. 1818, November 1977 (New York: The Conference Board, 1977).

(8) "Party's Over – Peru's Economy Sags," Los Angeles Times, November 3, 1977.

(9) "U.S. Predicts Another Slow Year for Europe," Los Angeles Times, January 27, 1978.

(10) "International Trade," Road Maps of Industry, No. 1819.

(11) "Russ Fall Short of Economic Goals," Los Angeles Times, January 28, 1978.

(12) Selig S. Harrison, China, Oil and Asia: Conflict Ahead? (New York: Columbia University Press, 1977) p. 17 and Fig. 12.

(13) Wall Street Journal, January 26, 1978, p. 4.

(14) "Borrowing in International Markets."

(15) Gilpin, "Political Economy," pp. 185-6.

(16) Ibid., p. 186.

(17) Cyrus R. Vance, "Foreign Policy Decisions for 1978" (Address to the Los Angeles World Affairs Council, January 13, 1978, Washington: Department of State, 1978).

(18) Reported in "Soviets Reaping Benefits of Capitalism; Expand Commercial Operations Abroad," Wall Street Journal, October 27, 1977.

(19) Ibid.

(20) Ibid.

(21) "China Seeks to Extend Its Influence in Southeast Asia," Los Angeles Times, December 11, 1977.

(22) Ibid.

(23) Lucino M. Rebamontan, "Peking Spurns Overtures of Foreign Oil Investors," Depth News (Manila: Press Foundation of Asia, 1974).

(24) Harrison, China, Oil and Asia, pp. 25-6 (emphasis added).

(25) Sam Jameson, "Japan, China Sign Major Trade Pact," Los Angeles Times, February 17, 1978.

(26) Ibid.

(27) "The European Community," Foreign Policy Outlines (Washington: Department of State, 1973).

(28) See Jean-Jacques Servan-Schreiber, The American Challenge (New York: Atheneum, 1968).

(29) John B. Rhodes, "The American Challenge Challenged," Harvard Business Review, September-October 1969.

(30) "Japan wants an airline to buy European instead of U.S. planes," <u>Los Angeles Times</u>, January 31, 1978.

(31) "Lockheed Faces European Threat in 3 Airbus Deals," <u>Los Angeles Times</u>, February 1, 1978.

(32) "China Initials 1st Trade Pact with Common Market," <u>Los Angeles Times</u>, February 4, 1978.

(33) William A. Dymsza, <u>Multinational Business Strategy</u> (New York: McGraw-Hill, 1972), p. 11.

(34) "Japan Expected to Sharply Boost US Investments," <u>Los Angeles Times</u>, October 31, 1977.

(35) "US, Japan Reach Agreements on Trade; American Side Gets More Than Expected," <u>Wall Street Journal</u>, January 16, 1978.

(36) Ibid.

(37) "Japan's Economics Inscrutable to West," <u>Los Angeles Times</u>, November 5, 1977.

(38) "Multinational Corporations," <u>GIST</u> August 1977 (Washington: Department of State, 1977).

(39) Nasrollah S. Fatemi, Gail W. Williams, and Thibaut De Saint-Phalle, <u>Multinational Corporations: The Problems and the Prospects</u>, 2nd ed. rev. (New York: A.S. Barnes, 1976), pp. 300-10.

(40) "Multinational Corporations," <u>GIST</u> 1977 (Washington: Department of State, 1977).

(41) "New Delhi Caps Coke But Desires Other Multinationals," <u>Depth News, Special</u>, October 3, 1977 Manila: Press Foundation of Asia, 1977.

(42) Ibid.

(43) "Multi-Nationals Come Under Heavy Fire From the Third World," <u>Depth News, Asia</u>, September 8, 1977 (Manila: Press Foundation of Asia, 1977).

(44) "US-Canadian Auto Pact May Be Scrapped," <u>Los Angeles Times</u>, November 14, 1977.

(45) "Indonesian Restaurant Shows How Firms Can Succumb to Threat by Foreign States," <u>Wall Street Journal</u>, October 13, 1977.

(46) For a detailed account of the Lockheed experience, see Robert Shaplen, "Annals of Crime Lockheed in Japan – Part I and Part II" in the

<u>New Yorker</u>, January 23, 1978 and January 30, 1978; see also Neil H. Jacoby, Peter Nehemkis, and Richard Eells, <u>Bribery and Extortion in World Business</u> New York: Macmillan, 1978.

(47) "Tax Position of House Panel Chief Spells Rough Sailing for Some Carter Proposals," <u>Wall Street Journal</u>, January 19, 1978.

(48) "Japan Expected to Sharply Boost US Investments," <u>Los Angeles Times</u>, October 31, 1977.

(49) "Foreign Investment in US Jumps," <u>Los Angeles Times</u>, January 25, 1978.

(50) "Iran Made Biggest US Buy of '76," <u>Los Angeles Times,</u> December 6, 1977.

(51) "Senator William Proxmire," <u>Los Angeles Times</u>, October 24, 1977, p. 2.

(52) Ibid.

(53) Ibid.

(54) Fatemi, et al., <u>Multinational Corporations</u>, Ch. 4.

(55) Vance, "Foreign Policy Decisions."

3 Controlling the Transnational Corporation: The Issue of Codes of Conduct*

P. G. Bock

The worldwide debate over the impact of transnational corporations, which has been raging for at least ten years, shows no signs of abating. It has produced a veritable flood of books, reports, pamphlets, articles, and speeches representing the views of a larger variety of interested parties than almost any contemporary international issue.(1) Even a casual survey of this enormous literature reveals the extent to which ideological, emotional, and partisan elements outweigh rational discourse based on systematically collected and carefully analyzed information.

In recent years the debate has increasingly turned from the general question of whether TNCs are the primary promoters of global peace and prosperity or the leading exploiters of mankind, to the narrower issue of ways and means for controlling their activities, in the apparent belief that one can, at least pragmatically, take a middle position on the general question. In other words, since TNCs exist and are supported by powerful interests, and since they seem to perform some useful functions, the best approach may be to regulate them in such a way that their contributions will not be offset by their harmful activities. The culmination of this line of thought is the current attempt by the United Nations to formulate a "code of conduct" for TNCs. The central contention of this paper is that, given the state of our knowledge about these firms and the vast conflicts of interest among the actors involved, this laudable effort is doomed to failure.

THE NEED FOR REGULATION

I consider it a laudable effort because there can be no doubt that the

---

*This article was published in slightly modified form in Peace and Change, vol. V, no. 4, Spring 1979. Reprinted with permission.

TNCs have created considerable difficulties for the other international actors, primarily the nation-states and the labor unions. These difficulties flow first and foremost from three structural characteristics (2) of the firms:

1. As is well known, the leading TNCs have enormous financial resources, comparing favorably with those of many nations.

2. By definition, these firms operate "transnationally," i.e., in a number of political jurisdictions, but are headquartered in one country (Nestlé, for example, operates in 114 different nations). This inevitably produces enormous legal and political difficulties for the parties. The firm has to deal with different and often conflicting national requirements, and the individual nations have to deal with an entity that is only partially within their control.

3. Because of the hierarchical and highly integrated nature of the modern corporation, it has the capacity to manipulate its resources with considerable ease, shifting them among jurisdictions and activities in accordance with a central plan which is not easily subject to national control. A recent, perhaps extreme, example is IBM's decision to dismantle its operations in India rather than obey the new Indian law which requires foreign companies to sell 60 percent of their equity to local shareholders.(3)

Of course, the impact of a particular TNC will depend on the way its management decides to use these resources and capabilities, what we might call its "corporate philosophy." And thus we find a full range of behaviors from ITT's notorious conduct in Chile,(4) to Lonrho's efforts to help black African nations,(5) to the divergent policies pursued by copper companies in Peru.(6) But collectively, the TNCs pose a triple challenge to the traditional notion of the supremacy (or sovereignty) of the nation-state.

In the first place, TNCs complicate the efforts of governments to control their own economies, polities, and even cultures. Since most of the major TNCs are United States based, this challenge was first recognized by host countries which experienced the large increase of American investment after World War II. Critics in Europe (most prominently Servan-Schreiber) and Latin America pointed out with increasing vehemence that these firms take over or replace domestic enterprises, thereby discouraging national entrepreneurship; use local credit facilities and repatriate profits, thereby impoverishing the host economy; determine the sectors and size of the investments according to their own plans, thereby interfering with national economic planning; introduce the influence of the home country in unacceptable ways, because they can be used as instruments of foreign policy; and undermine the local culture by introducing alien, unwanted (and perhaps harmful) products, labor practices, and managerial styles.

Before long, however, critics emerged who pointed out that the problems are not confined to host countries, and that TNCs are not necessarily an unmixed blessing for the nations in which their headquarters are located. Thus it was pointed out that these firms, by transferring operations abroad, can export jobs, diminish tax revenues, have a negative impact on the balance of payments, and threaten the stability of the national currency by shifting their considerable liquid assets in a speculative manner. In short, even the home country seems to lose some control over its domestic institutions and policies. And both sets of critics pointed with alarm to the ability of TNCs to circumvent certain national laws and regulations.

The transnational corporations also challenge the nations' ability to achieve external goals, i.e., to implement foreign policy objectives. It is well established by now that there is at best a very imperfect fit between the objectives of TNCs and the foreign policies of their home countries. There are simply too many examples of corporate behavior that conflict with national objectives, ranging from such extremes as United States oil companies' actions during the 1973 Arab oil embargo to lesser refusals on the part of companies to follow "their" nation's guidelines in host countries.(7) Furthermore, it is also clear that the activities of TNCs can embroil their home countries in foreign disputes that are not of their own choosing, or at a minimum exert great pressure on the home country to accommodate its foreign policy to the needs of the firms.

The third challenge of the TNC is to the nations' collective efforts to control the international system. Although it is quite common nowadays to emphasize the emergence of nonstate actors in world politics, and the importance of environmental processes in shaping the international system,(8) it is still true that nations believe that they have the exclusive right to determine the structure and functioning of world order. They must, therefore, view with some misgivings the increasing role played by TNCs in such areas as regional integration – where company investment patterns can facilitate or retard cooperative national policies; production and distribution of natural resources (oil, copper, etc.); and the structure of the international economy (especially the contribution of TNCs to the growing North-South gap). Thus it is well known that approximately two-thirds of direct foreign investment is to be found in the developed countries; and beyond that, nearly 50 percent of such investment is made by eight of them (U.S., Canada, U.K., Switzerland, FRG, France, Japan and the Netherlands) in one another. Of the investment in the Third World, only a tiny fraction finds its way to the poorest countries.(9) To the extent that this growing imbalance among nations, attributable in no small part to the activities of TNCs, sharpens global conflicts and adds to the instability of the international system, it becomes the concern of all nations.(10)

Organized labor, both on the national level and through its various international federations (ICFTU, WFTU, and WCL), has repeatedly expressed its awareness of the challenge posed by the TNC, focusing, quite naturally, on such issues as the firms' ability to resist collective action, to impose a particular system of industrial relations operating in the home country on their foreign subsidiaries, to fight unionization especially in developing countries with weak union movements, and in general to control working conditions without regard to workers' legitimate interests.(11)

The TNCs and their defenders have, of course, responded vigorously to any and all criticisms. Articulate spokesmen for individual corporations like Jacques Maisonrouge of IBM, trade associations like the International Chamber of Commerce, and a variety of academic scholars not only deny assertions that the firms have harmful impacts (with only a few "exaggerated" and highly unusual exceptions), but make a good case for the beneficial effects of the TNCs in promoting industrialization, raising wage levels, transfering technology, improving economic and social infrastructures, promoting economic and social welfare, and, through their global activities, increasing international understanding and eliminating barriers between peoples, nations, and blocs of nations.(12)

But underlying this spirited defense is a growing awareness of certain areas of friction and conflict. Corporate officials are often heard to complain that they cannot operate efficiently because governments impose excessive restrictions upon them; that, although they try to be "good citizens" in every country in which they operate, the wide variation in what constitutes good citizenship makes it impossible to satisfy all of them; that many potential host countries, particularly the less developed ones, are so <u>politically</u> unstable that they make investments too risky; and that if the international political system could only be made less anarchic, the economic and social contributions of the TNCs would indeed be maximized and universalized.

EXISTING REGULATORY MECHANISMS

As the awareness of frictions and conflicts of interest among the major participants grew, so did their efforts to find mechanisms for alleviating them. Initially each of the parties tried to devise individual mechanisms so that the controls would be within their control: nations through legislative measures, companies through management guidelines (or "codes of behavior"), and unions through transnational collective bargaining. A brief examination of national regulations and company codes should help us understand the current drive toward international regulation.

National Controls

National governments have long been aware of the benefits of foreign investment (capital formation, industrialization, employment, etc.), and even today it is not unusual to find them offering a variety of inducements to TNCs in order to attract their operations. Nevertheless, as some of the less desirable economic consequences of TNC activities became apparent, nations began to pass a variety of restrictive laws on <u>inward investment</u>. Prominent among them are the following.

Terms of admission and operation

A growing number of both developed and developing countries have closed certain industrial sectors, usually those considered of special national interest to foreign investment. For example, India and Canada have excluded banking and insurance; Brazil and Canada exclude broadcasting; Indonesia, the United States, and Japan exclude nuclear energy; Brazil and the United States exclude coastal shipping; Algeria excludes all "basic sectors" (construction, mining, mineral processes, etc.); and Libya excludes all retail, wholesale, import, and export trade.(13)

Canada, with its widespread concern about United States domination of its economy, has established the Foreign Investment Review Agency (FIRA) which must approve all foreign takeovers and major new investments regardless of sector.

Form of foreign ownership and participation

All governments assert the right to control the extent of foreign ownership of their economy, but a growing number of countries, particularly in the developing areas, are legislating specific ceilings for ownership of individual enterprises. As was mentioned, India's Foreign Exchange Regulation Act, which requires most foreign companies to sell 60 percent of their equity to Indians, led to the withdrawal of IBM (and Coca Cola). Mexico and Iraq also require majority local participation, and other countries have similar though less stringent regulations. Gabon even requires an automatic transfer of 10 percent of the shareholding to the state.(14) Several countries also have regulations on company personnel, i.e., requirements that a certain proportion of the management and labor be nationals.

In addition, there is a proliferation of national regulations in such areas as: restrictive business practices, transfer pricing, taxation, capital movements (particularly the amount of profit that may be repatriated), financing (the ratio of capital that must be brought into the country to local borrowing), and disclosure of information (so that nations can know the condition of foreign subsidiaries and not merely the consolidated state of the mother company.)

In light of recent well publicized discoveries of incidents of political interference and corrupt practices, there will undoubtedly follow a series of varied and uncoordinated national laws to prohibit and punish such activities.

All of these regulations amply illustrate the profound concern of the nation-state, not only about "foreign intrusions" into its sovereign domain, but more broadly about its ability to exercise control over its territory, population, and economy.

But as the activities of TNCs expanded into an ever increasing number of countries, and as they shifted investment from their home base, or at least preferred to invest abroad, home countries too became concerned. And while this is a newer and less obvious development, a trend toward national regulation of outward investment can also be seen.

These regulations often take the form of restrictions on capital export and a variety of tax provisions (for example, the withdrawal of tax incentives intended to <u>encourage</u> foreign investment). An interesting recent development is the effort by Sweden and the United Kingdom to bring the activities of their TNCs abroad into line with their government's political objectives. The Swedish Export Credit Guarantee Board will only guarantee investments in countries to which the government assigns priority, and only if the intended project will contribute to economic and social objectives. The British government is trying to convince British companies to adopt voluntary codes of behavior which would require them to improve the working conditions of blacks in their South African subsidiaries or else pull out of that country.(15)

Company Controls

Confronted by this array of national restrictions and by a rising tide of public criticism, some transnational corporations adopted the strategy of drafting and publishing codes of behavior for their managers. Companies (national as well as transnational) have, of course, always had rules and procedures by which they operate, and which are transmitted to their managers in training programs, memoranda from headquarters, and informal briefings and discussions. A part of this control system includes instructions regarding relations with significant actors in their environment – governmental agencies, union, suppliers, customers, and consumer groups. But as the tensions mounted, corporate leaders and their trade and professional associations decided that it would be useful to formulate guidelines focusing on these matters, and also useful, as executives readily admit, to publicize these guidelines in order to demonstrate that the companies are doing something to control their activities and to minimize the friction between them and the other actors.

The most elaborate (and most widely distributed) company document is Caterpillar Tractor's <u>A Code of Worldwide Business Conduct</u>, issued in 1974 and revised in 1977.(16) It is worth a closer look because in its principles it is quite typical of all such business efforts, and reflects, I believe, the attitudes of most TNC managers.

Addressed to all Caterpillar employees by the Chairman of the Board, the code "is an attempt to capture basic, general principles to be observed by Caterpillar people everywhere" (p. 2). Each officer, subsidiary head, and plant or department manager, is instructed to prepare an annual memorandum affirming that he knows and understands the code, and reporting activities that might suggest the code has been violated (p. 10).

The code is divided into seventeen sections under such headings as: ownership and investment, relations with employees, sharing of technology, finance, business ethics, relations with public officials, disclosure of information, and reporting code compliance.

Many of the principles would be totally unobjectionable to governments or unions, e.g., the emphasis on a single, worldwide standard of fair treatment of employees, the acceptance of unionization, the lack of racial, religious, or sexual discrimination, the desire to share technology, the avoidance of unfair competition, the encouragement of ethical business conduct well above the minimum required by law, and the assertion that "the basic reason for existence of any company is to serve the needs of people," and that, therefore, "the public is entitled to a reasonable explanation" of business operations (p. 9).

But even this document, which is (at least in part) also a public relations instrument, could not avoid listing a number of principles, objectives, and demands which are not likely to be universally endorsed. A few illustrations will suffice:

1. Caterpillar supports full ownership of operations by the parent company (p. 3).
2. Caterpillar facilities are to be located wherever in the world it is most economically advantageous to do so, from a long-term standpoint, and location decisions will be based in part on political stability and demonstrated governmental attitudes.
3. Since technology transfer depends not only on the donor's willingness to give but also on the recipient's ability to utilize, Caterpillar "encourages" developing countries "to create an environment of law and custom that will maximize such utilization. . . ." (pp. 5-6).
4. There are business differences among nations regarding competitive practices, boycotts, labor standards, and repatriation of profit which should be made more uniform and harmonious through multilateral action (p. 6).
5. While Caterpillar will obey all laws, no matter what they may be, it intends to offer, where appropriate, "constructive ideas for changes in the law" (p. 8).
6. Payments to public officials are prohibited, but where payment of gratuities to public officials are "customary," and "as a practical matter unavoidable," they must be limited to customary amounts, and paid only to facilitate correct performance of duties (p. 8).
7. In general, while Caterpillar affirms that its investment must be "compatible with social and economic priorities of host countries, and with local customs, traditions and sovereignty," it is also asking such countries to provide for its stability, growth, and success and to avoid discrimination against multinational corporations (p. 3).

Needless to say, neither governments nor unions found such codes sufficient to allay their fears about the impact of the TNCs and, as even this brief analysis of the Caterpillar code shows, the TNCs are far from convinced that national regulation can overcome all their misgivings.

Indeed, a consensus seems to be emerging among the major participants that there are serious and growing conflicts among them, that existing regulatory mechanisms are inadequate, and that something should be done to improve the situation. The evidence for such a consensus can be found in the repeated calls by all the parties for a "New International Economic Order," and, more to the point here, in what I consider a genuine willingness by them at least to discuss international regulatory devices such as codes of conduct. In fact, representatives of TNCs, nations, and labor organizations are actively participating in the current UN efforts to draft a universal code. The most concrete expression of this development can be seen in the OECD "Guidelines for Multinational Enterprises" adopted by the 24 leading industrialized nations in June 1976.

THE OECD GUIDELINES

The negotiations within the OECD began in 1975 and after 18 months of "arduous negotiation, with marathon sessions," in the words of United States Ambassador William C. Turner,(17) they produced a three-part document consisting of a declaration on international investments and multinational enterprises, a set of guidelines for multinational enterprises, and three decisions regarding future governmental consultation.

Although the formal negotiations took place among representatives of the member states, extensive inputs were provided by business and labor groups not only through informal contacts with home country delegations but more directly through two specially accredited groups: the Business and Industry Advisory Committee (BIAC), and the Trade Union Advisory Committee (TUAC) (both of which prepared briefs and attended conferences with the negotiators). The two committees are composed of some of the most influential corporate and labor entities. (BIAC's American membership, for example, included representatives of Caterpillar Tractor, Eastman Kodak, E.I. duPont, and Exxon).

The result has been described by one close observer as a "heavily American-inspired balanced investment package."(18) It is indeed an attempt to balance the conflicting interests of the parties. Thus the preamble to the declaration starts by affirming that TNCs make positive contributions to economic and social progress, and that it is, therefore, in the common interest of the member governments to provide them with a liberal investment climate. Furthermore, the declaration states that even though the governments reserve the right to control foreign investment, they undertake to treat foreign controlled enterprises in a manner similar to national ones. And finally, although guidelines for business conduct are attached to the declaration, these are merely recommendations within the framework of this nondiscriminatory, liberal investment environment.

In short, great care was exercised to make the guidelines palatable to the firms. Nonetheless, the guidelines are the core of the package and do attempt to construct a framework for TNC business practices. Specifically:

1. TNCs should have due regard for the social and economic goals and priorities of host countries, e.g., industrial and regional

development, environmental protection, employment, and technology transfer.

2. TNCs should permit "parts of their enterprises" to develop their national and international competitive advantages as much as possible given the requirements of specialization and good management.

3. In the appointment of managers to responsible positions, TNCs should not discriminate on the basis of nationality.

4. TNCs should undertake all efforts to encourage fair competition and avoid restrictive practices.

5. TNC's financial and commercial transactions, especially short-term foreign currency transactions, should consider the balance of payments and credit policies of host countries.

6. TNCs should provide nations with proper tax information and should avoid transfer pricing which departs from the "at arm's length" principle.

7. TNCs should encourage technology transfer and licensing under reasonable terms and conditions, with due regard to patent protection.

8. Within the legal framework and prevailing labor-management relations in each host country, TNCs should respect the rights of workers to unionize, should bargain collectively, should provide sufficient information on the situation of their subsidiaries to enable unions to negotiate intelligently, should pay wages no lower than prevailing rates in comparable domestic firms, and should inform unions of all planned activities that could have major consequences for the workers, especially the closing of parts of the enterprise or mass discharges.(19)

9. TNCs should, with due regard to business confidentiality, provide governments with information on the structure, activities, and policies of the entire firm as a supplement to information about subsidiaries required by the laws of individual countries. They should publish, at least annually, data on the home and location of the parent companies and its affiliates; the geographic areas where they operate; and the capital investment, sales, and operating results in these areas.

10. TNCs should refrain from bribing or improperly influencing public officials, should not engage in improper political activities, and, except where permitted by law, should not make contributions to political parties or other political organizations.

Since the guidelines are, at this stage, merely recommendations by governments to TNCs, minimal provisions for enforcement were formulated. In fact the package provides only for intergovernmental consultations about the guidelines, and permits the OECD's Committee on International Investment and Multinational Enterprises to review specific issues of particular concern to specific enterprises, at which time those enterprises may be allowed to express their views if they wish to do so.

Even this brief description of the OECD package shows that it contains a number of ambiguities and can by no stretch of the imagination be considered a tough regulatory mechanism. Some of the weakness and ambiguity must be attributed to the conflicting positions of the member states, and in particular the desire of the United States to protect its foreign investment on the one hand, and the desire of certain European countries (e.g., Sweden) to control the operations of TNCs on the other. A few examples will suffice.

On the issue of enforcement, the United States strenuously objected to a draft provision which <u>invited</u> individual TNCs to discuss matters affecting them, arguing that such an invitation would be tantamount to pressure. The result was the weak wording cited above. As Gerald Parsky (Assistant Secretary of the Treasury for International Affairs) put it, "we don't want any international legal structure, each nation should deal with any alleged misdeeds of its own corporations."(20)

Similarly on the question of binding versus voluntary guidelines, while Sweden and the Netherlands felt that moral persuasion is so ambiguous as to become inoperative, the United States felt that domestic and international business transactions are so closely tied that they are not conducive to international rule-making. Again the United States view prevailed.

Regarding the type of information TNCs should disclose to governments and the public, the United States favored minimum disclosure on geographical lines, arguing that this would unnecessarily hamper corporate operations, whereas the European countries wanted country-by-country financial statements. A peculiar compromise was finally reached with the main body of the guidelines calling for "geographical area" breakdowns, but a footnote stating that the term "means groups of countries or individual countries as each enterprise determines is appropriate in its particular circumstances."(21)

On the issue of bribery, however, the United States, under the pressure of the indignant publicity given to the practices of some major corporations (e.g., Lockheed), called for tougher provisions than the other members who were not as vulnerable at that time. The result was the rather weak provision listed above.

In addition to these politically induced weaknesses, there is a serious problem stemming from the code's lack of a clear definition of what constitutes a "multinational enterprise." Thus it is by no means clear which provisions apply to which legal entities. For example, the recommendation that "parts of enterprises" (subsidiaries?) be given sufficient autonomy to expand their domestic and foreign markets, is virtually meaningless unless the legal and structural relationships among components of TNCs are clearly understood.

In spite of these shortcomings, the OECD package was received with general approval. Ambassador Turner (United States representative to (OECD) called it "an important step in international cooperation" and "a major accomplishment."(22) The other governments seemed at least satisfied. Officials of transnational corporations (American and European) in press releases, public statements, and interviews expressed very few misgivings about the OECD guidelines, admitting that they were quite fairly treated and usually adding that their company has always lived up to all these standards and more. International labor was, of course, considerably less enthusiastic, but even its spokesmen felt that the guidelines were a beginning. And early in 1977 TUAC began to present to the IME committee a number of cases where TNCs apparently infringed the labor-related guidelines. International labor's hope is that these guidelines will be a "first step towards a more far-reaching, global agreement of a legally binding nature."(23)

THE PROSPECTS FOR INTERNATIONAL REGULATION

We have seen that there is a broadly shared "felt need" for the harmonization of TNCs' activities and national goals and policies, and that the OECD has taken a step in that direction. But it can hardly qualify as a giant step. It must be noted that the OECD started with a number of advantages. Its 24 members contain all the major industrialized market economies in the world with long experience in international trade and investment. They are the home countries of virtually all the large TNCs, and they host most of their activities (perhaps as much as 70 percent of global direct investment). Therefore, they are the most likely countervailing power to the TNCs. Yet all they achieved so far is a series of voluntary guidelines that are vague, ambiguous, and far from inclusive – a result of serious differences which could only be resolved by compromising to the lowest common denominator. If we consider that the formulation of a global code would require the participation of socialist and developing countries, we see that the difficulties will obviously multiply and thus the outlook becomes gloomy indeed.

These difficulties are not simply the result of the tendency of each nation to pursue its selfish interests (protect its TNCs) and its reluctance to give up any part of its sovereignty (exclude foreign influence). They flow primarily, I believe, from certain differences in the structural characteristics of the parties, in the interactions between them, and in a broader sense, from the discontinuities (to use Oran Young's term) between the economic and political dimensions of the global system.

The well-known differences among nations in ideology, social structure, economic system, and political organization have led to a wide range of relationships between them and TNCs. In home countries we find the following continuum: state ownership – e.g., certain European airlines; state participation – e.g., the British and French automobile industries; state coordination – e.g., the close consultation and even joint planning between German and Japanese firms and their governments; and state regulation (albeit usually supportive) – e.g., in the United States.

In host countries, on the other hand, we find an equally broad range of policies toward TNCs: "open door" – major financial inducements to foreign investors and minimal regulation (e.g., Israel, the Philippines, Germany); moderate regulation – short-term financial inducements, local participation quotas, exclusion from certain sectors (e.g., Saudi

Arabia, Iran, U.K.); <u>strict regulation</u> – limited or no financial inducements, prior authorization, majority participation (e.g., India, Mexico, Canada); and <u>virtual exclusion</u> – licensing agreement, joint ventures, control of operations (e.g., USSR).

It is not hard to see that such fundamental differences in policy attitudes and structural relationships make it extremely difficult to achieve interstate consensus. But above and beyond such political differences, there are also major variations in the nature of the contributions that TNCs make in different countries. The issue here is not merely number, size, and profitability, but the role the TNCs play in various economies.

For home countries it makes a difference whether the firm makes a direct or indirect contribution to its economy. The United States and Switzerland are both strong defenders of their TNCs, and yet it is clear that their interests do not totally coincide, because while Swiss-based firms have always had most of their operations abroad, American-based ones have a very large domestic component (few are more than 50 percent foreign). The potential impact on the home economy of transnational resource shifts is thus much greater in the United States case.

For host countries the issue again is not simply the size of the investment, although for developing countries this is, of course, enormously important. It is, rather, the degree to which the TNCs' operations are integrated into the national economy. In the developed countries (the United States and Western Europe), subsidiaries of TNCs are readily absorbed; are often staffed by local nationals (even at the top management level); and (particularly when they adopt local names) are hard to distinguish from domestic firms in the same sector. Occasional conflicts with host governments do arise, but it is generally difficult to attribute them to the firms' transnationality. In the underdeveloped host countries the situation is radically different. Here the subsidiaries usually stick out as symbols of foreign intrusion, often dominate the most advanced industrial sectors, employ foreign managers, introduce divisions into the labor force, and pose serious problems for governmental economic planning. In short, they are not integrated, and even if the government pursues an "open door" policy and wants the benefits of foreign investment, it must handle its relations with the TNC in special ways.

Even if the conflicts of interest attributable to these differences in the relationships between nations and firms could, by some miracle, be reconciled, there still remains the issue of the diversity of the TNC. The problem of defining a "multinational corporation" has stumped executives, public officials, and scholars alike. The OECD guidelines go so far as to say that a precise legal definition is not necessary, and then proceed to define a multinational enterprise as one consisting of companies or other units in private, public, or mixed ownership which operate in different countries, and are linked to each other in such a way that one or more of the parts can influence the others, and in particular that they can jointly dispose of knowledge and resources. They go on to say that the relationships among the parts vary widely by company and area of activity, and that the guidelines, therefore, apply to all parts of the enterprise according to the actual distribution of responsibility.

The confusion in the preceding paragraph underlines my point. There is no good functional definition of a TNC, because we are discussing a universe of very different entities. The modern corporation is above all adaptive, and TNCs have adapted their structures, management styles, and operations to the needs of the enterprise and to the requirements of their environment. Thus we find firms which are vertically integrated (the oil companies), and others which concentrate their activities at one level (automobile firms). There are firms with a narrow product line (Caterpillar Tractor), and others with hundreds of products (Nestlé). Most TNCs stay within a single industrial sector, but some are giant conglomerates with operations in many manufacturing and service industries.

The diversity of activities has produced a no less diverse panoply of corporate structures and management styles. There are highly integrated, hierarchical firms which pride themselves on the uniformity of their operations (Caterpillar's Belgian factory is indistinguishable from its Illinois plant), and others which allow subsidiaries maximum autonomy (the extreme case, perhaps, is the oil companies' assertion that they can do nothing about the behavior of their Rhodesian subsidiaries). Some TNCs are geographically organized, some by product line, and some by function (marketing, manufacturing, financing), with various permutations and combinations also found.

True, there are some elements common to all TNCs. They have production or service facilities in several countries; they shift resources across borders; and central management almost invariably reserves the right to make all the major decisions regarding top-level staffing, major investments and acquisitions, and major product changes. Nevertheless, this is a very limited degree of uniformity, and on such a high level of abstraction, that it makes the formulation of a single, meaningful set of guidelines, not to mention a single effective regulatory mechanism, impossible to conceive.

CONCLUSION

In a recent paper, Werner Feld concluded his analysis of the beginnings of UN involvement in the issue of transnational corporations with the following remarks: "Only a balanced set of rules taking into consideration the legitimate interests, traditional practices, and natural spheres of responsibility of MNE's and governments will produce beneficial results and make United Nations involvement a productive enterprise."(24)

As the foregoing discussion shows, it is necessary to regard even such a carefully worded and circumscribed assessment with great skepticism. Given the great diversity within each of the two sets of actors (nations and firms); the radical differences between them in structural characteristics, objectives, and modus operandi; and the complex and varied relationships of interdependence that they have formed; is it possible to formulate any set of rules that would be acceptable to the parties and produce "beneficial results," i.e. be effective?

The conceptual difficulties which such an enterprise would entail are compounded by the state of our knowledge about TNCs and their relations to nations. Although there is by now a truly vast literature on foreign investment and on "multinational corporations," it, unfortunately, does not contain a solid base of integrated data. Studies on foreign investment are usually based on statistics aggregated to the national or regional level (i.e., flows among nations or groups of nations) and do not provide systematic data on the impact of individual (or even groups of) TNCs. Systematic studies of TNCs, on the other hand, usually focus on their structures or management styles, and rarely touch on their relations with governments. The few studies that do tackle this dimension tend to be case studies of specific TNCs in single countries, or histories of a single firm. Similarly, our knowledge of national attempts to regulate TNCs is still episodic and impressionistic. The UN Centre on Transnational Corporations is attempting to remedy these deficiencies, but is far from having an adequate collection of systematic information.

In spite of all these recognized difficulties and deficiencies, the United Nations is forging ahead in its endeavor to formulate a code of conduct for TNCs. Even if we accept the idea that such an instrument need not codify accepted international rules and practices, but can embody an international consensus on desirable rules and practices, it seems evident that only the most general exhortations are likely to be included. They would culminate in a code that is even less specific than the OECD guidelines, urging upon the TNCs such unexceptionable behavior as due regard for national sovereignty, aspirations, and socioeconomic policies; fair competition; good citizenship; abstinence from political influence peddling and corrupt practices; and maximum disclosure of information.

As for the creation of an effective regulatory mechanism, it is instructive that the UN's document on material relevant to a code, which merely lists a large variety of possibilities without choosing among them, does contain one strong assertion: "Legal regulation of (TNC) activities is most effective when carried out through national legal procedure."(25) If that is a generally held view in national governments, and chances are that it is, the prospect for an international regime seems very remote. Indeed, it is hard to find supporters for a regulatory regime among the major actors, since all of them, quite naturally, want to maintain a maximum degree of freedom of action. Specifically, developing countries would be reluctant to surrender their potential power to control guest TNCs; socialist countries have never been favorably disposed to international regulation; and developed countries would certainly object to any regulatory mechanism that could put them under the control of countries other than themselves.(26) TNCs, on their part as we have seen, would prefer self-regulation through their own codes, and even unions would object to an agency that could bind them.(27)

For the foreseeable future, the controls on TNC activities will continue to consist of a complex and haphazard mélange of company rules, national regulations, and narrow international agreements (e.g., bilateral tax treaties). Only as our knowledge about the phenomena we have discussed grows, can we expect to find areas of sufficient consensus for broader international regulation. The chances for specific regulatory conventions regarding bribery, technology transfer, and disclosure of information – all of which are being discussed in various forums – are far better, and deserve greater attention than a universal, multipurpose code which, like the Universal Declaration of Human Rights, will at best be a summary of worthy aspirations to be realized in the distant future, and not an enforceable code of proper contemporary behavior.(28)

NOTES

(1) It is impossible to present even a tiny fraction of this literature here. An indication of its scope can be found in the 450-page Multinational Corporations: The E.C.S.I.M. Guide to Information Sources, Joseph O. Mekeirle, ed. (Brussels: European Centre for Study and Information on Multinational Corporations, 1977).

(2) In this paper attention will be focused on the large TNCs, primarily those on the Fortune lists of leading corporations. Not only do these firms control the bulk of international production, but, furthermore, they are the ones at whom the regulatory efforts are directed.

(3) New York Times, November 16, 1977, p. 51.

(4) P.G. Bock, "The Transnational Corporation and Private Foreign Policy: The Case of ITT and Chile," Society, January/February 1974.

(5) S. Cronjé, et al., Lonrho: Portrait of a Multinational (London: Penguin, 1976).

(6) Charles T. Goodsell, American Corporations and Peruvian Politics, (Cambridge, Mass: Harvard University Press, 1974).

(7) See Bock, "Transnational Corporations."

(8) For a more detailed analysis of these challenges, see P.G. Bock and V.J. Fuccillo, "The Transnational Corporation as an International Political Actor," Studies in Comparative International Development, vol. X (Summer 1975), 51-77.

(9) Financial Times (London), October 30, 1975; see also Maurice Williams, "Development Cooperation," DAC-Review, OECD, Paris, 1975.

(10) Andrew M. Scott, "The Logic of International Interaction,"

International Studies Quarterly, vol. 21 (September 1977), 429-60.

(11) For the sake of brevity, the labor position will not be extensively treated in this paper. However, see the excellent summary in Carl Wilms-Wright, Transnational Corporations: A Strategy for Control (London: Fabian Society, Fabian Research Series 334, September 1977), and the seminal work of Ernst Piehl, Multinationale Konzerne und internationale Gewerkschaftsbewegung (Frankfurt: Europäische Verlagsanstalt, 1974).

(12) See, for example, the various publications of the International Management and Development Institute, Washington, D.C.

(13) United Nations, Centre on Transnational Corporations, Transnational Corporations: Materials Relevant to the Formulation of A Code of Conduct (United Nations E/C.10/18, 10 December 1976), pp. 29-30.

(14) United Nations, Transnational Corporations, p. 31.

(15) Wilms-Wright, Transnational Corporations, p. 22.

(16) For an example of a highly structured control system, see Anthony Sampson, The Sovereign State of ITT (New York: Stein & Day, 1973).

(17) William C. Turner, "Multinationals and the OECD," International Herald Tribune, June 30, 1976, p. 6.

(18) Henri Schwamm, "The OECD Code for Multinational Enterprises," mimeo, September 28, 1976, p. 2.

(19) The section on employment contains the most detailed guidelines, a clear indication of the desire to "balance" labor interests and the influence of TUAC.

(20) New York Times, April 17, 1976, p. 29.

(21) Schwamm, "OECD Code," p. 5.

(22) Turner, "Multinationals and the OECD."

(23) Wilms-Wright, Transnational Corporations, p. 31; see also International Confederation of Free Trade Unions, Multinational Charter (Brussels: ICFTU, 1975) and Free Labour World, July-August 1976, pp. 18-19.

(24) Werner J. Feld, "U.N. Supervision over Multinational Corporations: Realistic Expectation or Exercise in Futility" (Paper presented at ISA Annual Meeting, February 25-29, 1976), p. 28.

(25) United Nations, Centre on Transnational Corporations, Transnational Corporations, p. 85.

(26) Rainer Hellman, <u>Kontrolle der multinationalen Unternehmen</u> (Baden-Baden: Nomos Verlag, 1974).

(27) Piehl, <u>Multinationale Konzerne</u>, p. 287.

(28) For a somewhat more optimistic prognosis, see Henri Schwamm and Dimitri Germidis, <u>Codes of Conduct for Multinational Companies: Issues and Positions</u> (Brussels: E.C.S.I.M., 1977).

4 The Transnationalization of Domestic Policy: Social Security in Western Europe and the United States*

Richard L. Siegel

This is a study of the continuing transformation of a sphere of social policy from a "state's rights" preserve of national sovereignty to an internationalized issue area. The coice of social security policy as the focus of this study is based primarily on the centrality of such programs as health, unemployment, employment injury, old age, survivor's, and invalidity insurance, family allowances, and public assistance in the social policies of most industrialized countries. Additionally, social security policies, with long and well-documented histories, have been identified as a major area of program and public expenditure variation between the United States and most Western European nations.(1)

The central questions of this study involve the evolution and manifestations of domestic and international influence, jurisdiction, and control. Is social security still essentially a domestic, state's rights policy area? Which aspects of social security have been transformed by the broad sweep of transnational and multinational relations?(2) Which transnational forces have contributed most to such transformations of social security and related social policy which have occurred? What differences exist in the way in which social security has been affected by such forces in Western Europe and the United States?

The focus on Western Europe and the United States provides an opportunity to compare such processes in two settings. Arnold Heidenheimer, Anthony King, and others have drawn attention to major variations in Western European and United States approaches to education and social insurance in terms of public expenditures, scope of services, and the underlying values reflected in the programs.(3) The American emphasis on expanding opportunity through education and its grudging and slow development of social insurance contrasts with

---

*A version of this article was presented at the Annual Meeting of the International Studies Association, Washington, D.C., February 22-25, 1978.

relatively elitist and less flexible educational systems as well as more advanced social insurance and other social protection programs in most of Western Europe.

A "great debate" in comparative social policy has focused on whether domestic political factors have had an independent impact on policy outcomes or have merely served as conduits for such socio-economic variables as income and urbanization. We ask here whether the external factor of transnational and transgovernmental relations may be a relatively neglected one. Could the differences between Western Europe and North America in their exposure to such processes have contributed to and presently be contributing much to social policy variations?

TRANSNATIONAL RELATIONS, INTERDEPENDENCE, AND REGIMES

In his analysis of foreign policy-making in Britain, William Wallace concludes that "foreign policy has ceased to be a discreet field, separated from domestic politics both in the nature of the issues and the management of policy."(4) The merging of domestic and foreign policy has now become a major theme of observers of world affairs. Yet how deep and broad is this merger? It remains to be determined what portion of domestic policy belongs to foreign policy and world politics. Are transnationalization and multinationalization of domestic policy limited to particular categories of policy that have the most obvious linkages to global economic, military, and environmental relationships?

Initial post-1945 international regimes were shaped in such areas as regional security and international economic interdependence. These goals were to be fostered by such organizations as the United Nations, the International Monetary Fund, the International Bank for Reconstruction and Development (World Bank), the General Agreement for Tariffs and Trade (GATT), and such alliance structures as the North Atlantic Treaty Organization (NATO).

Other sets of international agencies emerged for the promotion of necessary international cooperation in a host of other areas. Regimes were shaped and are being reshaped around spatial-physical dimensions (Antarctica, outer space, oceans), technical developments (nuclear energy, space satellites), particular resources (energy, food), and new offshoots of policy areas given priority earlier (economic development, multinational corporations).(5) Regime characteristics for the most obviously transnational of policy areas have been dissected and advice concerning the further evolution of such regimes has been offered from the various viewpoints of national governments,(6) international organizations,(7) and avowed advocates of mankind as a whole.(8)

The concept of international regime has rarely been applied to substantial aspects of social policy, except in relation to the programs of particular international organizations.(9) Yet key elements of the paradigms and models of regime analysis regarding such spheres as oceans, outer space, weather, and money are clearly adaptable to multinational social policy regimes.

For Keohane and Nye, regimes are "the more or less loose set of formal and informal norms, rules, and procedures relevant to the system."(10) For Ruggie and Haas, they are "international arrangements for jointly managing a resource," serving such functions as "problem search and definition," "harmonization/standardization of national responses," "defining property rights," and "collective elaborations of welfare choices."(11)

Each of Ruggie and Haas's functions are theoretically compatible with actual or potential social policy regimes. One of the constraints on the internationalization of social policy has been the reluctance of authorities to recognize underdeveloped human capabilities as resources or social rights as property rights. Yet such recognition is growing and the determination to protect social rights as well or better than physical resources and economic systems could well follow.

Other works have emphasized the choice of organizing policy regimes on a global and/or regional basis and in relation to socioeconomic affinity. Social security is a policy area that is highly dependent on levels of national income and involves considerable responsiveness to regional models. A global regime for social security can exist only in a skeletal form. The potentialities for harmonization, standardization, and "collective elaborations" of social security programs are greatest in advanced industrial states and, especially, in Europe.

Joseph Nye's "law of inverse salience" suggests that:

. . . the less important the task politically, either because of its technical nature or limited impact, the greater the prospects for the growth of the (international) organization's authority vis-à-vis the member states. Conversely, the more important the task by nature or impact, the weaker the authority of the organization will be.(12)

Yet the establishment of international regimes and the form of such regimes appears to have less to do with political salience than suitability for multinational management.(13) Most aspects of social policy lack certain attributes that have pulled other policy areas toward multinational control. The most obvious candidates for multinational regimes tend to involve one or more of the following factors: a lack of clear national jurisdiction; a need for international cooperation in the deployment of technology to make possible effective development of resources; and direct association with aspects of economic integration or the pursuit of expanded international economic relations. In contrast with the policy areas that appear most ripe for multinational management, in most areas of social policy the legitimacy of multinational management is not fully established and both public and governmental support for creation of international regimes are limited.

Despite such differences in apparent suitability for multinational management, the two categories are not in practice as wide apart as might be suspected. Most international policy regimes that have been discussed as natural ones have not developed as broadly (scope) or as far in relation to extra-national authority (level) as could be expected. Correspondingly, social policy has not been as much of a state's rights enclave as our original dichotomy suggests.

Various barriers to regime development affect obvious candidates for international regimes. Space satellite and weather modification regimes are responses to relatively recent technical developments. Critical national interests may be at stake (e.g., oceans and money) and initial control by one or a few states may have to be overcome before effective alternative arrangements are established (e.g., nuclear energy and telecommunications). The politics of regime creation and modification must also overcome the barriers of conflicting domestic interests in major states and the quagmires of intentional linkage of policy issues (as energy and military security). Such supportive forces as the expansionism of international bureaucracies, the dynamism of political and economic integration processes, and the demands of the increasingly numerous and united Third World states have all failed to overcome fully the fundamental problems of moving beyond national sovereignty and the power of the rich and strong.

Correspondingly, various aspects of social policy have been affected by many transnational, transgovernmental, and intergovernmental influences. Such factors have contributed to the tendencies of Western European states to develop increasingly similar social insurance systems in the present century and to promote reciprocity in regard to eligibility of nationals of other states. The involvement of the United States in such processes has tended to be less extensive and more negative in character. This has contributed to a situation in which American social insurance has been less developed in most aspects, including coverage, benefits, and reciprocity, than that of most of Western Europe.

Examining social security systems of the early 1970s, Kaim-Caudle found that culturally and geographically linked pairs of European nations had markedly similar social security programs in relation to expenditures, standards of benefits, organization, and other provisions.(14) In contrast, that study revealed few similarities in the specific features of the United States and Canadian social security systems while confirming continuing differences in the American and Western European approaches.(15)

The question remains as to the contributions of various kinds of international interactions to such variations. William Wallace has asserted that "The Atlantic system, overlapping, interacting, and conflicting as it does with the still-primitive and underdeveloped political system of Western Europe, is as yet still more primitive."(16) It is the comparison between Atlantic and European relations that is at the heart of any analysis of the internationalization of social insurance in Western Europe and the United States.

TRANSNATIONAL INFLUENCES ON SOCIAL SECURITY

Transnational interactions have been defined as flows of nongovernmental contacts, influence, and movements across national lines.(17) Such relations have been measured in terms of investments, communications, trade, and prices.(18) Various writers have analyzed "transnational organizations" – corporations, churches, revolutionary groups, and others – that pursue their own interests and perform specialized functions across national boundaries.(19)

How broad and intensive is the transnationalization of such a social policy area as social security? The development of an internationalized social security regime can be expected to be related to flows of people and resources across national lines. The present investigation suggests that growing transnational movements of workers and multinational enterprise as well as the development of transnational organizational ties among academics, trade unionists, employers, and social service providers contributed to the internationalization of social security. However, these factors rarely influenced social security in simple or direct ways. The orientations – geographical and ideological – of relevant organizations were often in conflict and quantitative indicators of interactions often underestimate or overestimate actual impacts.

Transnational Social Science

The first transnational organizations influencing social security centered on politically oriented academics. In the first decade of this century the International Association for Labor Legislation (IALL) and International Unemployment Association were among the spearheads of efforts to promote the still new concept. The United States affiliate of the IALL, the American Association for Labor Legislation, was strongly influenced by political scientists and both academic and nonacademic economists.(20) No organization contributed more to the early stages of the difficult struggle to establish social insurance in the United States.

Individual and group ties between academics and national governments expanded considerably in much of Western Europe as well as in the United States throughout this century. Particularly strong ties were formed between the emerging British "social administration" discipline and that country's governmental developers of the welfare state. With reputations for somewhat greater objectivity than labor or management advocates, academic views have often been far more influential than other indicators of group power would suggest.

The International Social Security Association (ISSA) and International Society for Labor Law and Social Security serve as vehicles for the continuation of organized research, discussions, and limited advocacy by jurists, scholars, and program administrators. Closely linked to the International Labor Organization, ISSA serves as a leading forum for international exchange of information and ideas regarding social security through its International Social Security Review and other formats.

Foreign Workers and Immigrants

Exchanges of European workers stimulated international agreements on reciprocity, harmonization, and standardization beginning in 1904. The impact of such flows on social security has clearly been greater in Western Europe than in the United States. The nine states of the European Communities utilized legal foreign workers (including nationals of other Community nations) as more than 8 percent of their civilian employees at the post-1945 peak of this flow in 1973.(21) More than one-fourth of these employees were from other Community nations or Scandinavia, these being potential transmitters of high social security standards.(22) Italy, the major Community export of labor, has had a well-developed social security system for several decades.

As compared to most of Western Europe, the United States has a much stronger tradition of receiving flows of foreign workers through immigration. More than 35 million Europeans have immigrated to the United States since 1820 and the countries that pioneered in the development of social insurance have always been strongly represented in these movements. Yet pre-1935 immigration was not a strong stimulus to American social security development due to factors involving both the immigrants and their adopted nation. First, massive immigration largely preceded the development of comprehensive social insurance in Western Europe. Second, the early American labor movement, with much of its leadership from immigrant groups, was ambivalent and often negative to social security initiatives.(23) Later generations of immigrants and descendants of recent immigrants did, however, provide crucial support for social security in the 1930s and after. Yet they had to contend with the continuing impacts of the absence of a tradition of state social protection, the reality of weak state bureaucracies, the lack of public support for values and programs in this sphere, and the power of employers and private service providers.(24)

Post-1945 immigration was modest by the standards of the first quarter of this century and the United States was quite sparing in its acceptance of nonimmigrant "temporary workers."(25) Legal and illegal movements from Mexico and other nonEuropean regions increasingly dominated the intake. Yet further exploration is needed of the effects of American social security on significant flows of immigrants from such countries as Germany, Italy, and Great Britain between 1945 and 1965.(26) These movements blended into a markedly increased American labor force and came at a time of sharply rising prosperity and the general acceptance of social security in the United States.   Such persons had far less opportunity to achieve positions of authority than their predecessors. Yet they came from increasingly more complete welfare states and could have been expected to bring some new orientations to a parochial America. The 1945 to 1965 period was one of progress in American social security, but also one in which U.S. programs fell increasingly behind those of the rapidly developing European welfare states.

In response to the difficult economic times of the mid-1970s, alien workers became increasingly unpopular in most of Western Europe as well as the United States and active measures to discourage such flows were combined with deportation in both areas. Yet the limited social protection of aliens in the United States continued to contrast with Western European efforts to include such workers in existing social security schemes and develop additional programs for their benefit. National and regional European trade union and social service associations have contributed substantially to the development of such benefits while also supporting reduced intake of foreign workers in response to rising unemployment.

Multinational Enterprises

The growth of multinational enterprise promises more for the future development of an international regime for social security than it has contributed in the past. The activities of these enterprises have been directly responsible for major policy changes throughout the developed world in such areas as taxation, exchange controls, employment, regional development, and counterinflationary efforts.(27) Yet by all indications the influence of the multinationals on social security in developed countries has been less direct than in these other policy areas.

Certain recent changes in the flows of multinational business investments suggest that their effects on social security may increase in the foreseeable future. Although the European experience has been influenced much more by international industrial and financial cartels than by multinational enterprises in their contemporary form, direct investments by European companies in the United States exceeded those of U.S. companies in Europe until 1956.(28) Yet in 1974, U.S.-based multinationals had more than twice the investment in the nine member states of the European Communities than vice-versa.(29) European direct investment in the United States contributed less than 1 percent of annual "nonresidential gross private fixed investment" as late as the 1960s.(30) However, in 1974 this proportion had more than doubled. Although the overall level of multinational investment in the United States could still be termed "not of major significance" by the U.S. Department of Commerce in 1976,(31) data support the widespread awareness of the United States public of a sharp acceleration of this phenomenon in the mid-1970s.

The impacts of the multinationals on social security can be expected to vary in relation to the size, direction, and motivations of the flows. One expectation is that European multinationals, with their long experience with high social security tax contributions and the generous characteristics of European benefits, would not flinch at the development of such systems in the United States and other Western European countries. Yet, as pointed out in a recent study by the U.S. Department of Commerce, such enterprises may be coming to the United States in part to flee from more costly fringe benefits imposed by European governments and trade unions.(32)

The proposition that the growth of European-based multinationals would promote higher standards of social security in the European Communities area could not be tested effectively until quite recently because almost half of direct foreign investment in the Communities' states was United States-based during the first fifteen years of the EEC.(33) However, the position of the American-based multinationals in the nine Communities' nations declined relative to other countries' enterprises in the mid-1970s and greater attention is being given in that region to the advent of European multinationals.(34) Unlike the present situation in the United States, much of Western Europe appears ready to utilize intergovernmental auspices to expand and harmonize at least some social benefits in response to the expansion of multinational enterprise.(35)

Because such pressures include widespread support for worker participation in industrial management and other fundamental alterations of industrial policy, the multinationals and national employer associations are increasingly defending their interests at an international level through such channels as the International Chamber of Commerce, the International Organization of Employers, and the Union of Industries of the European Community. These channels have proven invaluable to these enterprises in the current era of intensive scrutiny and rule-making concerning multinationals by such intergovernmental organizations as the Organization for Economic Cooperation and Development (OECD), the United Nations, and the European Communities. International employer associations are integrated into the policy-making processes of these and other intergovernmental organizations.(36)

International Trade Unionism

Long before the post-1945 expansion of multinational enterprises, trade unions were playing major roles at the national and international level to improve social security systems. Activity at the international level is evident from labor's contribution to numerous International Labor Organization conventions and resolutions concerning social security beginning with that body's founding conference in 1919. However, wars, democratic-fascist divisions, and subsequent cold war struggles sharply restricted the effectiveness of international trade unionism ever since the first general trade union International, the International Federation of Trade Unions, was established in 1913.

The present structure of trade union Internationals includes three major bodies: the "free world" International Confederation of Free Trade Unions (ICFTU), the Communist-directed World Federation of Trade Unions (WFTU), and the Christian-oriented World Confederation of Labour (WCL). The two major organizations were formed in 1945 (WCTU) and 1949 (ICFTU), respectively, and have been embroiled in constant political struggles that have minimized their effectiveness as catalysts for improvements in working conditions. Notably, the dominant United States national labor federation, the AFL-CIO, withdrew from the WFTU in 1949 and the ICFTU in 1969. As such, United States interests are no longer effectively expressed through these channels and these organizations are unable to influence United States approaches to social security. American unions remain active in industry-based international trade secretariats that have recently developed considerable dynamism in response to the accelerated growth of multinational enterprises.(37) The United States-based United Automobile Workers pioneered efforts to achieve wage parity and uniform working conditions on both sides of the United States-Canadian border.(38) However, such efforts have focused on traditional areas of collective bargaining rather than social security.

Western European unions remain affiliated with each of the international confederations and various international trade secretariats. Such associations have made significant efforts to influence social security policies in Europe in recent decades. For example, the May 1976 European Automobile Conference sponsored by the International Metal Workers' Federation demanded increased social security benefits for laid-off automobile workers.(39)

Western European unions are now developing new transnational organizations that promise to have even greater influence on social security than the more established structures. The European Trade Union Confederation (EFTC) represents more diverse unions than any other in Europe and has taken the lead for labor in discussions within the European Communities' institutions and in wider contexts. At its April 1976 Congress, the EFTC called on all Western European governments to extend the duration of unemployment benefits to the longest period then existing in Europe.(40) The EFTC has also supported a series of "tripartite" conferences on employment that have dealt with social security issues in the context of broader discussions of the developing recession. Social security also had a central place in a series of conferences of European and Mahgreb trade unions. The May 1976 Third Conference called for new bilateral and multilateral agreements in social security for foreign and migrant workers "so as to assure equality in law and in fact" and also promoted additional compliance and more effective implementation of ILO and European Communities' actions in this area.(41)

Western European transnational trade unionism is functioning in an institutional context that is also promoting ties among European social workers, academics, political parties, farmers, students, and many other groups. In the majority of cases these linkages function without substantial United States group participation.

Conclusions: Transnational Flows and Organizations

It appears that transnational flows and organizations have grown in actual and, especially, potential impact on international social security regimes since the launching in 1906 of the International Association for Labor Legislation. In the early decades of social insurance, relatively small organizations and informal groups of academics, trade unionists, or service providers had major impacts on national policies and encouraged essential international coordination. Today the Western European trade union movement, responding to unprecedented flows of foreign workers, multinational investment, and opportunities to influence national policies through intergovernmental organizations, is organizing considerable power regarding aspects of social security, other social protection issues, and broader issues of participation and co-determination. Many of the most significant movements are essentially internal to Western Europe and exclude the involvement of American groups and organizations. Yet the United States can expect some impact on its social benefit structure from both rapidly expanding European multinationals and the strong role of American unions in industry-based international trade union organizations.

BILATERAL RELATIONS AND SOCIAL SECURITY

As in most policy areas, bilateral intergovernmental contacts regarding social security preceded multilateral ones and those fostered by international organizations. Bilateral relations have involved both high level diplomacy leading to formal agreements and "transgovernmental" interactions among subunits of governments described by Nye and Keohane.(42)

James Rosenau's categories of penetrative, reactive, and emulative "linkage processes" offer a useful approach to bilateral relations.(43) In penetration, the stress is on participation by externally based actors (including, but not limited to, foreign governments) in the determination of critical choices by a given nation. Emulative processes are said to occur when policy makers copy or adopt elements of policy demonstrated in another country. Reactive processes can be observed when developments in one nation prompt a policy response in another.

Various problems emerge in distinguishing these processes. When penetration exists, as in a situation of military occupation, infiltration of civilian bureaucracies, or electoral interference, no neat line can be drawn between emulation and penetration. Further, penetration is usually disguised by both the penetrated and penetrating regimes. Even emulation that is fully or largely free of penetrative influence is often disguised by governments that prefer to exaggerate their own originality.

The numerous bilateral social security agreements have been products of both emulative and reactive processes. While primarily reactive responses to particular flows of migrants, they have also been instruments for emulating favorable aspects of policy in the more progressive signatory states. The first intergovernmental social security agreements, signed in 1904 by France and Italy, provided for reciprocal payment of certain workmen's compensation and employment injury pensions.(44) Germany and Italy initiated aspects of old-age pension coordination in a 1912 convention. During the interwar period, bilateral social security agreements gradually became more detailed and inclusive.(45) With the encouragement of intergovernmental organizations,

Western Europe led the way in a new flurry of post-1945 bilateral agreements that reflected still higher standards.(46)

Bilateral agreements have contributed much to the principle that benefits should be tied to the person regardless of the location of work or residence. Yet they are less likely than multilateral instruments to extend broad principles or utilize effective enforcement machinery.(47) Commitments are usually extended to only one other country and can be tailored to weaknesses in the programs of either signatory.

Of greater significance in the pre-1914 era were efforts at informal emulation. Visits, studies, and other contacts proceeded from the 1880s at the civil service, ministerial, and parliamentary levels. Studies of the German experience contributed significantly to the development of the Swedish and British programs in the decades following the 1883 initiation of German social insurance.(48) In turn, Sweden and Britain were "among the first innovators in what became known as a worldwide diffusion of social programs."(49) Intra-Scandinavian governmental cooperation in social insurance was making significant progress by the first decade of the present century. Between 1900 and 1914 Swedish, Danish, and Norwegian officials and private experts were holding regular meetings in regard to such areas of social protection as accident insurance, cooperating in management of unemployment funds, and developing procedures for "harmonized" social legislation.(50)

Bilateral agreements and emulation have continued to develop in Europe up to the present time. Governments continue to recognize the need to study other nations' experiences with social protection programs. The social security area has been infused with numerous new "schemes" that were experimented with in one or a few countries, lauded as international innovations, and ultimately superseded by still newer approaches. Proximity and cultural affinities clearly contributed to the communication of information about programs and the formulation of comparable demands for new programs and improved standards in Northern and Western Europe. Common experience of war and a growing welfare ideological consensus among government bureaucrats, parliamentarians, trade unionists, academics, and even industrialists contributed to the acceleration of this positive emulation process in the 1950s and 1960s. At the close of the 1960s, Britain was sending more labor attaches.(51) Direct formal and informal contacts between social policy ministries became routine throughout most of the region, especially in Scandinavia and in such intensive relationships as the Anglo-German.(52) By 1960 such bilateral processes had contributed much to agreement among Western European states on the risks requiring insurance or grant protection and some of the goals to be achieved through eligibility and benefit schedules.(53) European trans-governmental cooperation set the stage for movement towards even more similar systems after 1960.

The involvement of the United States in such bilateral processes was remarkably slow to develop and was dominated by negative responses to most efforts at social security emulation. As early as the 1890s there was no dearth of studies of European social insurance by American academics and by both federal and state labor bureaus.(54) The competent nongovernmental studies of the American Association for Labor Legislation augmented these throughout the subsequent decades. Yet contrary information and propaganda from other groups such as physicians and manufacturers fed on and augmented mass xenophobia and value preferences that were incompatible with the social security movement. By the 1920s it was clear that associations with Europe were an albatross around any social insurance proposals in the United States.(55)

A turning point for greater American acceptance of foreign models may have been the inclusion of a reference to the role of social security in the Anglo-American Atlantic Charter of 1941.(56) Presidential leadership combined with the emergence of new federal social service bureaucracies to create new inclinations toward and capabilities for transgovernmental emulation in the postwar decades. The U.S. Departments of Labor and Health, Education, and Welfare (HEW), as well as Congress, developed substantial programs for research and publication concerning foreign developments in such fields as social security and health services.(57) Statistics on reported "international personnel" in various U.S. government departments reveal that HEW has recently been among the most "internationally involved" federal agencies as indicated by number of "international personnel," amount of overseas travel, overseas expenditure, and employees stationed abroad.(58) However, although HEW compares closely with the Treasury Department in terms of these indicators of transgovernmental involvement, it does not appear that this activity is focused on Europe and other developed regions.

The American legacy of negative transnational and transgovernmental relations has not disappeared in the present era of searching for appropriate new systems of health insurance, social security financing, and public assistance. The stumbling British welfare state continues to be painted with broad negative strokes while neither Canadian nor successful Northern European programs have been effectively brought into American public discussions. Nonetheless, the growing extent of organized research and North Atlantic transgovernmental and academic contact and study has already helped make United States policy development much more rational and objective in the 1970s regarding such issues as national health insurance.

Although not comparable to emulation in its impact, penetration also played a role in the development of social insurance. The rise of Nazism brought on an era of markedly increased penetration that reflected strong emphasis on social and cultural policies. Effective penetration was also exercised within Western Europe in the decade after 1945 through Allied occupations of Italy, Austria, and West Germany; the policies of the Marshall Plan administrators throughout the region; and the activities of foreign intelligence agencies and Communist party liaisons. Certain of these penetrative activities persist to this day, with adaptation of strategy and tactics, in much of Europe.(59) However, it is clear that penetration had much less of a positive impact on Western European social security than emulation did. German occupation forces had far greater priorities than social security. American official representatives helped to deflect much of Western Europe from expanded social benefits to investment in economic infrastructure and defense in the decade after World War II.(60) Finally, the formal and informal agreements that accompanied direct foreign loans to struggling European countries in the decades after World War II often involved restraints on Western European public expenditures generally and social benefit allocations in particular.

Taken together, bilateral relations were of great value in the earliest decades of social insurance and have continued to play an important role in the development of reciprocity and progressive expansion of social insurance in Europe and North America up to the present time. Penetrative processes were rarely as important as emulative ones and the United States was involved later and in a less professional manner in efforts to utilize the experience of foreign governments in this policy area. Bilateral relations increasingly came to be viewed as an inadequate basis for the development of the necessary levels of cooperation among Western European and North Atlantic nations or for the creation of a genuine international social security regime.

INTERGOVERNMENTAL ORGANIZATIONS AND SOCIAL SECURITY REGIMES

The national governments responsible for the previously discussed developments have also promoted numerous intergovernmental organizations that have had varied impacts on social security. The activities of such organizations as the International Labor Organization, Council of Europe, European Communities, Organization for Economic Cooperation and Development, and Nordic Council have done much to promote transnational flows of workers, investments, and organizations that have in turn stimulated international cooperation in social security. Their staffs have also contributed to the development of bilateral and multilateral cooperation outside of the organizations' settings. These agencies have ensured the continuing leadership of Western Europe in this policy area and have contributed to a distinctive Western European sub-regime while also influencing developments elsewhere. Further, such organizations have both extended and limited the international social security regime in functional terms.

The OECD, Council of Europe, Nordic Council, GATT, European Free Trade Association, and, especially, the European Communities have contributed from their inceptions to the free movement of labor and capital in their respective territorial spheres. Increased interdependence in the cause of economic and political integration has opened new opportunities for cooperation in social security and has made necessary some degree of harmonization in this policy area. Although no reliable data exists to indicate the precise contribution of these and other intergovernmental organizations to interdependence at the European or global levels, the post-1945 era of creation and expansion of such agencies has coincided with major expansions of worker migration, multinational investment, and other aspects of transnational relations. Further, despite major differences in their original orientations and goals, various specific actions of intergovernmental organizations can be linked directly to the expansions (and occasional contractions) of such flows. Free movement of labor has long been an explicit priority of the Nordic Council, other Scandinavian intergovernmental bodies, and the European Communities. Freer flow of capital is noted in the founding documents of such organizations as the OECD and the European Communities. New transnational organizations for employees, employers, farmers, social workers, and political parties have been organized by intergovernmental organizations or have been founded in response to their actual or anticipated power to shape international and national regimes.

Intergovernmental organizational concern for social protection may develop in several ways. In the cases of the European Communities, International Monetary Fund, and OECD, it was largely a by-product of the overwhelmingly economic concerns of the organization. They have each tended to view social security as a factor in the costs of production and trade, as a contributor to the stability of common labor markets, and as an increasingly important element of national macro-economic policies and restraints on public expenditures. Other organizations regard social security variously as an aspect of social justice (Council of Europe, ILO); a source of political support for broader programs of economic and political integration (European Communities); and as a suitable vehicle for cooperation short of integration (Council of Europe, Nordic Council, and Nordic Council of Ministers). A close look at each of these organizations suggests that most, regardless of their founding charters, combine economic with other motivations. For example, the Court of Justice of the European Communities, citing the founding documents of the Communities, stated in 1976 that it is "not merely an economic union, but is at the same time intended, by common action, to ensure social progress and seek the constant improvement of the living and working conditions of (the peoples of Europe)."(61)

The central role of Western Europe in the intergovernmental development of social security and the largely isolated position of the United States in this regard have undoubtedly contributed to disparities among North Atlantic states. Two of the three intergovernmental organizations that have contributed most to the development of social security in industrialized countries are European and have never included the United States (Council of Europe and European Communities). As to the third, the International Labor Organization, the United States government was absent in its early years (1919-34) and withdrew in 1977. For much of the period of its membership, American governmental, labor, and employer representatives constituted what Ernst Haas termed "a deviant client with respect to the ILO consensus."(62) Haas contended that the United States used efforts to combine Cold War advocacy through the ILO's human rights program with continuing support for the ILO social security program.(63) Yet from 1934 to 1976, the United States government ratified only 7 of 147 ILO conventions on all subjects and none of these dealt with social security to a major extent.(64) Washington helped install an American, David Morse, as postwar ILO Director-General and supported advancement of social security in the organization's important Philadelphia Declaration of 1944.(65) Yet its main thrust was in opposition to legislated international labor standards.

In contrast, the strong ILO emphasis on social insurance beginning with its first conference reflected the considerable dedication to this field in much of Europe in the aftermath of World War I. Western European leadership in the ILO has been exceptional during all eras of that organization's work in terms of both quantity and quality of input.(66) As indicated by ratifications of ILO conventions and resolutions, Western European support for the output of the organization has also been comparatively strong.(67)

The disparities in United States and Western European roles involve both cause and effect. It has been relatively easy for those Western European states with the leading social security systems in the world at any given time to support standards that required only limited further modifications of their own programs.(68) In order to ratify various ILO social security conventions, the United States would have had to make major additions in such areas as family allowances and health insurance. Furthermore, Western European states share concerns over comparability of social security benefits paid to foreign migrant workers that do not involve the United States to the same extent. As to social security as a factor in production and distribution costs, the United States has enjoyed some advantages in relation to Western Europe and has had little incentive to close the gap. It remains to be seen whether the European Communities' greater costs in this sphere will lead its members to promote North Atlantic comparability or whether recent increases in United States social security taxes will avert such pressures.

Disparities in values, traditions, bureaucratic competence, party and trade union support, and class and income structure may all be playing declining roles as determinants of social security variations between the United States and most of Western Europe as at least some "postindustrial" trends affect both areas.(69) In contrast, the activities of intergovernmental organizations have reinforced some previously established variations and may well nudge Western Europe towards even greater relative advancement.

International regimes vary in terms of the aspects of the policy area subject to international rules and norms (scope) and the distribution of powers among the regulating and allocating authorities (level). Ideal type alternatives for an international social security regime could range from a single system of benefits and complete reciprocity directed by a centralized international bureaucracy to one in which few norms, rules, or procedures affect the autonomy of national government. Among industrialized nations, the extent of need for comparable and reciprocal programs has been debated extensively. Further, choices have been made concerning the stringency of enforcement of accepted state responsibilities and the use of intergovernmental resources for persuasion and technical assistance.

Although the scope of the international social security regime has gradually become quite broad it still bears the stamp of the original emphasis on employee security. Only gradually did the ILO and the major European organizations move beyond concern for particular categories of industrial and transportation employees to deal with other employees, the self-employed, and finally such nonemployed groups as homemakers, youth, and the handicapped.(70) The founding charters of both the ILO and the European Communities focused on the employment relationship. Yet the ILO, the Communities, and the Council of Europe have all been able, with both staff and national government support, to adopt recommendations and rules that extend beyond the social protection of employees. This has been easiest for the broadly chartered Council of Europe and most difficult for the Communities.(71) The European Social Charter, signed by the member states of the Council of Europe in 1961, represented a major step toward generalization of beneficiaries with its emphasis on families and the disabled.(72) The Council's leadership continued into the 1970s with its 1974 convention on the social protection of farmers and its 1975 resolution on social security for women at home.(73) However, various categories of nonemployed persons will continue to be protected, even in Western Europe, only by public assistance and other alternatives to social insurance.

Concern for foreign and migrant workers has spurred multinational action in social security since World War I. Beginning with its initial 1919 conference the ILO pioneered international standards for equality of treatment for such persons through its own conventions and resolutions as well as by promoting other multilateral agreements among its members.(74) The ILO, Council of Europe, and European Communities have cooperated very closely since 1953 to legislate increasingly broad equality of treatment for foreign workers. By March 1977, 32 states around the world had ratified the most comprehensive ILO Convention on the subject (Equality of Treatment (Social Security) Convention, 1962, No. 118).(75) More specific obligations have been promulgated for their member states with ILO assistance by the Communities and the Council.(76) The Communities followed up actions to guarantee equal treatment for workers from member states with a series of agreements with other countries that supply large numbers of "guest workers."(77)

The protection of various classes of persons depends on a broad approach to the range of risks and conditions to be protected against and the adequacy of benefits. Just as industrial and transportation employees were the first concern of the international regime as beneficiaries, their work-related risks were the first to be dealt with by national and international authorities. ILO efforts to protect against employment injury and occupational diseases (narrowly conceived) in the 1920s were followed in the 1930s by attention to the risks of old age, invalidity, and death. By 1952 an omnibus ILO Convention covered nine "branches" of social security, adding family allowances to the programs dealt with in previous conventions.(78)

Future additions to the branches of social security cannot be forecast with great confidence. Paternity leave is being pioneered in

Sweden and new connections are being made between social security and both taxation and labor market policies. Obligations to the physically and mentally handicapped are being broadened in many highly industrialized countries. Social security will not be utilized for all such new benefits and stress on social insurance funds in Western Europe and the United States makes short-term expansion of benefits problematical. However, a pattern has emerged in which programs developed in a few advanced states are being adopted in many others with the assistance of intergovernmental organizations.

The norms of the international social security regime have centered for decades on equality and reciprocity of treatment, cited first for nonnationals and then for women. A usually complementary but conceivably conflicting norm is the "right to protection," generally stated in relation to children and both employed and nonemployed women. Various instruments of intergovernmental organizations also cite the broad goal of progressive improvements of national systems.(79)

Since 1952 the interaction of the ILO with the Council of Europe and the Communities has helped to promote higher standards in each of the nine branches of social security. The Council's 1964 European Code of Social Security was a notable step in this direction.(80) The ILO, Nordic Council, and the Communities have each promoted earnings-related insurance and "dynamic" benefits that keep up with growth in national income.(81) In 1977, the Commission of the European Communities was studying minimum guaranteed incomes.(82)

The movement to set standards reflects what Ruggie and Haas have termed collective elaboration of welfare choices. In their view this occurs when regimes emerge "in which the disparate purposes of national policies are redefined in terms of the larger collectivity" and trade-offs are calculated among different national activities when not all can be pursued.(83) A social security regime lends itself to such allocational policies even more easily than the environmental and physical resource regimes emphasized by Ruggie and Haas. National policies in social security can easily diverge in relation to treatment of nonnationals and effects of policies on economic competition. The Western European sub-regime for social security has progressed quite far in delimiting choices concerning the scope and standards of social security programs. Another regime function, the definition of property rights, has been extended to much of the world through the efforts of the ILO. The modern conception of social insurance involves clear legal entitlement to benefits rights, whether through insurance or grant programs.

One of the most difficult issues in the shaping of an international social security regime concerns the ultimate goals of the on-going process. Should the ends simply be the strengthening of broad norms and principles and general efforts at improved benefits, or should it involve such goals as harmonization, standardization, coordination, and approximation of programs? As noted by Alan Dashwood, even in the treaties of the European Communities usage of these terms is not consistent. He adds:

The current view is accordingly that for legal purposes nothing turns on the precise wording. . . . However, in political terms the shift from "harmonization" to "coordination" may still be taken to indicate a significant increase in intensity.(84)

The most ambitious goals have been debated and sometimes acted upon within the European Communities and the Nordic Council states. Yet even in these groupings variations in existing national systems, the limits of intergovernmental organizational charters, and the inherent ambiguity of such terms as harmonization and approximation have proven to be considerable barriers.

As ˙recently as 1972 an official publication of the Communities stressed that the social security systems in the member states varied widely in respect to objectives, organization, and resources and that the Economic Community's treaty mandated only close cooperation in this field. It was stated emphatically that "there are no plans to bring about complete unity of practice in this field."(85) Although the Nordic states had by then achieved even more similar national systems, no active plans for full unity have been promoted. Still more modest statements of intentions were put forward in the early 1970s by the ILO and Council of Europe.

Yet in the mid-1970s a new thrust at effective harmonization and coordination was articulated in several European organizations. The major organs of the Communities, at the urging of the German Federal Republic, increasingly looked to apply to the social sphere their general power to promote harmonization and coordination of national law and policy. By late 1976 the EC Commission was actively promoting what its former director-general for social affairs termed its first venture in mandatory harmonization of certain categories of social protection.(86) By 1977, the EC Commission had moved far enough in this direction to refer to a broad approach to harmonization and a future "Community social protection policy."(87) Contemporaneously, the Council of Europe, with ILO assistance, was elaborating a medium-term program for the harmonization of social security in its larger region.(88) The new acceptance of the concept of harmonization involves a less rigid application of that term than in earlier years. Yet new momentum toward greater equivalency of programs is evident.

The instruments of the international social security regime vary widely in terms of their rule-making authority and the accompanying efforts to implement them. A given international regime may have any degree of dependence on regulatory legislation. Hargrove has written that in regard to international environmental problems "the problems on which major law-making can be expected in the near future are only a handful at most."(89) Yet the international social security regime involves virtually the entire gamut of legal instruments.

International social security legislation can be found in such major instruments as treaties, conventions, codes, and compacts, as well as narrow and specific devices. Unfortunately, such terms tell us little about the rule-making authority invoked. Broad instruments vary widely in terms of the specificity of obligations as well as their power to bind governments and citizens. Nevertheless, their broad scope and articulation of principles make pivotal such documents as the European Social Charter, Code of Social Security, and European Convention on Social Security, each developed by the Council of Europe, the ILO's Social Security (Minimum Standards) Convention (No. 102) and Equality of Treatment (Social Security) Convention (No.118), and the Nordic Convention respecting social security. Of these, the ILO's conventions have achieved the broadest applicability and those of the Council of Europe have done most to elevate standards in Europe in recent decades.

The nature of the obligations of member states in the European Communities tend to differ markedly from those of the ILO and the Council of Europe. Regulations, directives, and decisions of the Communities' organs bind all members or the specified targets of the action. Even its recommendations, under the European Coal and Steel Community treaty, are binding with respect to objectives to be achieved (Article 13).(90) In contrast, the ILO and Council of Europe depend primarily on ratifications by member states to trigger legal obligations and allow partial acceptance of conventions. Both the ILO and the Council have patterns of fairly slow and distinctly incomplete acceptance of major obligations.

Implementation and adjudication of rules poses difficult problems for each of these international organizations. Each relies on consultative processes, though the Communities' Commission and Court are blessed with unique powers. Its Court of Justice reviews actions of the Commission and other structures and affects obligations of individuals, corporations, and governments through interpretations of the founding treaties as well as other sources of law.(91) Community law is also enforced through national courts.

In contrast, the ILO relies on compliance reports from member governments that are reviewed by committees of experts and ministers with limited participation by labor and employer representatives. In regard to its European Social Charter, the Council of Europe expanded this procedure to involve committees of experts, representatives of the Consultative Assembly, official "representatives of States Parties to the Charter," and ministers in the review process.(92) The ILO Committees' considerations result in recommendations for changes in the laws and policies of ratifying states and the Council of Europe's committees produce "conclusions" and "views" as well as recommendations.(93)

The effectiveness of the Communities' authority in its limited sphere of involvement with social security is considerable. In contrast, the ILO and the Council of Europe depend more on persuasion and other informal action and have taken many years to achieve only part of the intended results. Yet their aims are broader and involve many more countries. A series of articles in the ILO's International Labour Review documents successful efforts of that organization to upgrade and regularize some of the most advanced Western European social security systems throughout its fifty-nine year history.(94) These and other studies suggest broad national legislative and administrative compliance with recommendations of the ILO's experts.(95) As noted by Haas, "the Committee (of Experts') persistence in demanding full implementation of ratified conventions is extraordinary."(96) Yet most of the experts' recommendations and opinions regarding compliance with ILO by Western European states have involved what one analyst terms "minor discrepancies" in national policies.(97) Luard is among those who have called for "some kind of inspection service to replace the present cross-examination system."(98)

The effectiveness of intergovernmental organizational efforts to upgrade and coordinate social security reflects a quite strong leadership role by international civil servants. As noted by Cox, "ILO officials dealing with standards have been even more influential in all phases of the rule-supervisory process than in rule creation."(99) Michael Shanks argues persuasively that the EC Commission has shifted to the social protection field some of the catalytic roles that have become increasingly difficult in most areas of economic policy.(100)

Yet this writer takes a cautious view regarding the prospects for spillover into other social policy areas as a result of the continuing development of the international social security regime. The ILO, increasingly oriented towards technical assistance in the developing world, can no longer be viewed as a dynamic organization able to implement functionalist objectives of a world political order or accomplish such a neofunctionalist aim as the spillover of organizational tasks at regional levels.(101) The Council of Europe has been a very useful instrument of cooperation in Western Europe, but it long ago abandoned the hopes of its founders for a role in European integration. Finally, the social policy activism of the EC Commission increasingly appears to be directed at bureaucratic survival and the provision of resources to be traded off among the increasingly contentious member-states. Some of the most important social protection actions of the Communities are being developed outside of its formal structures, thereby weakening the institutional development of that organization. Improvement of national social security systems and the increased coordination of programs owe much to these organizations and prospects for further progress are bright. Yet these developments should not lead to any great amount of optimism concerning short or medium-term prospects for the development of intergovernmental organizations, European integration, or regional harmonization of numerous policy areas.

CONCLUSION

The international community has agreed that, in regard to social security, international standards and reciprocal benefits serve the best interest of the individual, most nation-states, and the world economy. Yet neither world trade nor social justice has been determined to be dependent on rigid enforcement of the highest possible social security standards.

An international regime for social security has been developing for nearly a century and has advanced quite far in terms of the elaboration and implementation of principles, goals, and rules. It has reacted to transnational flows of persons and capital as well as to transnational development of trade unionism, social science, and employer associations. Bilateral contacts and agreements spurred the early progress in this policy area but have been largely superseded by efforts coordinated and promoted through intergovernmental organizations. Insofar as this regime goes far towards fulfilling Ruggie and Haas's functional tasks of collective elaboration of welfare choices and defining of property rights, and has made progress toward harmonization and coordination, it could serve (and to some extent already has) as a model for other policy regimes. However, variations in national resources and other national attributes have set limits on the development of this regime even as it affects relatively homogeneous groupings of Western European states. No adequate justification has been put forward for full standardization of national systems despite pressures of economic and political integration and interdependence.

The social security regime is not fully autonomous. Its development has been closely associated with the broader effort to assure basic human rights in the political and social fields. Further, it is increasingly intertwined with aspects of economic interdependence and environmental concern.

The evolution of several critical types of transnational forces and trends reflects and reinforces the relative isolation of the United States from Western Europe in regard to social security. Separation of the United States from new groupings of Western European trade unions and such organizations as the European Communities and Council of Europe has evidently contributed to the continuation of notable disparities in American and Western European social security systems. Washington's in-and-out relationship with the International Labor Organization and its reluctance to accept the rules and guidance of that organization have also reinforced transatlantic variations and a distinct Western European sub-regime in this policy area.

As some of the long-standing domestic factors that have contributed to a less-developed American social security system as compared to Western Europe have faded, variations in transnational flows and intergovernmental organizational influence have become more significant. Comparative analyses of national social policies should take greater account of these external variations.

Trends toward harmonization of numerous policy areas can be expected to promote the further development of the social security regime. Yet taken alone the advancement of this particular regime is not likely to go very far to promote regional or global economic/political integration or pave the way for comparable protection of other social and political rights.

NOTES

(1) Arnold Heidenheimer, "The Politics of Public Education, Health, and

Welfare in the USA and Western Europe," British Journal of Political Science 3 July 1973: 315-40.

(2) Definitions, again, are weakly established and in flux. Keohane and Nye originally applied the term "transnational" to "the movement of tangible or intangible items across state boundaries when at least one actor is not an agent of a government or an intergovernmental organization" as well as "relations between governmental actors that are not controlled by the central foreign policy organs of their governments." Robert O. Keohane and Joseph S. Nye, Jr., eds., Transnational Relations and World Politics (Cambridge, Mass: Harvard University Press, 1972) pp. xiv-xv. They subsequently separated out the latter pattern of relations and termed it "transgovernmental relations." Keohane and Nye, "Transgovernmental Relations and International Organizations," World Politics 27 (October 1974): 40-2. Nye and Keohane's perspective is broadened by aspects of Kaiser's concept of "multinational politics." See Karl Kaiser, "Toward a Theory of Multinational Politics," International Organization 25 (1971): 790-817. Burton's concept of "World Society" also offers a broader perspective than Nye and Keohane's. See John W. Burton, World Society (London: Cambridge University Press, 1972). The present study refers to a broad grouping of relations and interactions that affect and involve both potential subjects of governmental policy and policy itself in processes that cross national lines.

(3) Heidenheimer, "Politics of Public Education"; Anthony King, "Ideas, Institutions and the Policies of Governments: A Comparative Analysis," British Journal of Political Science 3 (July and October 1973): 291-313, 409-23; Phillips Cutright, "Political Structure, Economic Development, and National Social Security Programs," American Journal of Sociology 70 (March 1965), 537-50; Harold L. Wilensky, The Welfare State and Equality (Berkeley: University of California Press, 1975); Frederick L. Pryor, Public Expenditures in Communist and Capitalist Nations (Homewood, Ill.: Richard D. Irwin, 1968); Gaston V. Rimlinger, Welfare Policy and Industrialization in Europe, America, and Russia (New York: John Wiley and Sons, 1971).

(4) William Wallace, The Foreign Policy Process in Britain (London: The Royal Institute of International Affairs, 1975), pp. 270-1.

(5) See Evan Luard, International Agencies: The Emerging Framework of Interdependence (Dobbs Ferry, N.Y.: Oceana, 1977); Robert E. Keohane and Joseph S. Nye, Power and Interdependence: World Politics in Transition (Boston: Little, Brown & Co., 1977); Seyom Brown, et al., Regimes for the Ocean, Outer Space, and Weather (Washington, D.C.: The Brookings Institution, 1977).

(6) John Gerard Ruggie, "Collective Goods and Future International Collaboration," American Political Science Review 66 (September 1972): 874-93; Report on the Organization of the Government for the Conduct

of Foreign Policy (Washington, D.C.: U.S. Government Printing Office,June 1975).

(7) Luard, International Agencies; David Leive, International Regulatory Regimes, 2 vols. Lexington, Mass.: Lexington Books, 1976; Robert S. Jordan, ed., Multinational Cooperation: Economic, Social, and Scientific Development (New York: Oxford University Press, 1972).

(8) Richard A. Falk, A Study of Future Worlds (New York: The Free Press, 1975); Scanning Our Future: A Report From the NCO Forum on the World Economic Order (New York: Carnegie Endowment for International Peace, 1976); Lester R. Brown, World Without Borders (New York: Random House, 1972); Miriam Camps, The Management of Interdependence: A Preliminary View (New York: Council of Foreign Relations, 1974).

(9) For a valuable study of an evolving social and human rights regime in Western Europe see O. Kahn-Freund, "The European Social Charter," in F.G. Jacobs, ed., European Law and the Individual (Amsterdam and New York: North-Holland, 1976), pp. 181-211. See also Luard, International Agencies, pp. 133-94.

(10) Keohane and Nye, Power and Interdependence, p. 21.

(11) John Gerald Ruggie and Ernst A. Haas, "Environmental and Resource Interdependencies: Reorganizing for the Evolution of International Regimes," in Appendix B, Report of the Commission on the Organization of the Government, vol. 1, pp. 218, 222-3.

(12) J.S. Nye, Peace in Parts: Integration and Conflict in Regional Organization (Boston: Little, Brown & Co., 1971), pp. 23-4.

(13) See Camps, Management of Interdependence, especially pp. 90-2.

(14) P.R. Kaim-Caudle, Comparative Social Policy and Social Security: A Ten Country Study (London: Martin Robertson, 1973), especially pp. 306-10. These pairs were Austria and West Germany and Ireland and the United Kingdom. Lesser similarities were found for the United States and Canada. Note that both of the European pairs were at one time joined in political union. For an alternative comparison of social security systems see Barbara N. Rodgers, John Greve, and John S. Morgan, Comparative Social Administration, 2nd ed. (London: George Allen and Unwin, 1971), especially pp. 236-40.

(15) Variations in Western European and United States expenditures on social security have been reduced in some respects since the late 1960s as United States spending increased for medical benefits, old age, survivors', disability, and unemployment insurance, as well as public assistance. Alfred M. Skolnik and Sophie R. Dales, "Social Welfare Expenditures, Fiscal 1974," Social Security Bulletin 38 (January 1975): 3-12.

(16) William Wallace, "Issue Linkages Among Atlantic Governments," International Affairs (London) 52 (April 1976): 175.

(17) For a review of the sources of this term see Karl Kaiser, "Toward a Theory of Multinational Politics," International Organization 25 (Autumn 1971): 790-817.

(18) Richard Rosecrance, et al., "Whither Interdependence?," International Organization 31 (Summer 1977): 427-9; Peter Katzenstein, "International Interdependence: Some Long-Term Trends and Recent Changes," International Organization 29 (Autumn 1975): 1024-34.

(19) Samuel P. Huntington, "Transnational Organizations in World Politics," World Politics 25 (April 1973): 333-68; Keohane and Nye, eds., Transnational Relations, pp. 93-168.

(20) Roy Lubove, The Struggle for Social Security, 1900-1935 (Cambridge, Mass.: Harvard University Press, 1968), pp. 29-34.

(21) The 7.8 percent figure offered in the Communities' own compilation excludes such categories as foreign Nordic workers in Denmark and British and Commonwealth workers in Ireland. Dependence on foreign workers varied in 1973 from 0.4 percent in Italy to approximately 11 percent in France and the Federal Republic of Germany and a high of 35.0 percent in Luxembourg. Report on the Development of the Social Situation in the Communities in 1976 (Brussels: Commission of the European Communities, April 1977). Even after retrenchment, the Federal Republic counted more than 2 million foreign workers in June 1975. Social and Labour Bulletin, no. 4 (December 1976), p. 386.

(22) On varied social impacts of foreign workers in Europe see Ernst Gehmacher, "Foreign Workers as a Source of Social Change," in Richard Rose, ed., The Dynamics of Public Policy: A Comparative Analysis (London and Beverly Hills: Sage, 1976), pp. 157-76.

(23) Arnold J. Heidenheimer, Hugh Heclo, and Carolyn Teich Adams, Comparative Public Policy: The Politics and Social Choice in Europe and America (New York: St. Martin's, 1975), p. 196.

(24) Heidenheimer, "The Politics of Public Education" and Rimlinger, Welfare Policy.

(25) The United States admitted only 55,766 legal "temporary workers" under its immigration laws in fiscal year 1975, the bulk of these from Canada, Mexico, and the Caribbean. 1975 Annual Report: Immigration and Naturalization Service (Washington, D.C.: U.S. Department of Justice, 1975), p. 70.

(26) For example, 477,765 Germans immigrated to the United States between 1951 and 1960. Ibid., p. 64.

(27) See Jack N. Behrman, National Interests and the Multinational Enterprise: Tensions Among the North Atlantic Countries (Englewood Cliffs, N.J.: Prentice-Hall), 1970, pp. 71-82.

(28) Christopher Tugendhat, The Multinationals (London: Eyre and Spottiswoode, 1971), p. 24.

(29) Obie G. Whichard and Julius N. Friedlin, "U.S. Direct Investment Abroad in 1975," Survey of Current Business, 56 (August 1976): 49; Foreign Direct Investment in the United States, vol. 1: Report of the Secretary of Commerce to the Congress (Washington, D.C.: U.S. Department of Commerce, April 1976), p. 48.

(30) Foreign Direct Investment in the United States, p. 12.

(31) Ibid., p. xiv.

(32) Ibid., p. 103.

(33) European Communities (January-February 1974): 16.

(34) Sixth Report on Competition Policy (Brussels: Commission of the European Communities, April 1977), pp. 152-4.

(35) Michael Shanks, European Social Policy Today and Tomorrow (New York: Pergamon Press, Inc. 1977), p. 61.

(36) See, for example, Diarmid McLaughlin, "The Work and Aims of the Economic and Social Committee of the EEC and Euratom," Journal of Common Market Studies 15 (September 1976): 9-28.

(37) Robert W. Cox, "Labor and Transnational Relations," in Keohane and Nye, eds., Transnational Relations and World Politics, pp. 213-14.

(38) Multinational Enterprises and Social Policy (Geneva: International Labour Office, 1973), pp. 66-7.

(39) Social and Labour Bulletin, no. 2 (June 1976): 230.

(40) Ibid., p. 143-4.

(41) Social and Labour Bulletin, no. 3 September 1976: 284.

(42) "Transgovernmental Relations and International Organizations," World Politics 17 (October 1974): 40-42.

(43) James N. Rosenau, ed., Linkage Politics: Essays on the Convergence of National and International Systems (New York: Free Press, 1969), pp. 44-9.

(44) Helmut Creutz, "The I.L.O. and Social Security for Foreign and Migrant Workers," International Labour Review 97 (April 1968): 351.

(45) Ibid., and Guy Perrin, "Reflections on Fifty Years of Social Security," International Labour Review 99 (March 1969): 249-57, 285-92.

(46) Bruce Reed, "Social Security and Medical Care in the Context of the European Community," in Roger Lawson and Bruce Reed, Social Security in the European Community (London: Chatham House-PEP, 1975), p. 51; Social Security for Migrant Workers (Geneva: International Labour Office, 1977), p. 10.

(47) See Chester Edward Jarvis, "International Efforts to Promote Social Security" (Ph.D. dissertation, University of Pennsylvania, 1957), pp. 85-9.

(48) Hugh Heclo, Modern Social Politics in Britain and Sweden (New Haven: Yale University Press, 1974), pp. 78, 60, 180-5; Lubove, Struggle for Social Security, pp. 68, 124, 150.

(49) Heclo, ibid., pp. 13-14.

(50) Frantz Wendt, The Nordic Council and Cooperation in Scandinavia (Copenhagen: Munksgaard, 1959), p. 60; Erik Solem, The Nordic Council and Scandinavian Integration (New York: Praeger, 1977), p. 32.

(51) William Wallace, The Foreign Policy Process in Britain, p. 39.

(52) Ibid., pp. 225-31; and Karl Kaiser and Roger Morgan, eds., Britain and West Germany: Changing Societies and the Future of Foreign Policy (London: Oxford University Press, 1971).

(53) In 1960 the nine present members of the European Communities together covered 87 percent of their populations for hospital and medical care, 72 percent of civilian wage and salary earners for unemployment insurance, and 88 percent of the civilian labor force for invalidity, old-age, and survivors' pensions. Report on the Development of the Social Situation in the Communities in 1976, pp. 220-3. In 1962 social security expenditure as percentage of gross national product (at market prices) varied among the then six members of the Communities only from the Italian low of 11.9 percent to the German Federal Republic's high of 14.5 percent. The United States was reported at 6.9 percent in 1962, a figure termed "only partly comparable." Basic Statistics of the Community, 12th ed., 1972 (Brussels: Statistical Office of the European Communities, 1972), p. 106.

(54) Lubove, The Struggle for Social Security, pp. 25-26; Samuel Mencher, Poor Law to Poverty Program (Pittsburgh, Pa.: University of Pittsburgh Press, 1974 reissue), pp. 298, 433.

(55) Ibid., pp. 112-13.

(56) Cited in Maurice Bruce, The Coming of the Welfare State, 4th ed. (London: B.T. Batsford, 1968), p. 296.

(57) See Social Security Programs Throughout the World (Washington: Social Security Administration, biennial); "Health Financing and Delivery Systems of Selected Foreign Countries," in U.S. House of Representatives, Committee on Ways and Means, National Health Insurance Resource Book, Part 3 (Washington: U.S. Government Printing Office, 1974); Jozef Van Langendonek, "The European Experience in Social Health Insurance," Social Security Bulletin, 36 (July 1973): 21-30; Joseph G. Simanis, National Health Systems in Eight Countries (Washington, D.C.: Social Security Administration, 1975).

(58) Raymond F. Hopkins, "The International Role of 'Domestic' Bureaucracy," International Organization 30 (Summer 1976): 422-5.

(59) See Edy Kaufman, The Superpowers and Their Spheres of Influence (New York: St. Martin's Press, 1976).

(60) Harry Bayard Price, The Marshall Plan and Its Meaning (New York: Cornell University Press, 1955), p. 98.

(61) Tenth General Report of the Activities of the European Communities (Brussels: Commission of the European Communities, February 1977), p. 304.

(62) Ernst B. Haas, Beyond the Nation-State: Functionalism and International Organization (Stanford, Ca.: Stanford University Press, 1964), p. 233.

(63) Ibid., p. 238.

(64) Conventions Internationales du Travail: Tableau des Ratifications (Geneva: International Labour Office, 1977).

(65) "Declaration Concerning the Aims and Purposes of the International Labor Organization," adopted May 10, 1944 by the General Conference of the ILO, in Haas, Beyond the Nation-State, pp. 514-6.

(66) Robert W. Cox has pointed to the charismatic leadership in the ILO of representatives from Britain, Italy, and France and documents the relatively high proportion of "Western" members of the ILO Council as late as 1967. "ILO: Limited Monarchy," in Cox and Harold K. Jacobson, eds., The Anatomy of Influence: Decision Making in International Organization (New Haven, Conn.: Yale University Press, 1973), pp. 115, 408-9.

(67) European Communities countries now average almost 70 convention

ratifications, more than any other region. Social security conventions are well-represented among these ratifications. Nicolas Valticos, "Fifty Years of Standard-Setting by the International Labour Organization," International Labour Review, C, 3 (September 1969): 226; Conventions Internationales du Travail.

(68) See in the International Labour Review, G.A. Johnston, "The Influence of International Labour Standards on Legislation and Practice in the United Kingdom," 97 (May 1968): 465-88; Gerhard Schnoor, "The Influence of ILO Standards on Law and Practice in the Federal Republic of Germany," 110 (December 1974): 539-64; Jean Morellet, "The Influence of International Labour Conventions on French Legislation," 101 (April 1970): 331-58.

(69) Some supporting and conflicting viewpoints appear in Michel Crozier, Samuel P. Huntington, and Joji Watanuki, The Crisis of Democracy: Report on the Governability of Democracies to the Trilateral Commission New York: New York University Press, 1975; M. Donald Hancock and Gideon Sjoberg, eds., Politics in the Post-Welfare State (New York: Columbia University Press, 1972); and Richard Mayne, ed., Europe Tomorrow (London: Fontana/Collins, 1972).

(70) See Perrin, "Reflections on Fifty Years of Social Security," p. 259.

(71) O. Kahn-Freund, "The European Social Charter," pp. 194-5.

(72) European Social Charter (Strasbourg: Directorate of Information, Council of Europe, 1967), art. 11-19, pp. 9-12.

(73) European Treaty Series, no. 83 Strasbourg: Council of Europe, May 1974; Social and Labour Bulletin, no. 1 (March 1976): 80-1. In addition, the European Communities' structures are presently considering a recommendation concerning the progressive extension of social protection to categories of persons not covered or inadequately covered by existing social security schemes. Report on the Development of the Social Situation in the Communities in 1976, p. 24.

(74) Helmut Creutz, "The I.L.O. and Social Security for Foreign and Migrant Workers," International Labour Review 97 (April 1968): 351-2.

(75) Equality of Treatment (Social Security): General Survey by the Committee of Experts (Geneva: International Labour Office, 1977), p. 2.

(76) See European Convention on Social Security (Strasbourg: Council of Europe, December 1972); Regulation 1408/71 of the Council of the European Communities in Journal officiel des Communautes europeennes. Legislation, July 5, 1971, pp. 2-50.

(77) Report on the Development of the Social Situation in the Communities in 1976, pp. 24-5.

(78) ILO Security (Minimum Standards) Convention, no. 102, 1952, in Conventions and Recommendations Adopted by the International Labour Conference, 1919-1966 (Geneva: International Labour Office, 1966), pp. 811-32.

(79) Each of these norms is contained in the European Social Charter signed in 1961 under the auspices of the Council of Europe.

(80) It is stated in the Code's preamble that the members were "convinced that it is desirable to establish a European Code of Social Security at a higher level than the minimum standards embodied in International Labour Convention No. 102 concerning minimum standards of social security." European Conventions and Agreements, vol. II (Strasbourg: Council of Europe, 1972), p. 124. Yet it is the protocol to the 1964 Code, rather than the main body of that document, that set notably high standards in such areas as coverage, duration, and levels of compensation.

(81) Perrin, "Reflections on Fifty Years," p. 259. The Social Action Programme of the European Communities was approved in January 1974.

(82) Report on the Development of the Social Situation in the Community in 1976, p. 12.

(83) Ruggie and Haas, "Environmental and Resource Dependencies," p. 223.

(84) Dashwood, "Hastening Slowly: The Communities' Path Towards Harmonization," in Helen Wallace, William Wallace, and Carole Webb, eds., Policy-Making in the European Communities (New York: John Wiley, 1977), p. 275.

(85) The Common Market and the Common Man, 4th ed. (Brussels: European Communities Press and Information, June 1972), p. 28.

(86) Shanks, European Social Policy Today, p. 61.

(87) Report on the Development of the Social Situation in the Communities in 1976, p. 149.

(88) Action of the ILO: Problems and Prospects: Report of the Director-General to the International Labour Conference (Geneva: International Labour Conference, 1974), p. 65.

(89) John Lawrence Hargrove, ed., Law, Institutions, and the Global Environment (Dobbs Ferry, N.Y.: Oceana, 1972), p. 170.

(90) For a discussion of social policy in the ECSC, see Doreen Collins, The European Communities: The Social Policy of the First Phase, vol. 1 (London: Martin Robertson, 1975).

(91) On the Court's decisions on social security, see K. Lipstein, "Conflicts of Laws in Matters of Social Security Under the EEC Treaty," in F.G. Jacobs, ed., European Law and the Individual, pp. 55-77.

(92) O. Kahn-Freund, "The European Social Charter," in ibid., pp. 202-3.

(93) Ibid., p. 203.

(94) See note 68.

(95) See statistical breakdown on governmental responses in Haas, Beyond the National-State, p. 258.

(96) Ibid., p. 257.

(97) Morellet, "The Influence of International Labour Conventions on French Legislation," p. 337.

(98) International Agencies, p. 148. ILO investigatory bodies have been used in a limited range of human rights cases.

(99) Robert W. Cox, "ILO: Limited Monarchy," p. 112.

(100) Shanks, European Social Policy Today, pp. 84-5. For the leading analysis of such a catalytic role in economic policy see Leon N. Lindberg and Stuart A. Scheingold, Europe's Would-Be Polity (Englewood Cliffs, N.J.: Prentice-Hall, 1970).

(101) Essentially pessimistic prognoses underlie the analyses of the ILO in Haas, Beyond the National-State, and Luard, International Agencies.

III

OPEC:
Focused
Transnational
Politics

5 OPEC:
The Basis of the Arab Developmental World—A Transnational Model*
Timothy W. Luke

INTRODUCTION

In the 1950s and 1960s both academics and policy makers divided the world of nations into three distinct blocs of nation-states whose ranking in each bloc depended upon their respective national economic, political, and social power.(1) By the mid-1970s, however, the events of the intervening years greatly weakened the accuracy of the "Three Worlds" schema. The "First World" of Europe, Japan, and North America, as well as their respective client states,(2) gradually were coming to pragmatic terms with the "Second World" of the Soviet Union and the other states that modernized through "socialist revolutions." However, the greatest transformation occurred within the "Third World" of less developed and so-called "nonaligned" states of Africa, Asia, and Latin America.

Historically, the Third World's distinguishing features have been political domination by and economic dependence upon the more powerful First, and, in some cases, Second Worlds. Yet, in the 1970s, certain Third World nations were making some considerable economic and political advances. A small group of "export platforms," states with high levels of foreign corporate investment in export-oriented industries which tied them into international trade networks (such as Mexico, Brazil, Korea, Taiwan, Hong Kong, plus the oil-exporting countries),

*This study is a continuation of an earlier paper, "Arabs, Africans, and the Limits of Realpolitik," which I co-authored with Professor Victor T. LeVine. Our research was funded, in part, by a grant from the Office of External Research of the Department of State. Also, previous versions of this paper have appeared in Leviathan   A Journal   of Middle East Politics and Culture/an Affiliate of the   University Professors Program of Boston University. (Spring 1978) and in Victor T.LeVine and Timothy W. Luke,   The Arab-African Connection: Political and Economic Realities. , ©Westview Press, Boulder, Colo., 1979. Reprinted by permission.

were slowly increasing their gross national product and political visibility.(3) Still, for the most part, the Third World states remained "dual" economies and societies that blended several small economic sectors rooted in modern corporate production with traditional peasant agriculture. In any case, the Third World states attained political independence, but not political autonomy; achieved economic growth, but not economic development; and they effected social change, but not social progress.

Plainly, the past five years have radically transformed this international hierarchy of states. A new Third World, a different development world, has emerged from the old dominated and dependent one. And, by its emergence, this upwardly mobile Third World is reconstituting the symmetries of global interdependence, thereby establishing new configurations in the international division of power and status. The states of the Organization of Petroleum Exporting and Producing Countries (OPEC) form the core of the new developmental world.(4) With the formation of this new bloc, the vast majority of the less developed nations in Africa, Asia, and Latin America also have undergone downward mobility to become the clients and constituents of the new "Fourth World."

Like the relatively self-sufficient First World, this new Fourth World rudely awoke in 1973 to the presence of a new set of dependency relations – those involving both the modern and the modernizing economies' oil supply needs, now largely under the price control of the OPEC states. Consequently, in this analysis, I will examine how the new Third World has turned this commands over most of the planet's petroleum resources into the economic, political, and social foundations of a new developmental bloc. Special attention will be paid to the Arab OPEC states as well as to Iran, and to the parallels in their developmental progress with the previous developmental patterns of the First and Second Worlds, in order to better comprehend the diverse motives behind their economic and political relations with the First and Fourth Worlds.(5)

Although conceived over a decade earlier, October 1973 marks the birth date of the Arab developmental world. In discussing the origins and operations of what amounts to an emerging developmental model, two very important facts must be kept constantly in mind. First, the emergence and maintenance of this developmental path necessarily depended on the existence of the developed First World. The autarkic development designs of the Soviet model were neither a desirable nor a probable course for Arab development given the natural resource poverty, the small population, and weak state apparatus of most Arab countries. In a very real sense, the Arab developmental world was largely conceived by the industrial states of Western Europe, Japan, and North America after World War II as their industrial economies shifted from coal to oil to satisfy their energy needs. And second, this developmental path necessarily depended upon the activity of the large transnational oil corporations which so eagerly engineered the First World's increasing dependence upon the petroleum they produced and marketed. So effective were the corporations that by 1973 Europe relied on oil to generate 60 percent of its energy, of which 98.7 percent was imported (some 69 percent of that supply came from the Arab states).(6) Japan depended on oil for 76 percent of its energy, nearly 100 percent of which was imported; 72 percent of its needs were filled by Middle East suppliers.(7) The United States used oil for 47 percent of its energy needs. Thirty-five percent was imported, and nearly 10 percent of these imports came from the Middle East.(8) The solid structure of these international oil markets, then, provides ultimate economic basis for the Arabs' developmental strategy.

Originally organized in Baghdad in September 1960, OPEC was designed to protect its members' mutual interests against the collective actions of the transnational oil corporations (TNCs) which have operated as a price and production "cartel" in the world market since the 1920s.(9) Initially, OPEC was ineffectual against the allied operations of the "seven sisters" of transnational oil,(10) but it grew slowly in strength during the 1960s under the political aegis of Iran, Venezuela, Iraq, Kuwait, and Saudi Arabia. OPEC's political potential became manifest in 1971 in Tehran and Tripoli as the OPEC nations successfully forced a limited price increase upon the hitherto united and resistant oil companies. Further clout was created and exercised in Riyadh during 1973 as the OPEC nations sought gradual full "participation" in the ownership and management of the TNCs' joint venture subsidiaries such as ARAMCO. Still, it required the Yom Kippur War and the ensuing OPEC oil embargo to fix the necessary conditions for the postnatal survival of this developmental world. The technical prerequisites preceded it by several months, but the events of October 1973 conjured up the suitable political climate for its final appearance.(11) With Arab armies "victorious" for the first time against Israel, with the transnational oil companies acceding to its directives, and with its often divided and diverse membership acting as one, OPEC unilaterally declared a 70 percent increase in the price of the globe's main energy source – OPEC, but especially Arab, petroleum.

The initial price hike from $3.00 to $5.11 a barrel was augmented on January 1, 1974 with an additional increase bringing the posted per barrel cost to $11.65.(12) The implications for the transfer of wealth implied by the new prices were traced in 1974 by the Petroleum Economist: "The producing countries stand to increase their revenues to well over $100 billion in 1974 if production goes ahead as planned before the cutbacks, compared with the $30 billion they would have received on the basis of the posted price level on 1st October, 1973, and $51 billion after the 16th of October increase."(13) Forecasts by the World Bank in July 1974 projected that "the OPEC countries would accumulate an exchange surplus of $643 billion by 1980 and of $1.2 trillion by 1985."(14) In juxtaposition to OPEC's net foreign assets of $20 billion in 1973 and of $5 billion in 1970, it became clear that the oil-producing states, especially the Arab countries, stood to control an unprecedented flow of financial resources for their respective developmental programs.

DEVELOPMENTAL PRECEDENTS AND
ARAB OPEC PRACTICE

Plainly, these early estimates of the OPEC states' financial windfall have proved exaggerated. Even with further price increases in 1975 and 1976, the OPEC economies are accumulating less financial power than was originally expected. And the cumulative effect of all subsequent OPEC price increases has only been to worsen the impact of worldwide inflation which the First World has exported successfully to all OPEC oil producers. Most of the funds they have gathered are being prudently recycled for industrial goods or are reinvested carefully in world commercial and financial centers; current estimates peg the total 1980 petrodollar surplus at only $200 to $250 billion.(15)

Nonetheless, OPEC's earnings through the manipulation of a strategic commodity's price is a new form of capital accumulation which, in turn, drives the development of an entirely new bloc of modernizing states. However, the Arab countries' developmental successes can be understood only by recognizing that they are and were Fourth World nations prior to or apart from their involvement with their primary developmental agents – the transnational oil corporations. In other words, their most characteristic quality is that of a dual economy. Outside of the commanding heights of their petroleum sector, in many respects the Arab OPEC states remain traditional economies and societies as poor as any in the Fourth World. And within their petroleum and industrial sectors as recently constructed export platform economies, the Arab OPEC states remain deeply dependent on outside expertise, technology, and markets for the continued growth of these modern sectors.

Much of this discussion, then, deals more with potentialities and tendencies rather than fully developed economic, political, and social accomplishments. Nonetheless, it is both interesting and instructive to form certain generalizations about the course of Arab development in order to better comprehend how Arab and other OPEC leaders so effectively have taken advantage of their present objective possibilities. And, in coming to better understand how the Arab states are dealing with rapid modernization, one can usefully compare their developmental practices to previously proven developmental strategies.

An instructive approach for explaining the structural tendencies in the Arab model of development can be taken from Alexander Gerschenkron's theories on "delayed industrialization." In his comparative discussions of national development in Europe, Gerschenkron suggests that historical instances of delayed industrialization, such as Imperial Germany and Czarist Russia, overcome their "relative backwardness" (vis-à-vis other developmental pioneers, such as England) because of the institutional substitutes they turned to for capital accumulation. England, as the first industrializing nation, accumulated capital through the activities of private entrepreneurs running family firms in the "market," or by the mode of "primitive accumulation." It also began its industrialization from a position of "relative advancedness" with a fairly skilled labor force, a considerable pool of technical expertise, and an established developmental ideology rooted in Protestant religious beliefs. Possessing this requisite core of ingredients almost by chance, England successfully developed by the activities of private entrepreneurs working through the open capitalist market.

For various historical reasons, neither Germany nor Russia enjoyed access to this unique constellation of developmental requisites. Hence, each of them had to politically construct structural substitutes for "primitive accumulation" in order to spark their industrialization in more "backward" sociohistorical situations. Germany's leadership contrived a system of giant interlocking banking and industrial cartels tied together by the large commercial banks, the high bourgeoisie, and the Prussian landholding nobility. Russia, in a situation of even greater backwardness, employed the state as its agency for capital accumulation by attracting Western European investment, establishing state enterprises, and gathering commercial capital through taxation.(16) Although they began from relatively backward starting points, both nations' structural substitutes soon induced extensive and rapid economic development without having to laboriously reproduce the "tried-and-true" English method of development, especially its very elusive social consensus and political constitution.

The German and Russian history of dealing with delayed industrialization indicates how relative backwardness can be played into effective economic and social development by finding the right structural substitutes to compensate for "barren" preindustrial histories. Clearly, the Arab OPEC states are even more backward than was Czarist Russia when it embarked on its economic modernization in the 1880s. The Arab states lack secure supplies of skilled labor, technical expertise, capital accumulation, and a cohesive developmental ideology. What is more, these nations historically have been dominated by the outside, first by the Turks, later by the Europeans, and most recently by the large TNCs. No modern market system or progressive entrepreneurial class developed natively. What little capital accumulation there was usually flowed into more profitable European holdings, and those states that resorted to the state apparatus as an instrument of development – Mehmet Ali in Egypt during the 1820s and 1830s, the Ottoman Empire at the turn of the twentieth century, or even Mossadegh in Iran during the 1950s – continually were countered by outside political intervention. Moreover, to reemphasize their potential Fourth World character, many Arab states lack a large labor force or a considerable agricultural sector to exploit for capital formation. Until quite recently, they lacked administrative state mechanisms to guide national development, and they lacked a native technostructure to provide skilled labor and managerial expertise.

Still, because of their oil reserves, the Arab nations, in a very real way, <u>did</u> <u>not</u> need to internally generate these requisites. All of these elements existed, and could be imported at least initially from Europe, Japan, North America, or even the Communist states. Hence a historical compromise for national development was struck between the more advanced and the more backward nations through the mediation of the TNCs. The newly independent oil-producing Arab states, prior to the

TNC penetration, were so "backward" – despite some initial developmental advances in education, agriculture, and infrastructure which they made as colonies or wards of England or France – that even their state apparatus could not serve as the foundation of development. Therefore their ruling elites turned to the oil-consuming nations' petroleum corporations as a structural substitute to spark their very much delayed industrialization.(17) The Arab political leaders granted the corporations generous territorial, political, and economic concessions, and, in turn, the TNCs provided the initial capital, the skilled labor, the technical expertise, and the outlines of a developmental ideology which detonated the explosive developmental process of these Fourth World economies.

The TNC is excellently adapted to act as the structural mediation of national development. The eight "major" oil companies and their former regional subsidiaries, which have now been "indigenized" as ARAMCO, INOC, NIOC, KNOC, and ADNOC, essentially are creatures of international corporate, not nation-state, activity and loyalty.(18) As such, they owed their organizational existence and economic success to operating in the oil-producing countries for their parent TNC combines, and not for the TNCs' ultimate customers, the oil-consuming nations. On occasion, the TNCs were pressured to advance the interests of their home base nations. However, given the powerful political clout of the TNCs' home offices in First World countries, such pressures were effective only when the home base nation's and the TNCs' interests were identical. Otherwise, the TNCs usually were given a free hand to develop their own corporate foreign policy which often contradicted their home base nation's national foreign policy. Or, even more interestingly, TNC foreign policy formed and guided national foreign policy.

The TNCs were, and to a certain extent still are, the Arab states' primary capital generators and accumulators. Through corporate internal savings and later through international commercial banks, the TNCs imported pump-priming capital into the Arab economies. By opening Arab resources to foreign development, the TNCs also imported skilled labor, technical experts, and capital goods which were necessary for refining, transporting, managing, and marketing these resources. And, as the TNCs' administration and production needs grew, these corporate structures necessarily drew upon native labor and talent. Whereas the Arab states, even the military-ruled states, had largely failed to mobilize their capital and labor resources, the TNCs easily mobilized capital investment and absorbed many native workers by training them to control and manage modern corporate and industrial structures.

The TNC trade and managerial schools, the on-the-job training in the oilfields, and the massive deployment of modern capital goods gradually allowed Fourth World nomads, peasants, and villagers to begin to transform themselves into drillers, pipeline engineers, industrial managers, and petroleum economists of the new Third World. In doing so, these newly trained native workers picked up many of the cues of TNC administrative practices and managerial theories to learn a new developmental ideology. As living examples of modern management, rational administration, corporate power, large-scale organization, technological entrepreneurialism, and transnational oligopoly, the TNCs tacitly projected the essentials of a growth minded, corporate designed and industrially oriented developmental ideology into the ranks of the Arab modernizing elites. In their years of expansion in the Arab states, the TNCs baited the Arab's desire for modern goods and services by exposing many to the privileges of their own welfare systems within the oil company communities in Saudi Arabia, Iran, and around the Gulf.(19) At the same time, the TNCs everyday practices taught the Arab and OPEC states' leadership a great many lessons in how to program collectively just as the corporations collectively administered the world's energy resources for their own corporate advantage.

As was the case in Imperial Germany and Czarist Russia, once the developmental substitute established the capital base and a minimum of infrastructure, the Arabs also experienced a "diminution of backwardness." Through nationalization programs or participation arrangements, the Arab states are transcending their historical substitute to enter a more sophisticated phase of development, namely, that of state organized and directed industrial development. The TNC presence over the past four decades helped to gather the finance capital, train the skilled labor force, transfer the technical know-how, install the capital goods, and stimulate the developmental ideology necessary for national Arab elites to exert their autonomous political control. And, just as the Czarist state in its short commercial bank phase after 1905 could again resort to state action, and the German marketplace could rely somewhat upon its underlying financial and industrial cartels in times of uncertainty, the Arab and other oil-producing states have built OPEC as their "safety net" to coordinate collective transnational corporate action on oil pricing and supply.

As the former TNC oil ventures were increasingly subject to nationalization in the 1970s to guarantee Arab control over oil production and exporting, OPEC gained immense importance as the oil-producing nations' device for rationalizing oil distribution and oil supply policies. The major TNCs performed this supply prorationing and market-sharing function prior to OPEC's rise. Yet, to maintain the collective control engineered by the TNCs, OPEC is crucial to the transnational solidarity of the newly autonomous oil-producing states in pricing, supply, and production policies. As Zuhayr Mikdashi comments,

In the nineteen-seventies, however, once full control over the oil industries had been achieved, the OPEC conference, the secretariat, and the common commission became as concerned about the 'business' of oil as they already had been with its 'politics.' The business of oil inter alia called for expert skills in devising optimal pricing, production, and financial policies. For these, the OPEC governments came to rely on the technical staff of their newly formed national petroleum companies and of their central banks. OPEC delegations began to be composed of national corporation executives and bankers rather than politicians and bureaucrats of earlier years.(20)

The fact that the Arab states had enough personnel and resources to manage their own national petroleum companies as well as to contribute to OPEC's operations suggests that the Arab states were quite capable of mastering their own developmental programs. Trained in the tradition of the TNC's operations, OPEC planning and Arab experts easily became the structural substitute for the historically-constructed TNC oligopoly. Obviously, the TNCs still play an important role in exploring for and marketing oil world-wide, but the Arab states now effectively determine and administer the production and exporting links in their national petroleum industries. Furthermore, their transnational control apparatus, OPEC, frequently has "proved its competence in both 'battling' and 'cooperating' with the transnationals."(21) And, by doing so, its operations anchor the Arab states' respective plans for further heavy industrialization.

THE ECONOMIC AND POLITICAL DIMENSIONS

The Arab states also are exhibiting many parallels to the structural tendencies observed in the earlier German and Russian models of industrialization. For example, Gerschenkron observes that in conditions of delayed industrialization capital is scarce, entrepreneurial talent is rare, and industrial activity is often distrusted. Consequently, to best insure economy and rationality in the deployment of these scarce resources, an infatuation with "bigness" forms which is reflected in an emphasis on large-scale industrial plants and capital intensive modes of operation.(22)

Partly the result of purchasing capital goods and advanced technology from the already industrialized countries, and partly the result of a backward state making the fullest use of its scarce resources in the shortest time, these trends also appear to characterize the Arab developmental model as the following eight points illustrate in greater detail. Basically, these trends can be subdivided into two sets: the economic traits relating to finance capital, entrepreneurialism, industrialization, and organization; and the political features regarding internal social forces, developmental time frames, developmental social costs, and embourgeoisement.

Finance Capital

Sustained capital accumulation is a most essential element of development. The Arab states are engaged in "oil drum accumulation" as their increasing share of posted petroleum prices swells their national savings. In 1957 the average price per barrel of Saudi crude was less than $2; it is now over $12. Saudi Arabia's annual revenues two decades ago were $300 million a year; 1977's revenues should surpass $40 billion.(23) Kuwait's oil earnings in 1977 should reach at least $20 billion.(24) To judge the extensiveness of "oil drum accumulation," for only Saudi Arabia in October 1976, total foreign assets were $46,669 million.(25) As Saudi Arabia's oil production has risen from 1 mbd in 1958, to 3.5 mbd in 1970, and to 8.2 mbd in 1976, a readily increasing supply of finance capital has accumulated as well.(26) The existence and exigencies of the world energy market let the Arabs accumulate vast supplies of capital with relatively few domestic social costs. The Arab peasants do not feel the hardest bite, but "average consumers" abroad — American commuters, European industrialists, and African farmers — do. OPEC's political ability to "assure the protection of their common oil interests, especially prices and oil-export revenues,"(27) has ended the Arab states' respective histories as Fourth World countries. The OPEC countries' total investable surplus as a percentage of revenue from oil exports fell from 59.7 percent in 1974 to 28.4 percent in 1977. Still, nearly $158,000 million of OPEC capital is invested worldwide with almost a third of this sum in the United States.(28) As a bloc of states, the Arab countries are no longer being "de-capitalized" by the dominant metropole of more advanced industrial nations. Instead, the Arab developmental world has turned the tables on the First World as Arab industrialization forms from the capital extracted by higher oil prices and reinvested oil revenues in the First World economies.

Entrepreneurialism

Equally essential to accumulating capital and controlling finance, the Arab states are producing scores of finance capitalists, or an entrepreneurial elite shrewdly capable of using Arab capital resources at commercial and industrial applications in the Middle East and worldwide. Oil monies no longer lay inactive in the treasure rooms of minor sheikhs, or in the bullion vaults of Western banks. The Arabs, beginning with the original lessons learned at the Middle East Supply Center during the second World War, have trained hundreds of students at schools ranging from the London School of Economics to the Harvard Business School and the American land-grant universities in order to gain the expertise necessary for aggressively investing their capital worldwide. The managerial classes trained to administer the oil pipelines and the oil fields in the 1960s are transforming themselves, in part, into entrepreneurial elites. As one Arab Gulf banker asserted, "to me, money is like an army. We deploy chunks of our money in certain areas of secure investment. Profit is our prime target. But if we ever lose — and loss is a fact of present-day markets, just as profit is — we plan our investment in such a way that the loss affects profits percentage alone, while capital itself remains intact for another round."(29) Beirut, and now Bahrain, are world centers of financial activity. In these financial markets, the Arabs have retreated from unstable gold and real estate buys to investing in common stocks, establishing joint banking agencies, purchasing large interests in industrial combines, and edging into international shipping ventures.(30)

These new reserves of finance capital are further developing the skills of Arab entrepreneurial elites and expanding Arab commercial structures. In 1975, Saudi Arabia earned over $35 million from her oil exports, but only spent about $6 million on its own national expenditures – the remainder must be reinvested.(31) Having taken command of their own oil production, the Arab states are working to control "downstream" distribution and transportation of oil. Here the unbalanced nature of the TNCs' developmental activities can be openly witnessed. Even though the Arab OPEC states control most of the world's production of oil, they refine only 12.6 percent of their oil output and maintain only 3.6 percent of the world's refinery capacity.(32) Thirty percent of world shipping is to and from the Arab states, 90 percent of that volume in oil. The Arab states, however, control only 2 percent of the world's fleet and carry less than 5 percent of all tonnage going to and from the Middle East.(33) Hence the Arab countries are beginning to diversify by financing tanker lines, crude carrier construction, and even some limited marketing ventures.(34) The Abu Dhabi Fund for Economic Development, the Saudi Monetary Agency, the Kuwait Investment Company, and the Kuwait Fund for Arab Economic Development are financial institutions involved in funding and managing both Arab and Fourth World economic development projects. The further industrialization of Arab countries now is being planned, financed, and administered by Arab financiers and entrepreneurs, not First World investing elites.   Such new developments as the Arab Monetary Fund and a commonly organized financial market to better allocate all the Arab states' growing capital reserves are additional indications of the Arab states' entrepreneurial control over their economic futures through their own devices.(35)

Industrialization

As they begin their industrialization, the Arab states enjoy important advantages by tapping directly into the present state of technological development. With mainly small populations that lack most industrial skills, the Arab states could not have industrialized effectively in more labor-intensive modes of industrial development. Thus these countries can more easily engage in industrialization by turning their surplus oil revenues into a highly capital-intensive industrial base.   Yet, at the same time, these highly mechanized capital-intensive modes of industrial growth have not mobilized large numbers of workers. Indeed, most if not all unskilled or semiskilled labor is imported (like their machinery) from Europe, Asia, and Africa. A rather small elite of highly skilled and largely white collar workers has formed to oversee the new Arab industries.

As the most recent case of delayed industrialization, the Arab states also are displaying the latecomer's clear preference for large-scale industrial undertakings, big industrial plants, and high capital intensiveness. Some variation exists, to be sure. Smaller countries like Kuwait and Saudi Arabia need high technology to compensate for their very small labor forces, while larger states such as Algeria, Iraq, and even Iran have been striving to build massive heavy industrial sectors to employ their larger populations. The Arab desire for large-scale industrialization, for example, is reflected in Saudi Arabia's $142 billion Second Development Plan and its Joint Commission on Economic Cooperation with the United States. In this plan, ARAMCO has undertaken a $16,000 million natural gas liquefication scheme for export and use at the Saudi's industrial centers of Jubail and Yenbo. This massive project will feed energy into a planned petrochemical, fertilizer, and steel mill complex in addition to supplying power stations and allied industries. Foreign contractors perform much of the construction, but Arab engineers and ARAMCO planners have set out the designs and specifications.(36) Additionally, the Saudis, in conjunction with the American joint commission, are plotting out the large-scale development of infrastructure and service industries: "the activities of the commission include planning the needs, and supply of electrical equipment, vocational training (particularly in engineering, agricultural and water resources planning, statistical assistance and data processing), creating a national park, the developing of food marketing and many other aspects of commerce, expanding radio and television networks, and advising on an intercity expressway road system."(37) Saudi Arabia's new international airport, costing $3 to $4 billion and planned to be as large in area as the District of Columbia, also indicates the Arabs' fascination with "bigness" in their rapidly progressing industrialization.(38)

For the Arabs, then, industrialization means heavy industrialization with a concomitant interest in large-scale plants, or indeed whole industrial cycles. Hence, a strong emphasis is played on turn-key operations and emplacements that can be fitted immediately into the productive process. Because of their capital resources, and unlike Fourth World countries, the Arab states do not think in terms of a petroleum refinery, a steel mill, a copper mine or a power station. Rather, they are planning for and developing entire petrochemical industries, whole steel sectors, full-blown copper and aluminum industries, and comprehensive power networks in order to make rapid and efficacious use of their obviously dwindling oil resources. Iran has allocated many billions of dollars for a nuclear-based electricity network. It has also invested in mines and refineries to tap its estimated three billion tons of copper reserves, while over $3 billion is earmarked for Iranian petrochemical industries by 1980.(39)

The joint inter-Arab commissions established to coordinate regional industrial activity, in addition to expressing the need to establish and rationalize an integrated market among the 130 million Arabs in the Middle East, also reflect the need for "bigness" and large-scale production. The Industrial Development Center for Arab States in Cairo is promoting investment in special and alloy steel industries to satisfy internal market demands up to 1990;(40) the OAPEC ministers have agreed to organize petroleum services for the Arab market through the Arab Petroleum Services Company; (41) and the Arab League has set up the Arab Union for Food Industries in Cairo to encourage regional production, distribution, and marketing of food product.(42) A crucial motivation behind all of these programs is the same − the greatly delayed Arab industrialization has prompted them to stress large-scale "big" industry and high capital-intensiveness in their industrial growth to overcome and to compensate for their previous lack of expertise, labor, and entrepreneurial skills.

Organization

A final economic trend characteristic of the Arab states is their tendency to plan and organize their industrial and commercial activities in terms of the TNC organizational model. The formerly a-national joint ventures constructed by the international oil industry in the Arab states are being absorbed into the Arab state structures, giving these former transnational corporate structures a national economic role. In doing so, however, these TNC agencies are strongly influencing the Arab states' economic and political activities. Many of the organizational forms, procedures, and practices of Arab economic development seem to be modeled along the lines of a modern corporate executive apparatus and technostructure. OPEC, OAPEC, and a bevy of other international councils and regional directorates that coordinate and mediate the Arab states' development attest to the impact of this inspiration.

On the basis of the TNC example, the Arabs have established the Arab Mining Conference to discuss joint mining ventures,(43) the Arab Economic Unity Council to collectively plan economic interactions until 1981,(44) the Arab Industrial Conference to organize regional industry,(45) the Arab Free Zones to promote inter-Arab trade,(46) the Arab Investment Company to manage public investments,(47) the Arab Monetary Fund,(48) and the Gulf Common Market to ease inter-Arab trade flow.(49) All of these agencies seem to impart the qualities of transnational corporate behavior to Arab economic organization. Through these organizations' activities, the Arab states' technical personnel bring collective management, rational administration, and large-scale organizational methods to bear on their common economic and social challenges much like the TNCs traditionally operated using their organization to solve the engineering and marketing challenges posed by Middle East oil. These structures also buttress the Arabs' cultural community with functional ties of industry, finance, technology, commerce, and planning, enabling these rather small separate states to behave more like a single united body. Of course, such cooperative efforts remain contingent upon political events and the goodwill of the diverse Arab regimes. Yet given these factors, the Arab states have begun tentatively to rationalize their regional and national economy by means of transnational corporate forms.

The four commonly developing economic trends, in turn, are closely related to an emerging set of political features which seem to be shared by the Arab OPEC states. Here the peculiar tendencies of Arab industrialization directly affect the Arabs' internal social forces, developmental time frames and social costs, and embourgeoisement.

Internal Social Forces

In spite of the fact that world economic conditions and individual national objectives enforce a degree of Arab unity, tremendous internal diversity also characterizes the Arab developmental world. Basically, two distinct classes of states, with two different internal alignments of social forces, coexist within this bloc's ranks: the "banker" and the "industrializer" nations.(50)

The "banker" states seem to share these common qualities: small populations, small agricultural bases, no significant peasant class, little previously established industry or infrastructure, small recently formed middle class groups, but immense reserves of petroleum. To date, these nations mainly have been ruled by conservative aristocratic governments with deep commitments to traditional Islamic culture. They have accumulated large capital and foreign exchange holdings and have a limited capacity for absorbing extensive heavy industrial development. Among this group of states are Kuwait, Saudi Arabia, the UAE, Qatar, and Libya (which, of course, is an exception to many of the generalizations advanced above).

At this time and in the future this tier of states can most likely be counted on to break into the commercial bank phase of development because of their large financial holdings, small populations and work force, and their ruling elites' commitment to traditional Islamic life. Financial and commercial ventures developing towards a white collar economy based on services provide the "banker" countries with their most effective path for modern economic success without the pitfalls and disruptions of full industrialization. Indeed, the fact that they have such large reserves of oil and money accounts in part for their continuing aristocratic rule. There is plenty of economic opportunity and social privilege available for the modernized middle class groups, and a plethora of benefits open to the entire population because of these states' large supplies of oil. Thus there has been little effective pressure to date for deposing the traditional ruling oligarchies as these states throttle most internal dissent.

The "industrializer" states, on the other hand, have a distinctly different configuration of internal social forces. Having already partially developed economies with large populations and sizeable agricultural bases, Algeria, Iraq, and Iran fit into this category. Because of direct and indirect Western influence, these states possessed some infrastructure and industrial emplacements prior to experiencing a jump in their oil revenues; and they have articulated investment policies rooted in these oil monies that aim at attaining much greater and more diverse levels of industrialization than those foreseen by the "bankers." Yet, their reserves of oil (with the probable exception of Iraq) are far more limited than the "banker" states, and they can easily absorb all of their oil receipts plus additional capital, as Algeria's and Iran's heavy foreign borrowing reveals.

The "social costs" of modernization in these states – calculated in terms of peasant dislocations, rural poverty, police repression, urban sprawl, and internal resistance by the intelligentsia – have been and are far greater than in the "banker" states. The "industrializers" middle, working, and technical classes are comparatively much larger than the "banker" states', but these urban classes are still heavily outnumbered by the rural peasant populations. To be sure, this greater internal class differentiation is reflected in the "industrializers'" civil-military governing alliances which are far more secular and radically oriented than the "banker" states. Iran, prior to the revolutionary events of 1978-1979, was surely a traditional aristocratic regime, but its earlier "White Revolution" and its goal of great power status clearly distinguished it from Saudi Arabia's puritanical Wahabbi regime. Ultimately all of these nations aim at complete and comprehensive industrialization within the next generation. And, to be sure, a much greater sense of urgency prevails upon the "industrializer" states because their grand industrial programs are predicated upon more meager reserves of petroleum.

Within both blocs of nations, however, a similar alliance of class forces appears to guide the process of development.(51) The Arab model of highly capital-intensive development has not necessitated the complete displacement of old ruling elites. In the "industrializer" states where more radical civil-military alliances of modern urban intellectuals and secularly oriented military officer corps succeeded colonial or aristocratic rule, the new rulers also have essentially maintained the same relations with the TNC structures. The TNC presence over the years has trained and employed a new class of managers, economists, engineers, and entrepreneurs which are allied with an equally small working class (the working class, due to the capital intensiveness and technical sophistication of the petroleum industry, behaves much like a privileged petty bourgeoisie) and modern, international, higher management groups.

Together this unlikely alliance formed beneath the rule exercised by either traditional aristocratic or civil-military modernizers within the Arab states as these rulers slowly prepared to assert national control over the TNCs' productive structures. Once nationalization or participation began, the corporately created middle and working classes allied themselves with their state's established ruling elites to operate the oil industries for native benefit. The traditional aristocratic regimes, such as Saudi Arabia, Kuwait, and Qatar, try to contain change to economic development to preserve Islamic culture, whereas the military-based rulers, such as in Algeria, Iraq, and to a lesser extent, Iran prior to deposing the Shah, aim at using their economic development as a means to attain full social and cultural modernization. Still, for both internal class alignments, a dual economy/society relationship has survived the nationalization of the TNCs as most of the Arab populations, with the exception of Kuwait, live without many of the everyday benefits of a modern economy. As the native middle and working classes have taken over the TNCs' operations in the Arab states, a good deal of the "separate utopia" syndrome persists as these new classes enjoy company housing, schools, and benefits, while the larger society of migrants, peasants, and nomads have received fewer social benefits. This question is one that the ruling internal social forces have to deal with increasingly as their national development accelerates.

Time Frames

The national leadership of states which have experienced a delayed industrialization impose a time constraint of their designs as they initiate development. Both Imperial Germany and later Czarist and Soviet Russia strove to industrialize within one or two generations. The ruling developmental elites usually set a limited time frame for industrialization because of the tremendous pressures rapid industrialization puts on the peoples' political loyalties and social unity. In their political gamble, one generation's satisfactions are postponed, hopefully, to insure greater material well-being for the next generation. The Arab elites sense an equal urgency in their industrialization, but for different reasons. Oil once lifted from their territory is gone forever; and oil that remains in the ground if and when the First World develops any of its wide range of energy alternatives will be wasted potential. Consequently, the Arabs are not striving to industrialize quickly because of the high social costs they incur to overcome backwardness, but because their future prosperity is dependent upon a presently wasting resource. If the oil runs out before their secondary and tertiary industrialization takes solid hold, the Arabs stand to fall back into the ranks of the Fourth World. As the now deposed Shah of Iran continually observed, "our oil is bound to finish some day – in 20 or 30 years."(52) Necessarily, then, industrial diversification and integrated economic planning are in the works to assure equal power and prosperity for future generations of Arab OPEC state citizens.

Only Algeria and Iraq have any kind of "balanced economy" at this time. Both, like Iran, have considerable agricultural potential and large populations which could support an autonomous industrial state. Therefore Algeria is stressing its metal and mineral sectors, machine tool and machinery industries to prepare for its nonoil based industrialization, while Iraq is striving to rationalize its considerable agricultural resources. The smaller, less populous states, Kuwait, Saudi Arabia, Qatar, the UAE, and Libya, are directed toward building more moderate industrial bases tied to petroleum: petrochemicals, fertilizers, food processing, shipping, and oil production. Also, commercial and financial services are projected as integral components of their economies: banking, common stocks, communications, and transportation industries. Having more oil in reserve for the future and more money presently in the bank, these states also hope to industrialize rapidly, but their urgency is plainly less pressing because of their relative financial security.

Social Costs

By and large, and quite unlike preceding forms of industrialization, the Arab's accumulation of finance capital and formation of a modern work force is imposing fewer social costs on their native populations. Of course, political repression and popular rebellion are familiar occurrences, but at a comparatively lower level than in Europe or the Soviet

Union. The plethora of oil monies in most of these states has seen the construction of a welfare state proceed apace with the creation of an industrial state.

Again, this turn of political events has come about largely because of the existence of the First World and its immediate concern for providing welfare services. Because the Arabs are developing under this distinctly different horizon of welfare priorities – social welfare benefits were among the last provided to the German and Russian working classes even though more significant down payments were made by Bismarck and Lenin than the English reformers made to the British working class – they have plowed a great deal of capital investment into social services such as hospitals, housing, health services, schools, and welfare payments. Schools and hospitals are willingly built by the Arab states and, "though sometimes they cannot function for lack of staff, equipment or even water, illiteracy among the young is being abolished and health care is much superior to a decade ago."(53)

Many of the benefits, to be sure, are reserved for the Arab states' citizens and many migrant Arab and African laborers receive few if any benefits, but the main trends are toward providing immediate material benefits to the population as the states industrialize. Indeed, such purchases reverberate the economic trends discussed above as social welfare services are planned for and provided on a large-scale capital-intensive basis to illustrate the Arabs' desire both to overcome their delayed industrialization and their delayed social modernization. Not only must they have the best industrial goods and technology available, they must also have the most up-to-date consumer, medical, educational, and health services.

The developmental substitutes deployed by the Arabs enabled them to greatly diminish their social costs in industrialization. Historically, the process of development has required a harsh redistribution from social consumption to industrial capitalization; the exploitation of rural agricultural production to fuel urban industrial expansion; and the delaying of social gratification for entire generations of citizens. In the Arab developmental world, however, the TNCs' importation of capital, labor, expertise, and developmental ideology has placed an easy down payment on the Arabs' developmental advance. The continuing interest accruing from the TNCs' principal investments in infrastructure, capital goods, and labor training programs has for the most part obviated the Arab states' need to borrow against their domestic population's future social consumption.

Again this course arises largely from the legacy of the TNCs willingly providing and importing considerable quantities of social capital to sweeten their essentially unequal exchange with the Arab states. At first the TNCs both owned and controlled their productive and social capital emplacements, but once it was fixed into place, the national elites began to assert a measure of national control and to claim national ownership to derive benefits for themselves. Private wealth and public consumption in the Arab societies were not tyranically expropriated by the ruling Arab elites from the peasants and nomads, but TNC productive forces were increasingly turned to public advantage through added royalty assessments, adding additional taxes, pressing for limited participation, and finally effecting full nationalization. Foreign capital, labor, and expertise were easily available, readily importable, and quite controllable once the Arab states worked in unison for their collective benefit.

Saudi Arabia, for example, has over 1.5 million foreign laborers working on industrialization projects and another .5 million will be required to finish the current Second Development Plan by 1981.(54) Over 200 American firms as well as innumerable West German, Japanese, French, Italian, and South Korean firms are fulfilling development contracts in Saudi Arabia as well as throughout the Arab developmental world. And so the task of constructing, training, and deploying a modern domestic labor force, technological sector, and industrial base can proceed without the excesses and waste associated with previous forms of industrialization.

Although the Arabs are experiencing a heavy dose of "future shock" as their purchases abroad inundate their countries with a torrent of needed and superfluous goods, their developmental social costs up to this point have been comparatively very low.(55) Moreover, the fact that industrialization has imposed few hardships on the Arab population and class structure is important for understanding their unchanged coalitions of internal social forces and ready acceptance of immediate industrialization. As long as industrial development continues with matching increases in material benefits, it is quite likely that the elite coalitions and their developmental designs will continue to command both economic power and political support.

Embourgeoisement

Up until the 1960s, the Arab states usually portrayed themselves as fellow travelers of the very poor but morally pure Fourth World nations. Together with the African, Asian, and Latin American nations, the Arab states confronted the First World with demands for development aid and assistance to redress partly the economic exploitation which resulted from their unequal exchanges in global markets. Yet, as the Arab states have moved into a phase of lessened backwardness, they also have acted like a group of nouveaux riches economically, diplomatically, and politically. Because of their newfound wealth and status, the Arab states have gradually begun to behave much more like the developed First World states and they are forgetting their former fraternity with the Fourth World nations. As they develop, in other words, the Arab states are displaying sure signs of "embourgeoisement."

The embourgeoisement represents the outcome of several political trends. First, and undoubtedly foremost, the Arabs' economic power since 1971 to 1973 has become awesomely important. The financial solvency of many First World nations is now dependent upon Arab financial assistance; the developmental future of much of the Fourth World rests upon Arab oil energy; and the entire economic outlook of the industrialized nations can be changed radically by decisions made in

Arab capitals. Plainly, the serious conflicts between Arab OPEC moderates and radicals over maintaining the U.S. dollar as their oil pricing currency and over the timing of new price hikes in 1978 and 1979 indicate the careful concern that the OPEC countries extend to the OECD bloc. This new power has been accompanied with a cautious, conservative, and more responsible foreign policy that has little place for moral purity on the questions of economic exploitation, unequal exchange, or underdevelopment because OPEC itself can be rightly seen as causing all of these ills.

Second, the Arab states' political "victories" in 1973 – both in the Yom Kippur War and the following oil embargo – have eased their defeat complex vis-à-vis the First World. They are now the equals to and partners of the First World nations who, in turn, have shown the Arab states that the new obligations, responsibilities, and behaviors in the IBRD, IFAD, and IMF that go along with such status do not easily fit with the Arabs' association with Fourth World states. The Arab radicalism which was possible in the 1950s and 1960s when the Arabs fought Israel with Western war surplus weapons and African revolutionaries trained in Algeria's old FLN camps is no longer affordable as the Arabs spend billions on advanced arms and industrial development. In the 1970s the Arab states have developed to the point that they have a great deal to lose unless they behave with restraint and caution. Indeed, one can quite sensibly suggest that the recent conservative caution shown by the OPEC states in their price programming during December 1977 and June 1978 in fact illustrates how the OPEC states are full partners in western industry and commerce. To raise oil prices in the West, OPEC would only injure the economic well-being of its corporate investments and recirculate added inflation into its own imports from the West, while an effort to move away from the dollar as the unit for oil pricing to check the OPEC countries' financial losses to inflation – now running $12,000 to $17,000 million a year – would immediately devalue OPEC's dollar investments and the economic vitality of the OECD region.(56)

And, third, the Arabs' embourgeoisement draws heavily from their mode of development. Transnational oil corporations served as the main model for Arab organization and policy as these states embarked upon economic development. The clearly "bourgeois" institutions of international finance and trade, transnational oil production and industrial planning and management have become the Arabs' prime fields of action in the 1970s. And this institutional base affords infertile ground for Fourth World radical politics.

Thus, as newly wealthy states, the Arab countries are revitalizing and even reproducing many of the dependency relations they once suffered under, only now they are the beneficiaries of others' economic dependence. The Arab states are striving to assert themselves hegemonically over the Fourth World, especially in Africa, through international aid programs, petroleum price relief programs, and moral leadership at international summits. In the Fourth World the Arabs seek higher prices on their oil, but low prices on Fourth World exports. Consequently, the current account balances of the NODC's are $26.5 billion in deficit largely due to increased Arab oil prices.(57) And the non-Muslim NODCs have received less than 10 percent of all OPEC concessional aid since October 1973. The African and Asian nations are being "decapitalized" by high Arab oil prices; in 1974 the NODCs received $11.3 billion in developmental assistance, but their oil bills increased at the same time by $11 billion.(58) Indeed, when the Arab states do make investments in the Fourth World, they seek guarantees from the host nations against the nationalization or sequestration of their assets – ironically, this requirement is standard operating procedure at the Saudi Development Fund.(59)

The Fourth World is becoming more closely tied to the Third World because of Arab oil and petrochemical imports. Yet, at the same moment, the Arab countries are not investing in the destitute Fourth World area. In breaking out of many of their old dependency relations, the Arab OPEC states have placed much of Africa and Asia into new sets of asymetrical dependency cycles. The Arab states' embourgeoisement denies their alleged membership in the planet's destitute "Southern" camp; it indicates that the Arab OPEC countries are the latest and most enthusiastic initiates of the affluent "Northern" region.

CONCLUSIONS

Obviously, many forces played a significant role in the creation of OPEC's new economic power and political capabilities. The ultimate anchor of OPEC's strength can be traced back to the high-energy industrial forms of the import dependent OECD nations. The entire post-World War Two prosperity of Europe, Japan, and North America has been predicated upon readily accessible and fairly cheap energy supplies derived increasingly from petroleum rather than coal. In the 1940s, the nationally based oil companies provided a concrete mediation between the oil-producing regions of Africa, Asia, Latin America, and the Middle East, and the industrial nations. Backed by colonial or quasi-colonial native administrations and substantial Western military power, these major oil companies maintained a steadily increasing supply and an acceptably low price for petroleum in the oil-consuming countries.

Yet, as the demand for imported petroleum increased almost exponentially, the once nationally oriented oil corporations re-organized their operations to assert and then to expand their corporate political autonomy. The enlarged dependence of the oil-consuming nations upon the oil-producing nations led to the greater dependence of both blocs upon the oil corporations and to their increasing interdependence as national economies. Hence the corporations became transnational, or corporate directed, in their operating policies, foreign relations, and organizational loyalties. This freedom of action, in turn, projected the organizational model for the OPEC states' international collaboration, and provided the financial wherewithal for Arab economic and social development.

The crucial outcome of October 1973, then, appears to be the formation of an Arab developmental world within the global economic system.   While still entangled in a number of asymetric and unequal exchange relations with the West, the emergence of this Arab developmental world, at the same time, has shaken the industrialized West down to its deepest political economic roots by marking an end to the post-World War Two era of abundance and affluence. In doing so, OPEC, and its Arab members, have gained immense international prestige, new political leverage, and tremendous economic power. These developments manifest themselves in the massive transfer of wealth from one bloc of oil-consuming nations to the bloc of oil-producers, in the new prestige of the OPEC nations in international summits and organizations, in the economic prosperity of their national economies, and in the creation of a new international tier of lesser-developed nations below them.   The OPEC states, in the eyes of OECD and Warsaw bloc nations, are no longer the brethren of Bolivia, Kenya, Burma, or Afghanistan. On the contrary, their new political and economic capabilities, both those already tested and those yet to come, promise to make them more equal to North America, Europe, Japan, the Soviet Union, and China.

New developmental worlds seem to differentiate themselves through cataclysmic changes in global relations of dependence and interdependence.   These catastrophic turning points lead them out of their former low estate and into a new international tier of their own making. Collective activity accomplished through common will along unprecedented political paths demonstrates the OPEC states' economic capacity, organizational integrity, and political ability. For the OPEC bloc it was no mean feat to become an international powerhouse, banker, and, potentially, workshop — all against the resistance of transnational corporations and the industrialized West.

Obviously the new OPEC developmental world will not necessarily last forever. Its internal contradictions, political differences, and organizational difficulties mix a strong element of fragility with its present economic and political successes. Some new cataclysm may once again transform the international status system. But, as long as oil continues as the world's prime strategic commodity, the new "Third World" composed largely of Arab OPEC states will continue to benefit from the massive redistribution of capital that has been the principal effect of its creation. In fact, a whole new cycle of dependency relations seems to be forming in which the relatively rich First and Second World states contribute to the coffers of the new "Third World," either directly through oil payments and capital transfers, or indirectly as aid from the First and Second Worlds' funnels through the new "Fourth World," emerging as payments for oil, interest on loans, commodity exchanges, or capital blight. The poor states, of which the African, Asian,and Latin American LDCs are the most numerous, must now suffer a new set of dependency relations — in addition to their existing ties to the OECD nations and the socialist bloc — under the new Arab developmental world.

NOTES

(1) See Irving Louis Horowitz, Three Worlds of Development: The Theory and Practice of International Stratification (London: Oxford University Press, 1965).

(2) The First World's allied and client states would include less industrialized and somewhat marginal economies which associate with the First World block, such as Portugal, Spain, Greece, Turkey, or Ireland.

(3) See Richard J. Barnet and Ronald E. Muller, Global Reach: The Power of the Multinational Corporations (New York: Simon and Schuster, 1974), pp. 132, 194, and 196.

(4) OPEC currently has thirteen members: Saudi Arabia, Iran, Iraq, Kuwait, Abu Dhabi, Qatar, Algeria, Libya, and Gabon, Nigeria, Ecuador, Venezuela, and Indonesia.

(5) This study will concentrate on the Arab states except for one important exception: Iran. Although it is not an Arab country, it nonetheless follows essentially the same developmental formula as its Arab neighbors. Thus this discussion includes Iran among the ranks of the Arab states.

(6) Oded Rmeba, "Arab Oil and Aerica's Energy Dilemmas," Midstream 12 (June/July 1976): 30-1.

(7) Ibid.

(8) Ibid.

(9) The leading international oil companies, or the "seven sisters," include Exxon, Mobil, Standard Oil of California, Texaco, Gulf, Royal Dutch Shell, and British Petroleum.

(10) John M. Blair, The Control of Oil (New York: Pantheon Books, 1976). See Part One for Blair's discussion of how the major international oil companies evolved their oligopolistic control of world oil supply, marketing, and distribution during the inter-world war period.

(11) King Faisal of Saudi Arabia ordered ARAMCO to increase oil lifting in Saudi Arabia in May 1973 in anticipation of the fall "oil embargo." Production from May to October 1973 averaged 18 percent higher than the first quarter of 1973, and it was this added production in 1973 that prevented the so-called "oil embargo" from crippling the industrialized West. Yet the supply situation was such as to make the increased prices stick. Blair, The Control of Oil, pp. 268 and 281.

(12) Ibid., p. 262.

(13) The Petroleum Economist, January 9, 1974, p. 9. Cited in Blair, The Control of Oil, p. 272.

(14) Blair, The Control of Oil, p. 273.

(15) Robert W. Tucker, "Oil and American Power: Three Years Later," Commentary 63 (January 1977): 33.

(16) On the continent, and especially in Central Europe, many of the preexisting economic and social institutions found in England were not present. Consequently, a nation like Germany presents itself as a case of "delayed industrialization." Because of its lack of national unity, its largely agricultural economy, and its multiple social divisions, Germany represented a "relatively backward" developmental situation when compared to England. Gerschenkron notes: "One way of defining the degree of backwardness is precisely in terms of absence, in a more backward country, of factors which in a more advanced country served as prerequisites of industrial development. Accordingly, one of the ways of approaching the problem is by asking what substitutions and what patterns of substitutions for the lacking factors occurred in the process of industrialization in conditions of backwardness." Alexander Gerschenkron, Economic Backwardness in Historical Perspective (Cambridge, Mass.: Harvard University Press, 1962), p. 42. Lacking the "rich" preindustrial history of England, Germany's developmental elites – the marriage of "iron and rye" – sought a substitute for primitive capital accumulation in the credit creation policies of the giant commercial banks forming at that time. Likewise, the Russian developmental elites of modernizing aristocrats sought a substitute for capital accumulation in the state apparatus which both gathered capital and then invested it in various state planned enterprises. For more information on Gerschenkron's theories see also Continuity in History and other Essays (Cambridge, Mass.: Harvard University Press, 1968) and Europe in the Russian Mirror: Four Lectures in Economic History (London: Cambridge University Press, 1970).

(17) After the final failure of European "gunboat" diplomacy in Suez during the 1956 crisis, the transnational oil corporation increasingly could act as an independent social force in the Middle East. While it was not in the best interest of the oil-consuming nations to build up the Arab states into autonomous political units, the TNCs pursued this development because it was in their corporate interest to satisfy the demands of the oil-producing countries in order to maintain their corporate profits.

(18) The Arabian American Oil Company, the Iraq National Oil Company, the National Iranian Oil Company, the Kuwait National Oil Company, and the Abu Dhabi National Oil Company.

(19) "Special Report on Saudi Arabia," Middle East Economic Digest, December 1976, p. 20. Such estimates, of course, vary considerably.

Morgan Guaranty Bank projected in March 1978 that the total OPEC surplus would reach $250 billion by the end of 1978, Middle East Economic Digest, March 10, 1978, p. 15.

(20) Zuhayr Mikdashi, "The OPEC Process," Daedalus 104 (Fall 1975): 205-6.

(21) Ibid., p. 206.

(22) Gerschenkron, Economic Backwardness, p. 14.

(23) Middle East Economic Digest, March 11, 1977, p. 11.

(24) Ibid., (March 3, 1977), p. 7.

(25) Ibid., "Special Report on Saudi Arabia," p. 27.

(26) Ibid., p.19.

(27) Mikdashi, "The OPEC Process," p. 203.

(28) Middle East Economic Digest, September 30, 1977, p. 11.

(29) The Arab Economist, (January 9, 1976), p. 28.

(30) Kuwait has founded the Kuwait Oil Tanker Company, the Kuwait Shipping Company, and has jointly established with Iraq, Libya, Qatar, Saudi Arabia, and the UAE, the Arab Petroleum Transport Company which has ordered six new large crude carriers from France and West Germany Arab Economist, (January 9, 1976), p. 31. Arab investors now hold 25 percent interest in Krupp Steel, 14 percent interest in Daimler-Benz, and 7.5 percent interest in Occidental Petroleum Newsweek, (February 10, 1975), pp. 60-2. Arab investments have also gravitated to Eurocurrencies, and United States and United Kingdom securities. Over $8 billion in stocks and bonds were purchased in the United States during all of 1975. New York Times, "International Economic Survey," (January 30, 1977), p. 11.

(31) Edward F. Sheehan, "The Epidemic of Money," New York Times Magazine, (November 14, 1976), p. 116.

(32) Middle East Economic Digest, (February 10, 1978), p. 17.

(33) Middle East Economic Digest, (January 20, 1978), p. 14.

(34) See V.H. Oppenheim, "Arab Tankers Move Downstream," Foreign Policy, no. 23, (Summer 1976); and "Plain Sailing for Arab Fleets," Arab Economist, (March 1977).

(35) Middle East Economic Digest, (December 31, 1976), p. 9. Of course,

these relatively rational innovations in Arab finance continue to balance themselves against the sumptuary consumption of the royalty, the nobility, and upper middle classes. Moreover, these elites do continue to engage in substantial private foreign investment which encourages capital flight and lessened domestic economic development.

(36) Ibid., "Special Report on Saudi Arabia," p. 20.

(37) Ibid., pp. 31-2.

(38) Sheehan, "The Epidemic of Money," p. 117.

(39) New York Times, "International Economic Survey," (January 30, 1977), p. 11.

(40) Middle East Economic Survey, (April 3, 1977), p. 13.

(41) Middle East Economic Digest, (January 14, 1977), p. 12.

(42) Ibid., (April 3, 1977), p. 13.

(43) Ibid., (March 11, 1977), p. 22.

(44) Ibid., (December 31, 1976), p. 9.

(45) Ibid., (January 7, 1977), p. 9.

(46) Ibid., (March 11, 1977), p. 22.

(47) Ibid., (December 3, 1976), p. 9.

(48) Ibid., p. 8.

(49) Ibid.

(50) These terms initially were employed by Blair in The Control of Oil, pp. 280-2.

(51) See Michael C. Hudson, Arab Politics (New Haven, 1977), pp. 395-401.

(52) New York Times, "International Economic Survey," (January 30, 1977), p. 11.

(53) Sheehan, "The Epidemic of Money," p. 118.

(54) Ibid., p. 130.

(55) To be sure, the impact of "future shock" on these traditional Islamic cultures should not be ignored. The "Jeddah" syndrome of transportation bottlenecks, building delays, bureaucratic tie-ups, and

the general congestion of rapid growth are exacting certain "social costs" in the Arab developmental model. Yet they usually remain uncalculated because of their disorganized character. What is more, the fact that the Arab governments are not milking their populations for finance capital should not blind one to the fact of their failing to fairly redistribute much of their national wealth to their tremendously poor populations.

(56) Middle East Economic Digest, (April 7, 1978), p. 15.

(57) The Banker, vol. 127, (March 1977), p. 92.

(58) Blair, The Control of Oil, p. 274.

(59) "Arab Funds for Economic Development," Arab Economist, (April 1977).

6 Netherlands Foreign Policy and the 1973-74 Oil Embargo— The Effects of Transnationalism*

Frederic S. Pearson

INTRODUCTION

The foreign policy of any country, whether a great or small power, is strongly conditioned by the "environments" its government confronts. Certain scholars dealing with crisis decision-making have begun to focus on the important interplay between decision makers and environments in explaining the decisions, reactions to pressure, and consequences of policies adopted.

The search for general theories of crisis decision-making is complicated because different countries will face different environments and different political necessities in a crisis situation. Also, a country's resources may determine the approach adopted and the success of policies. Thus, in the long run it is necessary to build theories which explain the behavior of small, medium, and large powers possessing various types of natural, economic, political, and social resources, located in certain geographical or political environments, and confronting military or economic threats.

Crisis is an extremely elusive concept; it depends on leaders' perceptions, as well as on the political gains and losses they expect. Thus, there are difficulties with crisis as a "scientific" unit of analysis. Some crises may stem from threats in the external environment, forcing leaders to defend their countries; examples might include invasion threats such as those confronting Netherlands' leaders in 1940. Other

*The author gratefully acknowledges the assistance of the Netherlands-America Fulbright Commission, the John F. Kennedy Institute in Tilburg, The Netherlands, and its director, Professor F.A.M. Alting von Geusau, Mr. R.E. Doerga, The Center for International Studies of the University of Missouri-St. Louis and Professor Peter Odell of Erasmus University of Rotterdam. Responsibility for the study and findings rests with the author alone.

crises are conditioned in part by leaders' political needs or experiences. President Kennedy reacted strongly to the presence of the missiles in Cuba partly because he was under intense pressure from political elements inside the United States to "do something about Cuba," and partly because toleration of missiles so close to the American border would diminish Washington's control over future events.

Michael Brecher has defined crisis as:

> . . . a breakpoint along the peace-war continuum of the states' relations with any other international actor(s). A crisis is a situation with four necessary and sufficient conditions, as these are <u>perceived</u> by the highest level decision-makers of the actor concerned: (1) a change in its external or internal environment which generates (2) a threat to basic values, with a simultaneous or subsequent (3) high probability of involvement in military hostilities, and the awareness of (4) a finite time for their response to the external value threat.(1)

Brecher goes on to note that crisis may exist in the economic as well as military-strategic foreign policy spheres. Presumably economic crises, while not necessarily entailing high probability of military hostilities, involve threats to basic values including the possible loss of productive capability, severe unemployment, poverty, starvation, or severe social problems. Leaders may have limited time to remedy these threats. Most crisis analysis has dealt with military issues, and it is important to explore the economic realm to determine whether actors with different resources and levels of power can effectively deal with threats. Indeed in the future, with decreasing world resource supplies and the leveling off of national growth rates, economic crisis may be perceived more frequently.

Transnationalism is one of the factors in the present international environment which is likely to condition responses to economic crisis. While the supposed revolution in international affairs which has created new networks and linkages between states has sometimes been exaggerated – nongovernmental organizations, multinational enterprises, foreign control of domestic economies, and so forth have all been present historically – the fact remains that many countries' sovereignty is diminished by foreign penetration and dependence on foreign economic connections. It becomes increasingly difficult for some countries to regulate their economies through domestic means alone, since foreign sources can supply considerable capital which affects the domestic market. Countries with relatively small populations or which depend on foreign trade for important resources and capital can be especially hard hit by changes in the external environment. The way such countries deal with unexpected change has not yet been fully explored; it is important to know whether they have effectively dealt with threats or whether improvements in dependent states' crisis decision-making can be suggested. In this connection, let us remember that no country is ever totally isolated or totally dependent on another; <u>interdependence</u> is a more usual condition in which even the weak country will have some influence. We seek to understand more about the ways such influence has been and can be used.

Thus, crisis decisions can only be understood in relation to patterns of dependence and interdependence in the domestic and foreign environments. Keohane and Nye have noted the distinction between states which are <u>sensitive</u> to changes in the external environment and those which are especially <u>vulnerable</u> to those changes.(2) Both states would be dependent on the environment, but the vulnerable state would be unable to rectify dislocations caused by changes in the external environment through policies of its own. Thus, for example, a state might be dependent on foreign oil imports and sensitive to changes in the international oil market, but might be able to deal with those changes through its own domestic allocation system. Hence it would not be very vulnerable to foreign pressure. It is likely that economic crisis, as perceived by national leaders, will depend in part on their projected ability to handle changes in the environment through their own policy, and thus on their perceived vulnerability.

It is likely that the same factors leading to dependence or interdependence among states, their sensitivity to outside changes, and their vulnerability will also afford the opportunity to diminish vulnerability. These factors include transactions between states: "flows of money, goods, people, and messages across international boundaries.(3) The subtle process by which a state manipulates its transactional ties to other countries in order to relieve international pressure and vulnerability needs elaboration.

In the present analysis we examine the tactics of a small to medium-sized advanced industrial state, the Netherlands, confronted by both oil price increases and a direct embargo of oil deliveries in 1973. We will determine how its connections to the international community affected perception of crisis and afforded opportunities to relieve the crisis. It should become clear that transnational linkages are both the strength and weakness of such advanced small to midsize powers.

ENVIRONMENTS OF THE NETHERLANDS

In October 1973 the Netherlands was singled out, along with the United States and Portugal, for a full embargo of oil shipments from the Organization of Arab Petroleum Exporting Countries. It is still not fully clear why the Arab exporters boycotted Holland, though a number of theories are dealt with below. Arab leaders said that they objected to the Netherlands' "pro-Israel" policy stance; Netherlands' government officials argued that Holland's strategic pivotal position in European trade through the port of Rotterdam was a more likely explanation. Whichever basic view is correct, the fact remains that the Dutch government was suddenly and unexpectedly confronted with possible interference in the normal flow of oil to Rotterdam. A detailed chronology of the ensuing events, some of which took on crisis proportions according to Brecher's definition, is contained in the

Appendix along with a designation of precrisis, crisis, and postcrisis phases. In order to understand the way the Dutch government used international and even transnational leverage in an attempt to relieve the crisis, we must note the geographic, political, and economic environments perceived from the Hague.

In 1973 the Netherlands was in some sense caught in the middle in four relatively separate though interacting geo-political and economic environments: United States-European; intra-European; Middle Eastern; and multinational business. The Dutch had maintained relatively close relations with the United States, especially in defense matters, while strongly supporting the concept of increased European unification and joint decision-making in economic matters through the European community. Within Europe at that time were significant conflicts between French and German approaches to European integration. Pompidou and Jobert, his foreign minister, carried on the Gaullist push for resistance to American penetration; an independent European foreign policy line especially with regard to the Arab-Israeli struggle; dirigisme in the regulation of major companies such as oil producers; and general advantages for the EEC Council of Ministers over the Commission in planning for the future of Europe. Germany, on the other hand, tended to favor more of a "laissez-faire" approach to economic regulation, more cooperation with American foreign policy efforts, and general advantages for the Commission of the EEC. The Dutch were linked to the German currency system, but had significant trade relations with both France and Germany (one might argue more significant with Germany). A Dutch-French dispute existed, for instance, over the question of EEC support of a French force de frappe nuclear fuel plant. Thus there were cross-pressures in the French-German European political environment, although as shown below, pressures were sometimes convenient for Netherlands' leaders who could cite the "necessities" of European politics in explaining certain Middle Eastern policy moves to Washington.

In the Arab versus Israeli Middle Eastern environment, the Dutch had traditionally strongly supported Israel, both for reasons of sentiment and guilt (in relation to the Nazis) and because of the NATO realization in the 1950s that Israel represented a relatively stable and friendly state in the Middle East. However, there had been a slow movement in Dutch public opinion and governmental pronouncements with increased recognition of Arab and Palestinian grievances. We must note, however, that this was a relatively remote political environment for a northern European country, and that Dutch economic and political interests had been centered since World War II in their immediate European environment. Prior interruptions of oil supply in the 1956 and 1967 Middle Eastern wars had, however, alerted the Netherlands' government to its sensitive dependence on Middle Eastern oil, though natural gas discoveries had somewhat limited that dependence by 1973. Nevertheless, the Dutch had only three people working on the Middle Eastern desk in their foreign ministry at the time of the Yom Kippur War. Thus, cross-pressures existed as well in the Middle Eastern environment, though they were not fully realized before October 1973.(4)

The world of international business also impinged on Dutch leaders' perceptions since a number of multinational enterprises centered their operations in Holland, an active and trade-oriented country. As seen below, relations between the government and Royal Dutch Shell were crucial to the solution of the supply problem in 1973-74. Dutch political leaders, and the economic ministry in particular, had to identify both with oil producers and marketers in the form of Shell, and with consumers whose supply of oil might be threatened — consumers including the vast oil refinery complex in Rotterdam, much of which was owned by the supplying companies themselves. Cross-pressures existed here because of the multifaceted nature of multinational enterprises and because the Netherlands was a complex society with an economy highly dependent on petroleum and the sale of transport of petroleum products abroad.

As a result of such cross-pressures in all four environments, a fifth set of environmental pressures developed: bureaucratic politics and conflicts between the economic and foreign ministries. The foreign ministry arranged Dutch foreign policies in the United States-European, French-German, and Arab-Israeli environments (as well as in international organizations), but the economic ministry had to confront possibilities of local energy shortages as well as handle the complex relations with multinational enterprises which were the main source of energy. Priorities in these four environments were not always the same, and hence the approaches of the Foreign and Economic Ministries did not always mesh.

Responses to policy problems in the various environments depend on options perceived available, and these in turn depend on the assets and liabilities of the country "in crisis," in this case the Netherlands. For a country like Holland, assets tend also to be liabilities and vice versa. For instance, the Netherlands' small geographical size means that relatively little international attention will be attracted, but it also means less "marginal impact" on other countries' policies. This is somewhat compensated by the relative vitality and assertiveness of the Dutch economy, but it is an economy built on foreign trade and thus dependent on the whims and fortunes of larger economic markets. Germany and England, two of Holland's primary trade partners, are unlikely to abandon the Dutch in crisis, but also are likely to pressure the Netherlands' government for cooperative economic and political policies.

Possession of significant natural gas deposits means that Holland has relatively low dependence on oil (40 percent of domestic energy consumption) compared to other Western European countries, as well as leverage on other European countries through the export of natural gas. However, the gas is also a focus of envy and suspicion, and as seen below, makes it difficult for other European states to take Holland's energy dilemma seriously. The Rotterdam port complex is one of the largest in the world and Europe's main entrepot, thus making it almost impossible to effectively boycott the Netherlands. However, this asset too has its drawback, since Rotterdam also becomes a convenient means for the Arabs to pressure Europe through a threatened supply interruption. The gigantic petrochemical refinery complex in Rotterdam also represents a vulnerable portion of the Dutch economy; unemployment quickly increases as oil companies reduce production.

Another in the long list of this rather remarkable "small" country's assets is the participation in multinational oil companies which facilitates the necessary supply reallocation to keep oil flowing. At the same time, however, the relatively uncontrolled information and power at the disposal of such companies in 1973 left Dutch leaders with little recourse but to accept price increases (while trying to control domestic price ceilings). With Dutch leaders sometimes viewed in European capitals as the "voice of Shell," there is also the resentment and suspicion of EEC governments to contend with.

Along these lines as well, the relatively cordial Netherlands-United States relationship, while affording promises of American aid in oil supply, also led to friction between the Netherlands, British, and French governments in 1973. EEC membership constituted an advantage, affording Holland remedial options; in 1974 the Dutch were in a position to veto Algerian association with, and Arab interests in, the community. At the same time, however, the Hague experienced considerable pressure from larger EEC states for conformity with the emerging community viewpoint on the Middle East, and lingering uncertainty about the extent of EEC aid in energy reallocation if the situation became serious. Finally, in terms of lesser but still not inconsiderable assets, NATO membership afforded the Netherlands access to a complex petroleum pipeline for military use in case of emergency, and by implication for other emergency uses as well, and also to Belgian pipelines normally carrying oil from Rotterdam to Antwerp.

Thus in 1973 there was a series of environments – many of them transnational in nature – confronting Netherlands' decision makers, and a series of assets and liabilities – some of them transnational in nature – with which to work. Successful policy in such circumstances depends on balancing assets and liabilities to relieve environmental pressures and achieve goals. This is complicated when there are multiple goals, as there almost always are when environments are complex and overlapping. In 1973 a relatively new Netherlands cabinet faced the Arab oil embargo; it had been in office a mere five months. It had to revise quickly some of its goals for Dutch society, in terms of economic expansion, while weaving others – especially in terms of conservation – into reactions to the potential crisis. It was also necessary for the Netherlands' government to maintain its stake in the EEC as well as obtain oil; to pay heed to pro-Israeli Dutch public opinion as well as maintain some working relationship with Arab states (with whom Dutch trade had increased 33 percent from 1966 to 1970, the second largest jump in the EEC); and to set priorities in approaching Middle East conflict as both an economic and strategic NATO concern. Therefore it was necessary to balance priorities in United States versus EEC relations. More specific goals came to include the establishment of joint

EEC sharing arrangements for the continued flow of petroleum and petroleum products, balance of payments maintenance through natural gas price revision, as well as domestic economic relief, reorganization, and control.

By some criteria the Dutch succeeded rather well. We will see that the oil shortage was not very severe and that effective alternate means of petroleum acquisition were employed. Nevertheless, the Dutch economy, like those throughout the industrialized world, suffered from the staggering price increases, and the EEC failed rather pointedly to formulate the kind of sharing agreement the Dutch sought in 1973. It took the intervention of the United States with its massive economic power to finally bring the International Energy Agency to react to future crisis. In this sense the limitation of Dutch influence and the sensitivity of the Netherlands to transnational forces became clear; Holland edged closer to the EEC political line on the Middle East in order not to attract too much future attention. As shown below, however, this sensitivity did not seem to entail excessive vulnerability, though it is doubtful that the Arabs meant to ruin the Dutch economy in the first place.

ANATOMY OF CRISIS

Precrisis Period

According to Brecher's criteria, most crisis situations are composed of three basic phases: a precrisis period in which tension mounts, a crisis period with a "measurably sharp rise in perceived threat and the salience of time," and a postcrisis period in which perceived threat and time salience decline to more normal levels. In the case of the 1973 embargo, these phases can be identified.

The precrisis phase began with the October 6 Middle Eastern war and the October 9 Netherlands government statement (see chronology). This was followed in mid-October by the imposition of the embargo. The seriousness and import of this embargo was not immediately clear, and in fact there was some confusion about whether an embargo had actually been placed by Arab governments. Thus the first phase was characterized in the Hague by confusion, increased wariness, and as we shall see, a switch in bureaucratic and political influence within the government.

The crisis phase began in late November with what looked like a threat to the Netherlands' economy and the possibility of oil scarcity after the tankers which had already been dispatched in October finally reached port in Rotterdam. Netherlands' industrialists were talking about production cutbacks – including Shell and other refineries in Rotterdam – and it was not clear whether new tankers would be getting through to the Netherlands. It soon became clear that oil companies would reallocate necessary supplies so that non-Arab oil could come to Holland in place of Kuwaiti and Saudi crude (EEC statistics show that some Kuwaiti crude continued to get through). However, threatened

Arab production cutbacks of 5 percent per month, in addition to an initial 25 percent, left Dutch leaders somewhat uncertain about available supplies. It should be noted, however, that Indonesia reportedly offered Holland five million tons of oil on November 7, which represented the full shortfall in reallocated supply from Nigeria and Iran.(5)

Thus, conceivably the threat was not as great as it seemed, and government leaders either overlooked this offer or had other worries or reasons — perhaps political reasons discussed below — for maintaining a sense of threat in Holland. On December 1, Economics Minister Lubbers and Sheikh Yamani met in Brussels, and reportedly agreed that oil could go through Rotterdam for export.(6) There would be little threat to Dutch exports, and supplies would be sufficient for domestic use. Companies' projected production cuts were the main worry, but with full reallocation to Rotterdam technically possible, we might wonder why companies would have to cut production by 25 to 30 percent. World petroleum supply would be reduced, but Rotterdam, as a main European refinery, could be kept fully operational if oil companies so desired; exports could be maintained even on the principle of "equal misery" (i.e., equal shortfall for all states regardless of Arab designations).

The Netherlands' cabinet officials accepted company projections and worried about unemployment even though full employment would not have violated Arab guidelines and seems to have been feasible. Note, though, that deliveries to Rotterdam decreased in December, and some companies — notably Esso Nederland — claimed to be short 50 percent and to have stopped direct exports to meet Dutch domestic demand. Professor Odell, of Rotterdam's Erasmus University, points out that the effect, and he claims the motive, of company policies was to "rationalize" the European market, parcelling out control of certain countries' supply to certain companies — in Holland and Germany's case, to Shell.

The crisis phase lasted only a month, and by the end of December officials in the Hague admit that the perception of long-term threat was diminishing with encouraging words from Secretary Kissinger on a disengagement agreement. Nevertheless, this diminished threat perception was not communicated clearly to the Netherlands public for another two months. The United States was removed from the embargo in March 1974, but Holland stayed on officially until May.

There were transnational influences in each of the embargo phases, although the direct impact of multinational corporations was probably greatest in the crisis phase itself. One of the transnational forces that caused problems for the Dutch in the precrisis period was the rather well-developed world communications system which allowed policies adopted in one region to have implication for a country's relations with another region. When the Arab-Israeli war broke out on October 6, Dutch cabinet officials and bureaucrats did not perceive much danger for Netherlands' relations with the Middle East. There is still some controversy in Holland about whether the embargo was preplanned; one report indicated that Holland was included with the United States by Arab strategists as early as June 1973.(7) The Foreign Ministry responded to events in the Middle East with a rather strongly worded statement, supported in Parliament, that Egypt and Syria had been responsible for breaking the peace and that the parties should return to their prewar positions; this request would have benefited Israel since Egypt had made initial gains in the war by crossing the Suez Canal. The statement appealed to the Cabinet since it would be popular with the Dutch public and would express genuine concern of Labor and other party officials for Israel's survival – concerns stemming from diverse factors including guilt over Jewish lives lost during the Nazi occupation of Holland. It did not seem to the Prime Minister or Foreign Minister that there would be serious consequences in Dutch-Arab relations, since previous Dutch governments had expressed support for Israel in other wars and had backed up such expressions with material aid as well. In 1973 Dutch response was mainly verbal, although it has come out that United States planes, on their way to supply Israel, were allowed to overfly Holland, a grievance cited by some Arab states, since other EEC states – notably Germany – refused such cooperation.

Pro-Israeli statements fit with Dutch efforts to resist British and French dominance in EEC at the time, a dominance which seemed to mean a weakening of the Commission's power in energy and other matters as well as a Gaullist approach resisting American leadership and making rather direct approaches to the Arabs. Thus, when EEC foreign ministers met in Copenhagen on October 13, the Netherlands and Danish governments effectively opposed British and French requests to speak for the EEC in the upcoming UN Security Council Middle East deliberations. The Netherlands' government, without a prior clearly articulated Middle East policy of its own, and with only three people working on Middle Eastern affairs in the foreign ministry (compared to roughly 30 dealing with Europe), approached the October war mainly from the standpoints both of domestic politics and European policy. Furthermore, leaders in the Hague could hope for little efficacy in bringing about a Middle East solution on their own anyway, due to Holland's size and remoteness from the area.

However, the international communications network brought about consequences which Dutch leaders had not anticipated. In particular, news of the Danish-Dutch opposition in the EEC was leaked to the press and to the Arab governments, evidently through the French or Italians, whose governments were reportedly irked by Netherlands' resistance in the EEC.(8)

The French press made much of the supposedly brusque treatment of Arab ambassadors and chiefs of mission who met with the Netherlands' Foreign Minister after news of the dispute in the EEC had been communicated. The Netherlands' foreign ministry has denied that these ambassadors were slighted, and slights in themselves do not seem grounds for an embargo. However, if the Arabs were strongly interested in changing European policy, and Holland along with Denmark were seen as impediments, it would not take much to convince certain Arab leaders that a boycott of Rotterdam would be an effective lever (in this context note that Denmark was not formally boycotted but was denied certain products by certain Arab governments in early 1974). The

Algerian government initiated the embargo against Holland, but was quickly followed by Kuwait – which was a far more important supplier of petroleum to Holland and Shell. Both Algeria and Kuwait may have been especially responsive to the priorities of resident Palestinians, and Algeria may have reacted strongly to news from France about Holland.

The general tendency of Netherlands' officials to make pro-Israeli statements or attend rallies also drew the attention of at least one prominent Arab representative inside Holland – the Consul of Kuwait, who was a Palestinian. Having resided in Holland for many years, this official concluded that it was time to "wake the Dutch up" and alert them to Arab perspectives. He claims to have personally urged the four ambassadors as well as the Kuwait government to impose an embargo.(9) Thus, it was impossible to isolate the statements and events inside a relatively small European country and prevent them from catching Arab interest. Of course, the fact that the world's largest port also was located in that country contributed to Arab interest.

Note that the source of the official Netherlands' statement criticizing Syria and Egypt seems to have been a secretary level official in the foreign ministry whose concern was basically with international organizations and security affairs. He was strongly pro-Israeli, but also reportedly staunchly anti-Gaullist. Sources in the Netherlands' press indicate that the relatively inexperienced Foreign Minister van der Stoel relied on this official for early advice in the conflict situation. Hence a more strongly worded statement than might have been diplomatically advisable was drafted.

The rest of the precrisis phase seems to have been characterized by a bureaucratic struggle in the Netherlands' government between the strongly pro-Israeli faction headed by this high official, and his critics who advocated a more restrained approach to the Middle East question and a more flexible EEC policy. Many of these critics were diplomats in the field who began to sense uneasiness in neighboring countries over the Netherlands' position. Some of these career diplomats may also have resented the foreign policy assertions of the Labor Party, in office for the first time in memory.

There are indications that the Netherlands' partners in the European Community, and especially Germany, began to put considerable pressure on the Hague to change its policy and move more in line with EEC statements calling for cease-fire, return of occupied territories, and recognition of borders. Dutch diplomats negotiating with EEC representatives became sensitive to this pressure and also seemed to push the Hague to change positions or modify the tone of prior policy. Although the Dutch government never admitted to changing positions, the fact that it finally subscribed to the EEC statement of November 6 indicates that the critical wing of the foreign ministry won out. In fact this "victory" seemed to come at the last minute, as the negotiations for the final wording of the statement were taking place and as heated phone calls were placed to the Hague to try and get permission to subscribe to new language. The Foreign Minister and Prime Minister were on the phone to the negotiators.(10) The EEC policy statement contained new wording which skirted the question of how much territory should be returned by calling for an "end to the territorial occupation" by Israel.

Thus, although the forces working on the Dutch government were not necessarily all transnational, they were extranational. Policy conceived largely in isolation was running into stiff opposition in the European Community and from the Arab world. European Community opposition was probably decisive since the Dutch were also contemplating requests for Community assistance in case oil supplies ran short. In this sense, European political institutions – while of dubious supranational power – represent pressures that can be applied across borders on small European countries to increase harmonization. It seems that the Germans were the most influential source of pressure on the Netherlands' government; the close economic relationship with Germany has strongly influenced Dutch approaches to the Community, and the Arabs undoubtedly knew this and used the embargo symbolically to pressure Germany – a country very dependent on Rotterdam.

The degree to which the Dutch government was responding to a number of audiences at once is revealed in their efforts to rebut charges of changing policy. It is true that changes in Netherlands' Middle Eastern policy had been made over a number of years, but the tone of the October 9 statement contrasts quite sharply with the tone of the November 6 EEC statement, and clearly a change took place. Netherlands' leaders were sensitive to the pressures of their European partners not so much because they necessarily hoped aid would result, but more because they no longer wanted to stand out as an easy target for the Arabs. There is "safety in numbers," and this is an important aspect of Dutch participation in international organizations. Nevertheless, the government anticipated that a domestic audience would be unsympathetic, and hence sought to isolate that audience from the European audience and the Arab audience.

CRISIS PERIOD

International agencies, along with multinational corporations, were to play an even greater role during the crisis phase, from the end of November to the end of December 1973. The crisis phase was characterized both by uncertainty in the Hague over possible oil shortage, and preparations for the important Copenhagen summit meeting which was to decide whether EEC aid would be available to energy-short countries. In this sense it was in the government's interest to stress Rotterdam as the sole reason for the embargo (ignoring the diplomatic conflicts) and stress the potential threat to Europe if Rotterdam were shut. The government also sought to push emergency economic control legislation through Parliament, legislation which fit in with prior interests in controlling prices, rents, and wages.

International leverage was applied by the economics ministry in threats to shut off natural gas exports if domestic energy supplies were greatly reduced. These threats had special reference for France, which imported 40 percent of its gas supplies from the Netherlands at a relatively low price. Le Monde reported these threats on November 16 and the same day editorially called for EEC aid to Holland. Interestingly, British newspapers reported (Guardian, November 19) that the UK was willing to see Netherlands gas shut off because this would increase British North Sea sales in Europe. Thus, London may have continued to oppose EEC aid to the Netherlands even after France began to relent. On November 20, the EEC Commission called for moderation in Dutch-French disputes, with concessions on uranium enrichment and quiet help if necessary (the French did not want the Arabs offended) for the Dutch. Thus, implied natural gas threats paid off to an extent.

It should be noted that government officials' worries about the embargo were somewhat tempered by the policy of linking natural gas to oil prices. Gas prices would rise automatically to petroleum price levels with a one-year time lag. Thus some incentives developed for the Netherlands to go along with oil company price increases as long as supplies would be maintained.

There was a traditionally close working relationship between the economic ministry and multinational oil companies in the Netherlands, with relatively frequent interchange of personnel; officials in charge of the petroleum price regulation commission were ex-oil company executives. Economic ministry officials maintained that the best way to approach such a crisis was through the oil companies since they had the most extensive worldwide connections and the abilities to make the necessary switches to provide oil to boycotted countries. The Dutch government stopped publicly reporting tanker movements in and out of Rotterdam in December to facilitate and cover such transfers. The Dutch again differ from their French and Italian Common Market colleagues who have been much more suspicious of private international oil companies and much more supportive of close scrutiny and state ownership.

Economics ministry trust in oil company policy also had strong influence in the Organization of European Cooperation and Development and in the London Policy Group of oil companies which met to discuss emergency provisions during the embargo. The only international crisis machinery available for oil sharing at the time was through the OECD. However, to invoke such machinery would take a vote of the members affirming that an emergency existed. The British and French, perhaps partly in retaliation for prior Dutch opposition and partly not to alarm the Arabs with too militant an approach, refused to vote such emergency powers. The Dutch saw this and the subsequent EEC refusal to establish a sharing agreement as signs of inadequate response to the transnational reality of international oil interdependence. The French could not understand Netherlands' alarm; with Rotterdam and Shell as resources, no emergency existed. However, in a meeting of OECD oil powers (the United States, Japan, Canada, Britain, and Holland) it was decided to allow the OECD Oil Committee to supervise informal sharing arrangements among the companies. It so happened that a Netherlands' economic ministry official was the chairman of the Oil Committee at the time. He came to view his function as essentially facilitating the communication necessary among the oil companies to parcel out the oil and, as a consequence, the markets in Europe. This could only happen with American cooperation as well, which necessitated justice department clearance and suspended antitrust enforcement (suspensions had been obtained since 1970). Secretary Kissinger strongly pressured the justice department to ease their standards of enforcement in these cases. Justice department and diplomatic officials joined company executives in London to arrange the "necessary" coordination. From reports of those present, it seems that there was little close scrutiny of companies' decisions. Economic ministry efforts to facilitate oil company operations did not rest with the OECD itself. The justice department was urged to support the cause of at least one American-owned company whose supply problems had the Dutch worried.(11)

We should not leave the impression that there was no supervision of oil company policy in Holland or of the oil flow through Holland. Investigations were made when newspapers reported interrupted deliveries to certain contractors and abundant oil flow to Germany. Because of complex contractual relations, "independent companies" were sometimes evidently allowed to use majors' names and trucks. In December Secretary Kissinger sent his assistant, Mr. Donaldson, to the Netherlands (whose Middle East policy Kissinger held up as a model of courage in contrast to the rest of Europe) partly to offer aid in meeting minimum Dutch needs (which it seems the Dutch could have met on their own), and partly to explain the policy of American majors in supply independents. Donaldson tried to make it clear that independents, not majors, took the oil to Germany. The Dutch government staunchly refused to allow Arab inspectors direct access to Dutch territory. The embargo was enforced through a system of vouchers signed by ship captains on their way out of port and on their arrival in port – a system which nevertheless allowed switching in midocean and evidently even barter or sale of oil from offshore ships. The Arabs could not have expected to seriously enforce the total boycott of Rotterdam and evidently winked at the improvised remedies. Oil states were probably more interested in symbolically threatening Europe and pressuring the United States while disarming their "extremist" Arab critics, than in strangling Holland and the United States. The oil companies obtained agreements from the Arabs to allow oil to flow to Germany as long as it was not destined for Dutch domestic use. Of course, it is very difficult to sort such oil once it arrives in Rotterdam, especially without the presence of Arab inspectors.

Thus the Dutch tended to see themselves as benefiting from the international linkages and transnational relations of the oil industry, and able, if not to manipulate such linkages, then to rely on the companies' interest in keeping Rotterdam going due to their heavy investment there. This open reliance on the companies, of course, had some negative consequences in the EEC environment in which French and Italian suspicions that Holland was the "voice of Shell" did not make sharing agreements likely at the Copenhagen summit of December 15. Reports indicate that the Germans gave some support to the Dutch and Danish efforts at the summit, but because of Germany's primary concern over the costs of British regional development policy and concessions obtained on this issue, there was little time or interest in pressing hard for the Dutch case. Furthermore, the French had surprised many of the delegates by inviting Arab representatives to testify, and the discussion was moved toward the creation of what came to be known as "Euro-Arab dialogue." This meant that there would be strong French opposition to measures which appeared designed to resist Arab pressure. The question of a sharing agreement was referred to the Commission for study and suggestion, and while such suggestions were eventually issued, they became essentially moot after the creation of the International Energy Agency with American leadership in 1974.

With so much reliance on the oil companies in the crisis, Netherlands' government statistics tended to reflect company information (a problem shared by other industrialized states as well and since remedied somewhat by the International Energy Agency's data gathering techniques). Company statistics tended to be rather pessimistic throughout December, citing probable production cuts in the Arab world (despite cancellation of the December cuts for Europe). Indeed, these projected production cuts and resultant unemployment probably worried Dutch leaders more than the embargo itself after it was clear that the companies could rearrange shipments. Storage tanks in Rotterdam were full, although some of these reserves were allocated for sale to Belgium and Germany and hence were not available for the domestic Dutch market. The Netherlands public did not easily pick up on such subtlety, but it was also not reported that while crude oil shipments may have been down somewhat, imports of finished oil products, mainly from England, were increasing – much to the displeasure of the British government which felt that the oil companies were under Arab orders to supply "friendly" states with a full measure of oil. The companies disobeyed British orders and continued to export products to embargoed Holland. In this sense, British-Dutch friction was probably worse during the crisis period than the French-Dutch conflict, especially after Netherlands' natural gas threats.(12)

Netherlands' officials cited pessimistic statistics, however, in part because these tended to justify the kinds of legislative initiatives that had been planned even prior to the crisis period. The government hoped to limit consumption while controlling the economy further by limiting prices, wages (in opposition to union demands), and rents in order to dampen inflation. With this in mind, the embargo represented an opportunity to push through such legislation in an emergency atmosphere. Prime Minister den Uyl cited a 30 percent drop in crude shipments to Rotterdam in the first week of December and forecast a possible further 40 percent cut. The Mayor of Rotterdam notes, however, that weekly figures always vary greatly, and do not constitute reliable trend indicators.

Unlike the French, the Dutch made few direct approaches to Arab states concerning special bilateral arrangements; missions were dispatched to the Arab states but mainly to explain Holland's political position on the Middle East question, although to little avail. Saudi Arabia wanted the Netherlands to call for the return of all occupied territory, but reassured the Netherlands envoy that other Dutch transactions (investments) with Saudi Arabia would not be threatened.

Thus, no complete break with Holland was signaled. A Netherlands foreign ministry spokesman was fired on December 5 for labeling Israeli territorial occupation as "illegal" and interpreting the November 6 EEC statement as calling for return of all territory. The New York Times reported that on the prior Saturday, Sheikh Yamani had demanded that Minister Lubbers make some "gesture" against Israel to end the boycott. If the foreign ministry spokesman was floating a trial balloon, it was quickly shot down by his superiors.

Common Market officials who studied the crisis situation concluded that the main effect was to raise world petroleum prices and equalize imbalanced prices. The Dutch Economic Ministry raised domestic price ceilings and did not much quarrel with the company price policies. EEC officials as well as Peter Odell have speculated that the United States and American companies benefited from the crisis, and Washington may even have ignored early crisis warnings because world oil prices would finally be forced up to domestic United States levels. At the time, with low foreign oil imports, the United States was relatively invulnerable to pressure through embargo.(13)

Company representatives point out, however, that profits were being taxed heavily and that they had to enter the new high-priced world oil market themselves to replenish stocks, thus being forced into the capital market. Dutch domestic prices were fixed, although rising in two steps due to decisions by the Oil Control Commission (which had been in existence since 1950 to advise the economics ministry and represented all refining companies in Holland with Shell representatives in the chair). Thus, there were incentives, especially for independents, to export gasoline to Germany where a free market prevailed. Because of rather nonuniform pricing policies in the Common Market, countries not especially friendly to the Arabs were able to attract oil products as easily as (and sometimes more easily than) France, Britain, and Italy, which enjoyed rather close relations with Arab states.

The EEC study commission which investigated oil company behavior during the crisis concluded that there was no indication of collusion to push up prices, except for one attempt to reduce stocks of crude oil and exert pressure on Belgium to increase maximum domestic prices to better conform with other EEC countries. Gulf Oil Corporation was also cited for charging exorbitant prices to certain independents. Companies were not above putting pressure on recalcitrant governments which attempted to keep prices "too low," but by and large got enough cooperation from European governments that such pressure was not necessary.(14)

In terms of overall crisis effect, Netherlands' average daily imports of crude oil, according to information furnished to the United States Federal Energy Agency and the Church Committee by thirteen United States oil companies (evidently excluding Shell), dropped by approximately 46 percent, and Holland lost $9.4 million in port duties.(15) Imports of oil products from these American companies decreased by approximately 52 percent during the embargo, although imports from West Germany increased slightly, those from the United Kingdom remained steady, and imports of oil products still came from Kuwait, and Iran, and the Netherlands Antilles or other Netherlands' possessions. When the impact of Shell is calculated, it seems that overall Dutch crude petroleum supplies were down by 13 percent which represents roughly the average world decrease. Netherlands' oil reserves at the end of the embargo in July 1974 were up nearly 30 percent over May 1973, and for the most part, reserves had not been touched throughout the embargo crisis. The 13 percent reduction may have been due in part to energy conservation measures as well as restricted world supplies. Substitutions of natural gas reduced Dutch fuel oil consumption and hence production in Netherlands' refineries, and while the refineries turned out increased levels of automobile fuel, because of the decrease in national consumption due to the fuel economy measures (e.g., carless Sundays after October), exports of petrol from Holland increased as a percentage of total production from January to March 1974. The situation had improved in January with stepped-up oil product imports from England. German crude oil imports through Rotterdam had increased during October and November in anticipation of possible shutdown at Rotterdam and also because of the free price levels in the German market. This market was saturated by January 1974 and imports tailed off; thus more was available for the Dutch market.

Refining activity for the entire eight months of embargo was down 13 percent in Holland, although it was also down 10 percent in Belgium which was not boycotted. Oil products – especially domestic heating oil – tended to move out of the Netherlands and Belgium, where the domestic market prices were controlled, and the supplies in these markets were down 10 percent in Holland and 8 percent in Belgium. Dutch oil product exports were also down 16 percent, so that the impact on Dutch trade was somewhat greater than on domestic supply. For a trading country, of course, this was damaging. Trade patterns were somewhat modified. At first, imports from England increased, and then British imports from the Netherlands rose; German oil product imports through Rotterdam were maintained and in fact increased slightly in 1973 and 1974 as compared to 1972. Thus, what could have been a major crisis in Dutch trade was averted.

Rotterdam represented a complex arrangement of transnational oil distribution, some of its under the control of the major companies, and some of it through what is called the Rotterdam "free market." Nearly 50 percent of EEC oil trade went through Rotterdam refineries and the major companies in 1973. The "free market," in which oil is transferred from control of the major companies to independents or other companies through the services of "jobbers," accounted for another 3 percent, but in the crisis period of uncertainty and stress, had significant impact in controlling dislocations and shortages. Much of this free market trade went to Germany, with some also going to the United States, Switzerland, and Sweden, and to other EEC countries with controlled prices. Through the mechanisms of the Rotterdam market, the Netherlands was able to keep its main customers supplied even though total exports and supplies diminished.(16)

POSTCRISIS PERIOD

United States initiatives were important factors in easing the long-term crisis threat — of reduced Arab production — confronting Holland. Secretary Kissinger was able to promote disengagement talks which encouraged the Arab states enough to suspend production restrictions for December (though the embargo of Holland would continue), and cease-fire arrangements looked more encouraging in January. We should note, though, that the Arab states probably had no intention of destroying the Western economies upon which they depended, regardless of Kissinger's success. They achieved their goals. The crosspressures felt by the Netherlands' government, with Common Market institutions and French demands on the one hand and American power and interests on the other, were largely resolved after the Copenhagen summit in favor of American energy initiatives and European political coordination on the Middle East. The Danish summit left the Dutch disappointed that no sharing arrangements were made. The EEC Commission was legitimized in entering the energy area in the fields of conservation and export licensing for better statistical compilations and sharing, but it was the United States proposal for the International Energy Agency which swept the day in energy organization beginning in February 1974. The Common Market countries (which had met early in 1974 to plan a joint approach for the Washington energy conference), with the exception of France, followed the American lead in fully backing the IEA. In fact, Dutch diplomats have expressed satisfaction at influencing the Washington conference toward a "North-South dialogue" on energy matters. The Netherlands foreign and economic ministries came to rely on the IEA for better information and a clearer commitment of aid in case of crisis.(17) The Americans, who had previously refused to commit national oil stocks to European needs, did so with the IEA initiative. Clearly, American power was irresistible (especially for the smaller European countries) on energy and economic matters; but interestingly this did not apply to the political questions. Since 1974 the Netherlands has continued to move toward the EEC position on the Middle East conflict, and toward recognition of Palestinian rights. In fact it is reported that the EEC refrained from issuing more pointed political statements in 1974 because of requests from Secretary Kissinger to quiet any dissenting voices that could interfere with his own initiatives toward a disengagement agreement. In 1972, an attempt at a common EEC Mid-East policy was scuttled when news leaked out prematurely, perhaps through the CIA or Israel, embarrassing some European governments.(18) Thus the crisis of 1973 ended with a certain disillusionment in the Hague regarding European institutions, although with a general willingness to go along with French initiatives for a "Euro-Arab dialogue."

The Netherlands' cabinet went ahead with domestic economic crisis controls despite the easing of tension on the international scene in January 1974, imposing automobile fuel rationing despite an acknowledged optimism about the overall supply picture. This optimism was not portrayed in public, and the economic ministry no longer supported the rationing program when it was finally introduced. It was introduced because of prior planning; because the procedures had already been established and the preliminaries set; and because the transportation and other ministries were geared for the rationing program – a case of bureaucratic momentum and bargaining. However, the public did not take rationing very seriously; transnational relations meant that Dutch people in the South and East of Holland could travel across the border to Belgium or Germany to buy unrationed gasoline, leaving a surplus supply in the South for Northerners. In this case, permeability of borders and lack of coordinated price policy in the European Community made domestic controls difficult. The Dutch government remained intent, however, on taking advantage of the crisis atmosphere to continue its push against inflation and excess consumption. Largely lost in the process were the government's early ambitions for economic expansion and a solution to Holland's unemployment problem. Reliance would be placed on support programs and social benefits for the unemployed and those hit by economic difficulties.

The Netherlands' embargo was not officially lifted until July 1974, although the effects had been eased by February. The Kuwaiti Consul had wanted it lifted in January, and the French called for an early end in March because of desires for Algerian-EEC association. However, while Dutch officials were no longer very worried by the embargo, they seemed to get caught in the middle of growing Saudi-Algerian friction over OPEC prices. While Saudi Arabia had been slow to impose the embargo (almost a month behind the others – indicating lack of prior planning), the Saudis delayed in lifting it. They claimed the Netherlands had not sufficiently changed policy, but in addition, their own oil supplies were already spoken for (production increases and reallocation might be necessary and take time) and the delay would inconvenience the Algerians. Finally, citing a more "positive" Netherlands' stance at the UN General Assembly meeting on raw materials and development in April, the various Arab states withdrew the embargo in June. The Algerians had unilaterally lifted the embargo on June 2.

Middle East policy and reliance on industry soured Dutch relations with two pivotal powers in the European community, France and England. News of this friction was leaked to the Arabs, worsening Dutch-Arab relations because of perceived Dutch-Danish threats to Arab-EEC cooperation. Subsequent Netherlands efforts to obtain European sharing agreements foundered on the resentment of Shell's influence in Holland and a disbelief in the seriousness of the situation. To French leaders it seemed that the Dutch were likely to undergo less supply disruption than France, given the advantages of Rotterdam and Shell, and the fact that Holland relied for only 40 percent of its energy needs on oil while French reliance was approximately 80 percent. The British, reeling under the impact of a coal strike and also experimenting with a neo-Gaullism, were suspicious of Netherlands' requests and resentful that oil companies continued to supply the Dutch market even while supposedly depriving Britain of some deliveries.

CONCLUSION

In general, a series of misperceptions contributed to the failure to achieve an oil sharing agreement in Europe and to the imposition of the Netherlands' embargo in the first place. Interdependence had increased enough that statements made in the Hague for domestic consumption or for the European contacts were picked up and magnified in the Arab world and, with the attractive importance of Rotterdam, brought the Dutch more notoriety on the world scene than they probably wanted. Arab states saw a chance to make a crucial political point without seriously hurting Dutch or European societies – a point which would be particularly clear to Germany.

On the other hand, complex interdependence also allowed reduction of Netherlands' vulnerability, since oil companies had a built-in incentive not to deprive Rotterdam and therefore their own refineries. The embargo also offered an opportunity for the Dutch government to pass emergency economic legislation which might otherwise have failed due to union opposition, although the long-term effect of such legislation in an era of rising oil prices and increased unemployment was questionable. Netherlands' energy consumption was drastically reduced during the crisis with the government-projected sense of urgency, a welcome reduction to ease import demands at least temporarily.

One other consequence of the impinging external environments was that the Dutch were forced to develop a more articulate, careful, and consistent Middle Eastern policy largely in conjunction with other European countries. Since November 1973 the Netherlands has subscribed to European statements dealing with the Middle East, the need for Israeli withdrawal, recognition of Palestinian rights, as well as secure and recognized borders. In this sense, the prior Netherlands' tendency to "go it alone" has been somewhat modified, although in the economic sphere there is still considerable reliance on Netherlands-oriented multinationals. However, with the development of the International Energy Agency, such reliance could also be merged with a growing internationalism and cooperation with the United States.

While the Arab embargo did not greatly diminish Netherlands' access to oil, it did cause a reevaluation of policy and a tendency to align political statements with the rest of Europe. By the same token, the government proved unable or unwilling to push for EEC oil price regulation; the Dutch were able to garner considerable influence on modifying IEA rules once the organization was formed but it was clear that a bigger world power, the United States, was necessary to have any impact on price. This required United States participation and influence with the major oil companies. Netherlands' influence applied mainly to Shell and even then mainly to Netherlands' branches of this and other multinationals and to supply questions. In essence, the Netherlands' government served the purpose of companies doing business in and through Holland by interceding with the American government to ease regulation attempts.

The Netherlands is certainly closely connected to the international oil network and strongly affected by price and supply changes in that network. It is not totally at the mercy of outside forces, but at the same time is only marginally influential in affecting those forces. This small to middle power, reaping the benefits of industrialization and world trade, proved to be no more, and probably even less vulnerable to Arab pressure (limited as it was) than its bigger European partners, notably Britain and France. However, Netherlands' leaders also had the limitations of their world influence clearly demonstrated.

APPENDIX
General Chronology of the Oil Embargo
in the Netherlands, October 1973 - July 1974

1973	
April-June	Arabs discuss use of oil as "weapon."
September	Arabs plan for higher oil prices and no production increases, though Saudis reported in favor of increases.
October 6	War begins in Middle East.
October 9	Netherlands government statement that Egypt and Syria had "broken the truce" and that parties should return to prewar positions.
October 13	Dutch and Danes oppose Britain and France speaking for EEC at UN Security Council. News leaked probably in Italy and France.
mid-October	Le Monde reports Arab ambassadors treated "badly" by Dutch foreign minister; Oct. 26 London Observer confirms that camouflaged El Al planes landed in Holland en route to resupplying Israel with U.S. arms.
October 16	OPEC Gulf Committee decides on 70% price increase, and OAPEC decides on 5% monthly production cuts.
October 18-21	Arab embargoes of US announced.
October 21-25	Algeria, Kuwait, Abu Dhabi and Oman announce embargoes of Holland; Iraq nationalizes Royal Dutch Shell holdings.
November 2	Saudi Arabia announces embargo of Holland.
October 30-November 4	Intense bargaining between Holland and EEC partners leading to foreign ministers' meeting.
October 30-November	Two Dutch diplomatic missions dispatched to key Arab countries to "explain" Dutch position and to see to it that Dutch business interests are not harmed. Foreign minister speaks in parliament about Israeli withdrawal to borders "approximating" those before 1967, with "small corrections." Arabs insist on statement calling for evacuation of "all" territory.

October 30-November 21	Reports in press and parliament of possible cutoff of Dutch gas exports to Germany and/or France. Government statements stress Rotterdam's importance for all of Europe.
November 4-5	Arabs decide to reduce production by 25% compared to September.
November 6	Netherlands subscribes to EEC statement calling for an end to Israel's post-1967 territorial occupation; no EEC agreement to share oil; no French agreement to mediate the embargo with Arabs.
November 7	The Times of London reports secret Indonesian offer of 5 million tons of oil for Holland per year — represents the expected shortfall, for domestic needs and perhaps export, in resupply by Iran and Nigeria.
November 14-December 5	The "Palestinians" appear in statements by minister president and foreign minister as "important political questions"; ministers refer to earlier statements as well.
November 15-21	U.S. statements of readiness to aid the Dutch with oil supplies if Holland cannot meet "minimum needs."
November 18-19	Dutch government reemphasizes ban on transport to Israel of weapons based in Holland; foreign ministry spokesman terms Israeli occupation of Arab territory "illegal"; foreign ministry spokesman dismissed by the minister.
	Le Monde editorial calls for aid to Holland, immediately below an article describing Dutch threats to suspend natural gas exports. UK reported unmoved by gas export threats. Major Rotterdam refineries schedule production cuts from 20-40% for November 26 (when full effect of embargo is expected).
November 20	EEC Commission proposes compromise on Dutch-French nuclear funding dispute, and quiet diplomacy on oil crisis solidarity without threats of gas export restrictions. Belgian economic ministry official promises "solidarity" with Holland. Dutch government expresses satisfaction with "common position" of the Nine.
November 21	OECD fails to invoke emergency oil sharing agreement (from 1956); UK and France oppose Holland. OECD Oil Committee given OK to supervise, with U.S. Justice Dept.

observer, informal oil company consultations in London.

November 23-28   VVD by-election win in Amersfoort. Report PvdA (Labor Party) criticism of government moves toward Palestinian support and of foreign minister's diplomacy.

November 28   Rotterdam storage tanks still full, but new shipments reported by companies down 15%. Government develops rationing plan for January, as well as emergency wage, rent, and price control bill.

November 30   Minister president reiterates that Israel's existence as a state would never be put in jeopardy.

December 1   Netherlands' government announces 150% increase in aid to UNRWA (Palestine relief); economic minister meets with Sheikh Yamani – little reported progress.

December 2   Netherlands' government reports 30% less oil received last week (importance of figure disputed by Rotterdam port director);government removes statistics on tanker movements at Rotterdam from public record.- Shell says new supplies down 17% with prospect for 25-30% reduction in refining. Dutch export licenses now required for oil and gas shipments.

December 3   Arabs agree to allow oil to go through Rotterdam as long as it is not "bound for" Holland. Dutch refuse to have Arab inspectors in Holland. Oil companies work for a compromise. Dutch economic ministry contacts U.S. to assure oil supplies for companies suffering shortages, and to relax antitrust legislation to allow companies to consult. 800 Dutch firms ask permission for layoffs or shorter work week. Amsterdam stock exchange down; investments remain high. Refineries reduce output.

December 5   Minister president mentions further possible 40% drop in oil supplies as emergency control bill is introduced in parliament. Arabs cancel planned 5% December supply reduction for EEC (except Holland).

December 10   Arabs plan to resume 5% production cuts in January.

December 12   Increased Dutch oil reserves and full tanks in Rotterdam reported by London Times; Iraqi oil continues to flow to Shell; Dow Chemical in Holland confirms receipt of

	Soviet oil; report that EEC partners, except UK, tacitly approve increased oil diversions to Holland to forestall natural gas supply reductions; tankers carry crude and oil products from UK to Holland; Dutch industry and labor criticize government oil statistics.
December 14-15	Copenhagen EEC summit. No formal oil sharing agreement. UK and France oppose Holland, Denmark, and Germany; EEC Commission instructed to develop proposals for energy conservation, alternate sources, cooperation with producers, etc. Euro-Arab dialogue endorsed.
December 15	Kissinger confident of disengagement agreement.
December 27	Dutch oil reserves remain untouched. Doubling of OPEC oil prices announced.
1974 January 12-February 4	Netherlands benzine rationing.
February 20	Washington Energy Conference creates IEA plan. Netherlands, along with other EEC states, except France, support U.S. position and push for consideration of Third World dialogue.
March 18	Boycott of U.S. lifted. Dutch reported ready to block EEC initiatives towards Arabs if embargo continues. Euro-Arab dialogue postponed at Kissinger's "request." France asks Arabs not to discriminate further against any EEC state.
June 2	Algeria and Abu Dhabi publicly support ending the Holland embargo; Algeria does so unilaterally, citing cooperative Dutch attitude at last month's UNGA Special Session of Raw Materials and Development (Algerian application to EEC still pending).
July 11	OAPEC embargo of Holland lifted. Netherlands' losses in port duties put at $9.4 million Netherlands' oil reserves up nearly 30% over May 1973; oil consumption down by 15%.

NOTES

(1) Michael Brecher, "Toward a Theory of International Crisis Behavior: A Preliminary Report," International Studies Quarterly 21 (March 1977): 43-4.

(2) Robert W. Keohane and Joseph S. Nye, Jr. eds., Transnational Relations and World Politics (Cambridge, Mass: Harvard University Press, 1972), Ch. l.

(3) Ibid., p. 9.

(4) H.A. Schaper, "Nederland en het Midden-Oostenconflict – Het Regeringsbeleid in de Jaren 1967-1973," International Spectator (The Hague) 29 (April 1975): 229-42.

(5) Times (London), November 7, 1973.

(6) Financieel Dagblad, December 4, 1973.

(7) A former senior official at the foreign ministry and Ambassador to Italy, Dr. H.N. Boon, has maintained that there was some indication of preplanning which he brought to the attention of the foreign ministry soon after the war broke out. The Foreign Minister then became involved in a heated controversy with Dr. Boon over the question of possible slights and affronts to Arab ambassadors called into the Hague during the early days of the war. The foreign minister argued that if there had been preplanning, the supposed slights could not have caused the embargo; Dr. Boon wanted a clear answer on whether there was preplanning and maintained that such slights could have aggravated the situation.

(8) H.N. Boon, Afscheidsaudientie: Tien Studies Uit de Diplomatieke Prakiyk (Rotterdam: A.D. Donker, 1976), ch. 10; also personal interviews in Netherlands' Parliament and foreign ministry, and with a political correspondent.

(9) M. Rabani, Consul General of Kuwait in Netherlands, personal interview (The Hague: February 1977).

(10) West German foreign ministry official, personal confidential interview (Bonn: April 1977).

(11) Oil Company executive, personal confidential interview (The Hague: March 1977).

(12) EEC Commission official, personal and confidential interview (Brussels: March 1977).

(13) Peter Odell, Oil and World Power, 4th ed. (London: Penguin Books, 1975), ch. 9.

(14) Commission of the European Communities, Report by the Commission on the Behavior of the Oil Companies in the Community During the Period from October 1973 to March 1974 (Brussels: December 1976), pp. 58-9.

(15) New York Times, July 11, 1974.

(16) Commission of the European Communities, Part IV.

(17) Indeed a dispute had evidently developed within the economic ministry in part over reliance on companies, and the official who had been influential in OECD was largely bypassed after the embargo. (Personal interviews, economic and foreign ministries, February 1977.)

(18) Personal confidential interview (Bonn: April 1977).

IV

Transnational Strains: Development, Imperialism, and Penetration

7 The Development Ethic: Experiences of the World Bank Group*

Charles W. Merrifield

INTRODUCTION

The address at 1818 H Street, N.W., Washington, D.C. is one of the most famous locations in the world. It is the central headquarters of the World Bank Group, a cluster of global financial institutions specializing in something called "development" – with special reference to the poorer countries of the world. As an exercise in applied ethics, it stands among its related institutions of the UN development system as a primus inter pares in pioneering the functional (problem-solving) approach to a peaceful world society. Its learnings, disillusionments, and its undoubted achievements merit a closer attention by all philosophers of the social process.

The sources of the Bank's(1) reputation and respect among bankers and investors in the private (profit) sector, as well as finance ministers and treasury officials of the several nation-states in the public (nonprofit) sector of the world politico-economy, provides us with a clue to its corporate ethics. Basically the strength of the Bank and its sister-agencies, the International Finance Corporation and the International Development Association, appears to derive from the fact that all three are voluntary agencies. That is to say, none of them have any power to compel their memberships. They have no armies, no police forces, no courts, no jails. Although member-nations can be expelled under the most serious conditions, even this (constitutional) right has never been exercised. What then might be the fundamental source of the World Bank Group's unique "determinant influence" in the global society?

---

*This article first appeared as ch. 14 in James John Jelinek, ed. Philosophy of Education, 1977-1978 (Tempe, Ariz.: Far Western Philosophy of Education Society, 1978), pp. 123-36. Reprinted with permission.

The answer to this apparently simple query leads the inquirer on an extended journey into the basic assumptions and the value-posture of the Western civilization, complete with its western optimism, belief in human dignity, and its abiding faith in "progress" – a body of beliefs and often inarticulate hypotheses not always shared by other nonwestern cultures. The Bank and its affiliates have just begun to be aware of some of the very real problems involved in deliberate culture diffusion on the western model. Fortunately, because they are voluntary agencies, the Bank Group members (like all functional entities) have not been permitted to relapse into the far easier role of policeman-enforcer. The Group has had to make its own ways on the much more difficult paths of obtaining understanding, will, and consent.

It is in this search for nonpower solutions to the problems of "development" that the major outline of an emerging development ethic is to be discerned. The effort to articulate a nonpower ethic is not complete; it has just begun. But even the beginnings forecast possibilities for the future – the subject of this brief essay.

THE VOLUNTARY PRINCIPLE

John Dewey's son-in-law, Eduard Lindeman, once defined the voluntary principle as the essence of the democratic type of society. "The health of a democratic society," he said, "can be measured in terms of the quality of services rendered by citizens who act 'in obedience to the unenforceable."(2) If Lindeman is correct, the motives of free men to undertake voluntary enterprises cannot be compelled. True voluntary enterprises appear to transcend the petty struggles for physical power – the squabbles of princes and power-politicians, dictators and dema-gogues, for prestige and differential advantages. The loyalties of free men derive from will (voluntas) and consent freely given to concepts and ideas which are correct because they currently have the ability to withstand all efforts to prove them false. Such ideas reach out and appeal to voluntary will and consent because their self-correcting qualities enlarge human responsibilities. There is no magic in such ideas; they are open, candid, and evidentially demonstrable for all to see (even the Missouri farmer whose nature of proof is "show me").(3)

When the world's financial leaders from 44 nations were called into session at Bretton Woods by President Roosevelt in 1944, there appeared to be an unusual – if not unprecedented – opportunity to mobilize the world's economic potential for postwar financial and monetary reconstruction and development. Parts of the world were in economic shambles: Europe, the Pacific Islands, Japan, China, South Asia, the Middle East, North Africa. The war had turned to the military advantage of the Allies (the United Nations) and the chance to set new ground rules to smooth the transition from war to peace seemed propitious. But everything depended upon what was needed and how it was to be done.

After much discussion, debate, and argument the Bretton Woods Conference agreed to set up a World Bank and an International

Monetary Fund. In the case of each organization, it was agreed that two voluntary gifts of capital funds would be pledged by the member-nations signing the respective Articles of Agreement. These were to be capital funds without strings. The Bank and the Fund were not required to pay any interest; there were no collateral requirements; there were to be no dividends. None of the usual restrictions required for financial "permission to proceed" were exacted.

In retrospect, the agreement at Bretton Woods was a voluntary act of unprecedented (and sometimes unappreciated) significance in economic history. These capital funds are, of course, still in existence and have been multiplied several times over.

As a result of this original act of foresight and generosity, there has now been put into place in the United Nations system a financial and technical facility that has become the centerpiece for development efforts of the world society. What was created was a conduit for the responsible sharing of the world's wealth and know-how. The effort of the Bank and its affiliates has been devoted to using their capital funds to reduce absolute poverty, enlarge the flows of international trade, and promote foreign investment to help needy nations build their infrastructure. So far the Bank Group has survived three decades with a record of financial integrity that is quietly eloquent. Its institutional modesty and low profile has earned it the solid – if sometimes grudging – respect and approbation of its states-members. It has never had an uncollectible loan.

THE BANK AND ITS BASIC ASSUMPTIONS

In searching out the reasons for the ethical posture of an institution, it is sometimes useful to examine some of its basic assumptions. In the World Bank Group's case, among the most instructive of these are its theory of progress; its theory of human nature and motivation; and its theory of social value. The original Bank was founded primarily by the victors of World War I. They were completing a successful defense of the western capitalist civilization, with the assistance of the USSR (but the latter did not sign the Article of Agreement created at Bretton Woods). It is therefore understandable if the Bank and the Fund and later the IFC and IDA reflected the traditional assumptions of Western European cultures and their overseas extensions.

The Theory of Progress

Of all the basic assumptions of western civilization, the theory of "progress" is perhaps most visible. Distilled from the classical Greek heresy that was successfully defended at Marathon and Salamis, the modern concept of progress postulates that not only is earthly life worth living, but improving. "Things can be made better than they are by human effort." Mankind is an imaginative tool-using and culture-building animal species. As such, he can alter his environment, bend nature to his will and purpose, add the amenities of life to the basic security base, and begin to release human energies and talents for the plowing of new furrows and the discoveries of new worlds. This is the basic, almost paralyzingly optimistic, western common sense.

It is not strange, then, that the World Bank Group, given the opportunity for a new beginning, should perceive its postwar tasks as redirecting the new world-society-to-be on the roads to rational re-development – a process which had been temporarily interrupted by the Axis challenge. All of the 44 nations which signed the original Bretton Woods agreements shared this consensus in one way or another. Indeed, the degree of unanimity seems effectively to have over-shadowed the disagreements on how it was to be accomplished.

The Theory of Human Nature and Motivation

A second basic assumption at Bretton Woods – and an essential component of the theory of progress – was the operational premise concerning human nature and its motivations. The doctrine that provides the model is that of "inherent traits," with which all humans are presumably endowed by "nature." In the economic realm, for example, it is simply assumed that men are born naturally acquisitive, selfish, aggressive, and capable in varying degrees of pursuing their own pecuniary and material advantage. What was perceived as needed by the Bretton Woods delegates was to restore the opportunities for human beings to follow their inherent drives. The motivation for progress (both of states and individuals) was presumed to exist as part of the biological inheritance.

Like the theory of progress, the doctrine of inherited behavior traits was not at issue. It was simply assumed as obviously unquestionable. Nature could be assisted by making available those "financial permissions" to war torn nations and developing territories in the form of loans and credits for capital improvements (the basic infrastructure) needed for economic growth and development. Capital funds were to be the dynamic for re-starting the great wheel of progress.

The Theory of Social Value

A third basic assumption that the founders of the World Bank Group employed was the utility theory of social value. The proposition rests upon the two previous assumptions. It is presumed that the pathway to progress by pecuniarily motivated individuals lies in an efficient "mini-max" of human effort: "minimizing" inputs which "maximize" the outputs that have utility (use) value in daily life. By using the maximization principles as a guide to social effort, it is presumably possible to escape the worst effects of nature's pervasive "scarcity," while rewarding the enterprising individual with the comforts and amenities afforded by the current level of technology and know-how. The principle also purports to explain how economic justice is combined with progress (every man gets what he is worth), through the impersonal price system through which everyone calculates what is useful to him. Thus, production of goods and services is guided by the rise and fall of prices, directing a society's productive effort in those directions most likely to satisfy human wants, desires, needs and/or fancies.

The unquestioned acceptance of the utility theory of value and the price system for allocating scarce goods amongst mankind's infinite wants provided the Bretton Woods founders with an apparently unassailable ethical position. They were simply to help administer a "natural system of economic justice" whose mechanism was the "unseen hand" (of God) working according to impersonal "natural laws." The proposition that is thus implied – that <u>price measures value</u> – was not to be seriously challenged.

With these three basic assumptions of the western commonsense in hand, the Bank could confidently proceed with its mission. Progress, growth, and development were synonymous terms. They designated the path to relief from war devastation, and from want, dawn-to-dusk toil, general misery, and a short life span of illness, illiteracy, and human degradation. The road ahead was clear – to help nations in ways that were both practical and humanitarian to help themselves along the road to progress that had served western industrialized nations in their great escape from poverty.

THE ROAD TO A GLOBAL DEVELOPMENT ETHIC
(SOME HALF-MILESTONES)

The social ethic of Practical Idealism is an attractive ideology. But in the three decades of the World Bank Group's existence, it has proven to involve some rather serious difficulties. Now, as the second United Nations development decade is drawing to its close, the Bank and its two affiliates appear to be groping toward some important modifications which merit the social philosopher's attention.

As described above, the World Bank Group understandably adopted the basic assumptions of the rich and advanced industrialized nations. These implied a generous outgoing (if somewhat patronizing) attitude toward the poor, less developed nations – many of whom had come only belatedly to national independence as the great colonial empires dissolved after World War II. As perceived through western lenses, the escape from poverty that had accompanied the western industrial revolutions was primarily a matter of <u>will</u> and <u>skill</u> combined. To share these things two requisites appeared necessary: the will and motivation to progress and the transfer of technologies of all sorts from the West to emergent cultures.

But, as the first decades of the UN development system began to unfold, it became increasingly clear that the same formula which had served the advanced nations was not necessarily that which can be exported intact to other nonwhite, noncapitalist, non-Christian, nonindustrialized cultures. In fact, it was somewhat disillusioning to find that in some cases the efforts of the developed world were neither understood nor appreciated – even viewed sometimes by developing cultures as culturally destructive.

Science and Technology as Articles of Faith?

The rise of modern science, with its myriad applications to the production of the means of life and experiences, has tended to become a basic tenet of western thought and attitude. The impacts of new ways – of innovation and novelty – on western cultures have proven generally capable of absorption and integration without undue dislocation, probably because for the most part they have been spaced over time and do not require a sudden wrenching of old habits and attitudes and values.

The same is not automatically true for many of the world's less developed cultures. The introduction of "inappropriate" technology may have serious disturbing effects on some cultures for which the germ theory of disease, computers, contraception, high-yield seeds, Rochdale-type cooperatives – even a money exchange system – can severely weaken the traditional social bonds.

The Bank, as an apostle of modern science and technology, and to maintain its financial integrity in the world money markets, adopted a methodology called the project cycle. What was required were procedures that would insure a loan's repayment on schedule, complete a development project, and make a profit for the lender. The steps of the project cycle are:

1. Identification: preliminary identification of high priority projects suitable to both the Bank and the borrower.

2. Preparation: entry of a project into the "pipeline," outlining in advance all the technical, economic, and financial feasibilities and potential problems.

3. Appraisal: Bank appraisal of the full package – the economic, technical, managerial, and institutional requirements for success.

4. Negotiation: discussion and negotiation between the Bank and the borrowing country on agreed measures for project success.

5. Supervision: field supervision of the project during construction in initial and subsequent stages, including necessary adjustments and changes as required.(4)

These are rigorous requirements based on western management experience. During the project cycle, the Bank (or IDA) is present at all stages; it holds the funds. It may insist on all measures for viability of the loan. It disburses the funds only upon evidence of actual accomplishment. In its supervision duties, the Bank oversees the procurement of goods and services on the agreed guidelines, including competitive bidding by qualified contractors and manufacturers.

The project cycle disciplines understandably tend to inject the Bank into the internal affairs of client nations. These affairs include such things as the government's borrowing policies, its tax and fiscal system, allocations of revenues received, and even the interest rates to be charged by the utility services developed. It is not surprising that on occasion the Bank has been accused of "neocolonialism," "capitalist arrogance," and "interventionism." The imposition of strict lending criteria, such as prevailing interest rates (on average about 8¼ percent), or a short grace period (7 to 10 years at most), and a relatively short maturity term (not more than 20 years), may well appear to developing nations as restrictive and high-handed – a vestige of attitudes of western superiority.

With the incumbency of George Woods, the Bank's third president, the development policies began to change in some important ways. Not the least of these was the discovery that the "demographic transition" as experienced in western nations was going to be long-delayed in many nations of the world – particularly those which, because of the rapid importation of death-control technologies, were now suffering an avalanche of population rate increase. Could it be possible that (with all the goodwill in the world) the Bank's efforts based on the "trickle-down" theory of prosperity were proving counterproductive? Was the realistic course, then, to contemplate Triage?

Triage – to Choose or not to Choose?

As Parson Malthus had predicted in 1798 (first Essay on Population) the infinite hopes for human happiness were inevitably doomed, for population growth always exceeds the growth of production of the means of life and experience. Now in the twentieth century we seem to be witnessing the full meanings of this dire prediction: famine, pestilence, illiteracy, and natural disaster, along with the misery, degradation, and desperation of perhaps 40 percent of the world's population. The ethical-moral dilemma of international organizations like the Bank, the IFC, and the IDA – the financial heart of the UN development system – could prove crucial in the further evolution of planetary civilization.

The case for triage, of course, is the Aristotelian-Malthusian proposition that, since population always outruns production, there are times when it is best to let nature take its course to ". . . prune the luxuriant growth of the human race."(5) South Asia, for example, can be perceived as beyond rescue or repair. Simply soothing the western conscience by donating food aid – thus creating a permanent welfare system – might well prove counterproductive by insuring the existence and further reproduction of even more welfare generations. If South Asia were to be cut adrift – thereby selecting who should die by doing nothing – only nature and the South Asians could be blamed.

The World Bank Group has, on the other hand, taken a most vigorous stand against triage. Beginning with the 1960s, both the Bank and IDA developed a modified set of lending criteria that would single out development projects which would directly assist the poorest of the poor. These new style projects and programs went far beyond loans simply for basic utility infrastructure. The purpose now was to help the poorest sectors of client states to improve their productivity and their incomes, thereby seeking "growth with equity." New style loans began to be made for such things as new job creation, labor-intensive intermediate (more appropriate) technologies, rural credit unions, improved food production methods, improved water supplies, farm-to-market roads, technical education facilities, health facilities, and family planning programs. The overall objective was to invest in "human capital," recognizing that without benefits to the lowest-income strata the meaning of "development" would be relatively hollow. Any development which left 40 percent of the poorest untouched would be an indirect choice for triage – and would render even the rich vulnerable to revolution.

The Bank's current president (now beginning his third term), Robert McNamara, put the World Bank Group's position in this fashion:

> . . . no amount of outside assistance can substitute for the developing member government's resolve to take on the task. It will call for immense courage, for political risk is involved . . . But if the governments of the developing world – who must measure the risks of reform against the risks of revolution – are prepared to exercise the requisite political will to assault the problem of poverty in the countryside, then the governments of the wealthy nations must display equal courage . . . by removing discriminatory trade barriers and by substantially expanding official development assistance.(6)

The rather blunt statement of the dilemma – "reform or revolution" – posed the more serious underlying question. Given access by desperate groups to weapons of mass destruction and atomic blackmail – what becomes of the stable and orderly process of development for rich and poor alike? Opting, as it has, for a global social ethic which links traditional "security" with development helps place the World Bank Group in a virtually unassailable moral position. As McNamara recently put it to the board of governors in Manila:

> Surely we cannot contemplate the stark realities of absolute poverty in our poorest member countries, and then turn our backs on the 750 million human beings there who are trapped in it. . . . By any objective standard, absolute poverty is an anachronistic tragedy in our century. A tragedy because it is a condition of life beneath the level of human decency; and anachronistic because there are now at hand the economic and technological means to end it.(7)

Sharing Development Potential: Can It Be Done?

Sharing the "economic and technological means" to end absolute poverty is no facile exercise as the World Bank Group has discovered. The simple "transfer of technology" from advanced to developing cultures involves enormously profound understanding of the ways cultures are built, the value-structures and assumptions that lie behind social institutions, and the ways institutions are modified and adjusted as new know-how becomes technically feasible.

The Bank and its affiliates are currently struggling to probe these dimensions of "development." The simplistic version of duplicating the western escape from poverty by substituting labor-saving machinery for hand production has obviously made little headway under the burdens of the population avalanche. Moreover, the suspicion and distrust that accompany western technologies (even, or especially, on the model of western management disciplines) have forced the Bank to realize that what is <u>technically</u> possible is not always <u>politically</u> possible.

What is now required is a much more sophisticated posture that recognizes the enormous importance of "culture conservation," and of the great habitudes (mental, manual, and moral) that perhaps control more than 90 percent of human behavior and conduct. These "cakes of custom" tend to freeze the conduct of successive generations into fixed channels of repetitive (usually unquestioned and unquestionable) behaviors. They can be changed only with the greatest difficulties, even with the utmost patience and understanding. To try to change them "from outside," from external cultural sources, may tend only to fix the foundations deeper in cement.

The Bank, along with other "development" agencies, has been pushed, in other words, back to the fundamentals of social change. It is the hardest problem of all: how to help people, with their consent and understanding, develop the <u>will</u> to modify their actual behaviors in order to choose more intelligently from among a newer and broader range of real choices. The problem is complicated by the fact that traditional forms of coercion – military, economic, financial – are irrelevant to the problem situation. Only the "power of ideas" that are capable of evidential demonstration – and can be made ceremonially legitimate with the prevailing cultural traditions – can serve as appropriate development tools.

Dimly recognizing the problem situation, the Bank has turned to something it calls "institution-building."(8) It is described as ". . . a process of change intended to strengthen local capabilities for achieving the goals of a developing society . . . a dynamic process, a largely indigenous process responsive to changing internal needs and based on internally shaped solutions to which outside contributions may be adapted."(9) Without some such methodology, the Bank is beginning to realize that "development" is at best a happenstance. In fact, without adequate institutions to guide and direct behaviors (without inhibitions of shame, guilt, fear, ostracism or punishment), sustainable social change is virtually impossible. But the puzzle still remains. How can it be initiated? How can it be made to come about while still protecting the dignities, pride, and self-motivations essential to its long-term viability?

The implications of this new posture are an interesting lesson in western humility. The (understandable) pride in western achievements has been brought up short in its efforts to transfer them cross-culturally. In the process some very important lessons have been learned, at least are being learned:

1. Development and its effects are not peculiar to new "emerging" nations; advanced nations too are affected by changes in technologies, demands for wider sharing of equities and amenities, environmental and resource limitations, and changing demographic patterns. All nations develop all the time, rich and poor alike.

2. Thus it is unnecessarily pretentious to hold out any of the industrialized models of development (western or socialist) as the best or only preferred models – especially for the absolute poor who live at the margins of all societies.

3. Therefore, indigenous institutions that serve particular development needs in particular cultures must be allowed to emerge out of their own settings, suited to their own psychological, religious, technological, economic, and resource assets and liabilities.

4. The key to institution-building lies deep within the cultural attitudes and existing value systems of any culture, which may be quite different from the western "impersonal and professional" bias of the industrial models of development.

5. The challenge is ". . . to diagnose problems properly and to adapt knowledge and advice into politically and culturally feasible solutions."(10)

In taking this position the Bank appears to be adopting a more universal stance of appreciating the wide range of ethical aspirations that formally motivate the many differing cultures it is seeking to assist.

SUMMARY
The World Bank Group and a Universal Development Ethic?

The World Bank Group purports to be a global, functional, change agent. In the three decades of its existence, it has, indeed, learned a great deal, and its own ethical positions appear to have been changed by the experiences. A brief review of some of its achievements is relevant here.

In the first place the Bank and its affiliates have performed a feat that is unique in economic history. That is, they have provided a means by which the voluntary principle (obedience to the unenforceable) can work through transnational organizations to share access to economic growth among advanced and developing nations. Though still in its infancy, this global enterprise is unique because it unites the interests of the free market economies of the western tradition with the emergent (often planned) economies of the developing world on terms helpful to both.

A second achievement of the World Bank Group has been its flexibility in adapting itself to changing economic and political conditions. The strict project cycle disciplines and the original hard terms of lending have now been supplemented by the "soft" or concessional lending terms of the IDA and adapted to the needs of poorer countries – but without surrendering financial integrity in the private money markets where the Bank's own bond issues must be sold. In fact, out of its "profits" the Bank has been able to assist in creating two new affiliates, the IFC and the IDA. In this instance, it has come to behave more like a cooperative credit union than simply a "bank."

Third, the World Bank Group has discovered the demographic transition, and especially some of the factors which tend to delay, lengthen, and amplify it in the developing countries. In this connection it has taken an unabashed moral stand against triage, and has sought to modify its lending practices to insure that the absolute poor will share in the development process. By thus stressing the global interdependence of both rich and poor (among as well as within) modern nations, it has assumed a dimension of leadership in the UN development system that appears to be as unapproachable as it is unassailable. Its current president has put it very directly in these terms: "The fundamental case for development is the moral one. The whole of human history has recognized the principle – at least in the abstract – that the rich and powerful have a moral obligation to assist the poor and the weak. That is what the sense of community is all about."(11)

It is perhaps not too much to expect that as the century closes the main outlines of a truly global ethic will come more sharply into view. Some half-milestones have already been reached. The pragmatic gropings of the past thirty years have provided a further verification of the functional hypothesis that the soundest base for peaceful and mutually rewarding social life are the commonalities – the things men share – rather than their cultural differences. The adventurs of the world bank group would tend to confirm that this is technically possible, if it can be culturally cushioned and made minimally dislocational.

NOTES

(1) The Bank's official name is the International Bank for Reconstruction and Development, established at the Bretton Wood's Monetary and Financial Conference in 1944, as World War II was coming to a close. The International Monetary Fund (FUND) was created by the same conference.

(2) Eduard C. Lindeman, The Democratic Man, ed. by Robert Gessner (Boston: Beacon Press, 1956), p. 217.

(3) W.W. Merrifield, Leadership in Voluntary Enterprise (New York: Oceana Publications, 1961), preface, p. 1.

(4) Warren C. Baum, "The Project Cycle" Finance and Development, June 1970, pp. 3-13.

(5) Howard B. Peterson, "Triage" (53rd Faculty Honor Lecture, Utah State University, Logan, Utah, 1976), p. 1.

(6) Robert McNamara, "Address to the Board of Governors," Nairobi, Kenya, September 24, 1973 (Washington, D.C.: The World Bank, 1973).

(7) Robert McNamara, "Address to the Board of Governors," Manila, Philippines, October 4, 1976 (Washington, D.C.: The World Bank, 1973).

(8) Jacques Roumani, "Institution-Building: A Position Paper and Work Program," Manuscript (The World Bank, March 4, 1977), summary, p. III.

(9) Ibid.,

(10) Ibid., p. 14.

(11) John L. Maddux, "Some Implications of the Development Philosophy of Robert McNamara," manuscript (The World Bank, January 1, 1976), p. 3.

8 Imperialism: A Transnational System of Privilege
Mansour Farhang

The purpose of this essay is to develop a conceptual framework for analyzing the evolving character of imperialism in contemporary international politics. Neither the orthodox Marxist theories nor the non-Marxist views that define imperialism as a relationship of domination/subordination between two nations provide an adequate model for describing the transnational realities of the present-day imperialist relations.

The term imperialism came into popular use in the 1840s, and since then its connotations have changed several times. The connotations of words which refer to dynamic realities change as the context and specific characteristics of the reality to which they refer change. The word imperialism has always been used to describe the dynamic reality of a system of privilege in international relations. A system of privilege involves exploitation, dependence, and inequality.(1) The suffix "ism" denotes principles of actions and intentions. A major contention of all theories of imperialism is that the actions and intentions in imperialist relations are more the manifestations of structural relations than the products of isolated ideas or conditions.

An imperialist system does not have to be formally constituted in order to be recognized as such. It is the actual exercise of its power, the nature of its objectives, and the practical consequences of its policies that define its reality. It does not particularly matter what the imperialist policy makers call their activities in the official proclamations. The British called their expansion into Africa and Asia the white man's burden; the French described it as their civilizing mission; the Soviet Union justified its domination of Eastern Europe in the name of international socialist solidarity; and the Americans defend their global counterrevolutionary activities in the name of freedom or peace.

The issue is not sincerity. What people think they are doing matters less than what they are actually doing. This does not mean that the thoughts, motivations, and intentions of the policy makers are not important in understanding their actions. To determine whether imperialism in fact exists one must focus on the conditions and relationships that constitute a system of privilege – namely inequality, dependence, and exploitation. But when it comes to the question of why a system of privilege exists, then a comprehension of the motives, intentions, values, and thoughts of the dominant and the dominated is indispensable.

Modern western expansion into Afro-Asian societies has an inexact but significant dividing line between the era of mercantilism and the period following industrial capitalism.(2) During the mercantile era, what mattered for the colonizers was trade in sugar, spices, and other tropical products grown by slave or semislave labor in the colonies. The colonizers had no interest in the hopes and dreams of the colonized. They were expected to work and accept their subsistence economy as normal. The enforcers of law and order were unconcerned with the natives' perception of reality. There was no need to alter the behavior of the colonized or transform the social structure of the colony because the objectives of the mother country were served in a static relationship.

After the industrial revolution the situation changed drastically. The colonies attained new significance as sources of raw materials for the home industries; and the output of the new factories needed ever-expanding markets. Thus the colonizers began to perceive the natives as potential customers and became interested in the economic growth of the colony. This development required at least some modification of the traditional socioeconomic structure in the colonies. The natives could no longer remain static if they were to modernize. Their buying power had to increase and their taste, values, and aspirations had to move in a direction compatible with the requirements of diversified production in the metropole.

However, the effort to modernize the material conditions and the consciousness of the natives could, at best, be a very slow process. In the feudal class system of the colonies, the change from slave or semislave labor to wage labor could not proceed without a heavy cost to the native ruling class. Thus from the very beginning the colonizers had a dilemma – how to expand the colonial market without creating political awareness among the natives. This contradiction ended in the explosion of the independent movements and the rise of nationalism.(3)

Since the establishment of national self-determination in the former colonies, imperialism as a system of privilege has developed a transnational characteristic. The term transnational is used here to describe those activities in world politics and economics which result from a confluence of interests by two or more nation-states. Such confluence of interests between states does not necessarily represent the existence of imperialistic relations. But when it does, the coalition resulting from it constitutes a transnational system of privilege.

The interdependency which underlies this development does not change the inequality between the states involved in the transnational system of privilege. For example, in spite of complex interdependencies that existed between the United States and Iran before the Shah's departure in 1979, the relationship between them was highly unequal because the ability of Iran to change or modify the interdependency was far more limited than that of the United States. Inequality is an indispensable condition of imperialism.

The conventional analysts of world politics view the nation-states as the only actors in the international system, and the pursuit of interest and/or ideology as the core of their interplay. Chiefs of state, soldiers, and diplomats − force or the threat of force − are the principal agents of the system; and the ability or willingness to compromise is the means by which war can be avoided in the unending struggle for power and privilege. The requirements of domestic order and stability are perceived as a motive in the formulation of foreign policy objectives and strategies, but they are not analyzed as a principal force in the interplay of the states.(4) This approach to the study of international relations could make sense if there were no actual domestic challenge to the power of the state and the socioeconomic structure it represents.

But we live in a revolutionary age, a period in which many states are threatened by those political elements that reject the foundation of their societies as unfair and illegitimate. In such situations, the requirements of domestic order and stability can create a confluence of interests between two or more states overshadowing their competitive relations as independent states.

It is due to the development of such a situation that today imperialist policies and actions increasingly subordinate the interests of the general public to the interests of the ruling elites in both dominant and dominated societies. The key concept is subordination, whether direct or indirect. The ruling elites of the subordinated societies are the junior partners of the elites in the dominant countries. In some cases such as pre-1979 Iran, Brazil, Indonesia, and the Philippines, the junior partners were chosen to form a subimperialist system. At times nationalism and conflict of interest create tension and distrust between the senior and the junior partners, the imperialists and the subimperialists; but the necessity of the partnership is not questioned because it is a response to the revolutionary challenge to the structure of privilege in the subordinated societies.

The imperialist policy makers perceive this challenge as much of a threat to their interests as those elites who have to confront the revolutionaries at home. Contemporary imperialism, therefore, does not have to involve impairment of national sovereignty. This situation does not change the reality of imperialism as a system of privilege. Transnationalism represents the ability of the privileged few in two or more nation-states to combine forces across national boundaries in their joint confrontation with the revolutionary challenge from below in the subordinated society.

Until recent decades, the ruling elites in the official or unofficial colonies of Africa, Asia, and Latin America did not need the assistance of colonial or imperialist powers in order to maintain their privileged position. In fact, in many cases the traditional rulers attempted to resist the Western penetration of their societies not only for political but also for cultural and ideological reasons. Until the outbreak of World War II, the cultural and ideological orientation of the typical traditional ruling class in the underdeveloped world was not too different from that of its own general population.(5)

To be sure, peasant life in the class-ridden underdeveloped countries was and is short, brutish, and nasty. But the landed aristocracy or its equivalent had constant contact with the exploited peasants. They all identified with the same religious symbols and justified their actions and intentions in similar fashion. The mode of transportation and communication used by the owners of land and capital was not a mystery to the peasants. The privileged children visited the village regularly and their education and attitudes were familiar to the villagers.

Today the situation is completely changed. The peasants are still living under the same conditions or have moved to urban ghettos, but the owners or controllers of the means of production have adopted a cultural and ideological orientation that is a mystery to the general population. The privileged few, whether they belong to the entrepreneurial, bureaucratic, or military sector of the ruling elites, have no sociocultural contact with the many exploited. In terms of their concrete aspirations and ambitions, they identify with the West to the point of being alienated from their own roots. Their children are educated in the West and their life-style, attitudes, and values mystify the general public.

Thus as the economic gap between the privileged few and the wretched many increases, so does the cultural gap. The enclaves of wealth and power in countries like pre-1979 Iran, Brazil, Indonesia, and the Philippines are also enclaves of imported cultures and life-styles. The presence of multinational corporations in such subimperialist countries benefits and strengthens the enclaves of wealth and power in the sea of misery. Of course the national elites who control the political and economic institutions of the country have their disagreements with the managers of the multinational corporations. But the disagreements do not involve the nature of the multinationals' operations. The concerns and questions of the native elites, when they arise at all, relate to tactics of operations and their share of the profits.

The multinational corporations operating in the subordinated or subimperialist societies often point to the increase in the aggregate national income which results from their operations. The national elites are the most unlikely candidates to question the appalling maldistribution of this aggregate growth because they, constituting no more than 2 to 3 percent of the population, are its principal beneficiaries.

Furthermore, the multinational corporations are producers of goods as well as transmitters of ideas and values from the advanced capitalist world to the poor countries. Thus Marx's notion that "the ideas of the ruling class are in every epoch the ruling ideas" becomes a transnational reality. "The class which has the means of material production at its disposal, has control at the same time over the means of mental production, so that thereby, generally speaking, the ideas of those who lack the means of mental production are subject to it."(6)

In their book Global Reach, Richard Barnet and Ronald Muller describe the leading executives of multinational corporations as "world managers."(7) These "world managers" need the active participation of the native elites in the poor nations in order to implement the corporate plans; the local elites need the resources of the multinationals in order to pursue their capitalist strategy for development. Richard Sklar has argued that this complex interdependency has led to

> the formation of a transnational class comprising at its core those who manage multinational corporations. To substantiate this thesis, it would be necessary to show that the members of any such presumed class tend to think and act as a collective entity. Social classes are sustained and strengthened by many different generators of vitality. A transnational ruling class would be especially difficult to overthrow inasmuch as its power would be fortified by the appropriation of diverse resources in many countries. Its significance as a power group might transcend the conception of imperialism.(8)

Thus corporate internationalism and the revolutionary threat to the class structure of the underdeveloped countries have led to the coalescence of dominant classes across national boundaries. The beneficiaries of this transnational coalition have more in common than their opposition to the revolutionaries.

The ostentatious life-style of the elites in the underdeveloped countries predates the multinational corporations or the confluence of transnational interests. But in recent decades this ostentatious life-style has been divorced from its native roots. The rapid growth of international finance, movement of goods and services, and travel and communication have led to a global standardization of values, goals, and aspirations among those who benefit from these activities. Since the technology and the ideology of this dramatic phenomenon are the product of organic socioeconomic growth in the West, the standardization of values, goals, and aspirations among the dominant elements in the transnational system of privilege has added a new dimension of cultural domination to the evolving character of imperialism in the contemporary world. Today even the liberal education, the manners, the dress fashion, the fads, and the consumptive norms of the elites in the subordinated countries are identical with those of their counterparts in the advanced industrial world.

The United States, as a chief imperialist power of our time, often justifies its actions in defense of the privileged elites in the underdeveloped countries in the name of stability, which is regarded as the prerequisite for economic development. Since World War II, United States officials have perceived the concept of development as a historical process by which societies have evolved from the primitive communities of the past to the industrial states of today. The term underdeveloped, therefore, is used to distinguish those societies which have fallen behind the countries whose quantitative progress remains uninterrupted.

An implicit contention of this view of underdevelopment is the equation of economic growth with qualitative advancement of the sociopolitical structures. This ethnocentric equation of aggregate/quantitative development with cultural/ideological advancement has been accepted by the elites in the subordinated countries.

Thus the dominant elements in the transnational system of privilege define underdevelopment by indices of traditionality, low per-capita income, widespread illiteracy, lack of political integration, a comparatively low degree of urbanization and industrialization, lack of institutional continuity, lack of national unity, particularism, functional diffuseness, and so on. This characterization may be useful as a first step in describing the conditions of some underdeveloped societies. But if the above variables are analyzed without inclusion of the class structure and imperialism, the result will be distorted both as an analytical tool and as a description of reality.

A meaningful conception of underdevelopment must include class rule and/or imperialism as its beneficiaries and perpetuators. Development requires structural change in both economic and sociopolitical institutions of the society. While economic growth can be defined as a steady accumulation of wealth and expansion of income, the process of development requires as a precondition the existence of a social structure in which wealth and income can be equitably distributed. The absence of this precondition in the dominated societies of the transnational system of privilege makes the initial step of the development process an act of revolutionary liberation, which includes the destruction of the traditional ruling class.

This historically inevitable feature of the developmental process is antagonistic to both the short- and the long-run objectives of United States imperialism. In the short run, the national liberation movements will not side with the United States in its ideological rivalry with the Soviet Union, nor will they favor the continuation of the dominant international trade and investment policies. They will not allow the multinational corporations to abuse their native resources or turn their countries into a market for United States surplus goods. In the long run, successful revolutionary governments might restructure their societies in ways that weaken the world capitalist order. They might give material support to other revolutionary movements in the underdeveloped countries and through the successful use of socialist methods of development become a source of inspiration for other subordinated societies.

Thus given the economic, the strategic, and the ideological objectives of American foreign policy, it is quite logical that United States policy makers are determined to strengthen the military and police institutions of their junior partners in the transnational system of privilege in their confrontation with the revolutionary challenge. The theoretical justification for this policy goes back to the post-World War II period. Dean Acheson, John Foster Dulles, Walt Rostow, Henry Kissinger, and Zbigniew Brezinski all maintained that the underdeveloped countries are going through the stage of development in which the traditional society is transformed into a modern political community. During this turbulent transformation the masses are vulnerable to revolutionary propaganda and they have to be protected from their own feelings and tendencies. The United States must give the national privileged elites military, political, and economic support against the revolutionaries but try to avoid overt military action if at all possible. The same people thought Vietnam was a mistake. Once the transitional stage of instability is ended by economic growth and the proper socialization of the masses, there will no longer be any need for American involvement in the internal affairs of the underdeveloped countries.(9)

It is quite logical that the United States has become a generous exporter of arms and repressive technology to the subordinated countries, particularly the subimperialists, in the transnational system of privilege.   United States military sales to the underdeveloped countries since 1970 amount to $41 billion, plus $13 billion in credit sales and $7 billion in commercial sales. United States military assistance in grants and credits to the underdeveloped countries between 1946 and 1976 amounts to $71 billion. United States assistance to police forces of the underdeveloped countries from 1961 to 1978 amounts to $322 million.(10) Beside bringing revenues to the arms industry, such vast transfer of arms and repressive technology is supposed to enable the junior partners in the transnational system of privilege to protect themselves against the revolutionary movements. While President Carter speaks of his "undeviating commitment" to human rights, some of the most insidious torturers of the world continue to receive weapons, repression technology, and intelligence training and advice from the United States. Such police states as Argentina, Brazil, Chile, Indonesia, pre-1979 Iran, Philippines, South Korea, Thailand, and Uruguay have been among the principal recipients of the United States weapons and repression technology.(11)

The formulators of United States foreign policies toward the underdeveloped world are not the only strategists of imperialism who have had to invent theories or justifications for international domination. The sixteenth century colonialists were not inhibited by any doctrine of the rights of man. If they treated any of their subjects humanely, it was because they were virtuous themselves and not because the subjects had the right to demand it. After the American and the French revolutions, the colonists found themselves in the position of having to justify the use of their power. Thus the nineteenth century colonialists contended that they were in the business of administering and advancing the masses. They often promised to end their rule as soon as the natives were ready to take care of themselves. Millions of Africans and Asians had to be killed and annual crops had to be burned year after year before the French gave up their civilizing mission and the British abandoned the white man's burden.

In our time imperialists once again fortify their actions with moral sanctions. They justify themselves by claiming to serve the people. Since imperialism harms the people and defies moral justification, the imperialists defend themselves by denying the very reality of their actions. When on occasion it becomes ludicrous to deny their domination of other societies, they claim that their actions are educative, liberating, and temporary. The brutal consequences of this development for the impoverished masses in the subordinated societies do not seem to catch the delicate eyes of the conventional analysts of multinational corporations or United States policies in the underdeveloped world. These "men of science" are acting in the long tradition of imperial scholarship. The distinguished scholars of British and French colonialism were also interested in questions of order and stability in the colonies more than the impact of colonialism on the natives.

If the study of politics is about who gets what, when, how, and why (if politics is concerned with the distribution of resources and its legitimizing ideology), then the study of international politics in the age of complex interdependencies must deal with the questions involved in who gets what, when, how, and why in interstate relations.   The material costs of imperialism come from the public treasury while its benefits go to private hands. And the human cost of imperialism is always paid by those who do not receive its material benefits.

Imperialism is harmful not only to the dominated peoples but also to the vast majority of the citizens in the imperialist society. Barnet and Muller demonstrate that by the use of exploitative/manipulative devices such as "transfer pricing," multinational corporations retard the economic development of the poor nations and at the same time cause retrogressive tendencies in their home countries as a result of the transfer of productive and distributive operations from the United States to low wage host countries.

The question of who pays the costs and who reaps the benefits form the interstate relations is an assessment of results rather than power. The native elites, who have control over the means of production, consumption, and compulsion, may or may not be an autonomous social force. The intensity of their nationalism could vary from one country to another. The degree of their dependency on or interdependency with the industrialized countries cannot be generalized. These are empirical issues which need to be investigated on a case by case basis.

What is clear in the present situation of international relations is the growing confluence of interests between the foreign policy elites in the industrialized world, particularly the United States, and the ruling elites of the class-ridden societies in the underdeveloped world. In confronting the revolutionary demand from below, these elites and their counterparts in the developed world have become interested in "revolution from above." The coalition of elites across national boundaries perceives economic development in the poor nations as a necessity not only in terms of market expansion for Western products, but also in the hope of enlarging the small middle class as a way of legitimizing the rule of the privileged few. This kind of economic development has nothing to do with justice or equity because the distribution of accumulated wealth takes place in the context of the existing class structure. In countries such as Iran, South Korea, and Brazil, economic development has intensified class differentiations and the maldistribution of wealth and income.

Thus, as transnational coalitions develop, the role of the state in managing the life of the nation expands. As the interests of the states in confronting the revolutionary challenge in the class-ridden underdeveloped countries converge, new issues enter the interstate relations and internationalize domestic politics. The consequences of these developments go far beyond the traditional questions involved in international politics and economics. In the age of revolutionary demand for equality, global standardization of elites' cultural values, worldwide dissemination of information, and the massive spread of sophisticated weapons and military technology, imperialism as a model of analyzing international relations must take into account the development of transnational interests and coalitions.

There are two primary questions involved in the study of imperialism as a transnational system of privilege: the empirical question of whether or not such a system in fact exists; and the theoretical question of what conditions and perceptions have led to its development.

The secondary questions of theoretical and empirical nature arise from the fact that the system of transnational privilege is not and cannot be monolithic. It is plagued by contradictions from within and challenged by forces from without. From within, the growing competition between Japan, the United States, and Europe in the markets of the world is disrupting the dominant position of the United States. The current balance of trade deficit of the United States is one manifestation of this development. If this trend continues, it could lead to disruption in certain sectors of the American economy and a growth of unemployment among the industrial workers.

So far the worldwide competition among the industrial capitalist countries has remained in the economic and financial realm, but sooner or later it will involve political and security issues as well. The Trilateral Commission symbolizes the desire of the competitors to deal with the situation within the parameters of their common privileged position.(12)

Another internal source of tension for the dominant countries in the transnational system is the moral opposition from a cross class segment of the privileged societies. This moral opposition is numerically small and as yet politically insignificant, but it plays a vital role in exposing the deceptive character of the system and analyzing its destructive consequences for peace and justice.

The moral opposition (not the entire opposition) to the war in Vietnam within the United States can be viewed as the most political manifestation of the moral opposition to the structure of transnational privilege. It was the second time in the history of imperialism that a significant number of the citizens in the imperialist country engaged in an intense and sustained struggle against the actions of their own government in a foreign country. The first example of such opposition to an imperialist war took place in France during the French-Algerian War, even though the French opposition to the Algerian War was much less intense than the American opposition to the Vietnam War. The current discussion of human rights as an aspect of foreign policy within the American government is in part a response to the pressure from the moral opposition. The most profound achievement of the moral opposition to United States imperialism is the level of public awareness which has made it extremely difficult for Washington to take overt or covert military action in defense of dominant elites in the subordinated societies.

A third source of tension within the transnational system lies in the frequent tactical disagreements between the privileged elites in the subordinated societies and United States foreign policy makers. Facing the revolutionary challenge to the structure of privilege at home is not the same thing as fearing such a challenge from Washington. Managing a political system based on fear and coercion is quite a different role than running an empire from within an open society with a democratic tradition.

The Shah of Iran could never understand why Richard Nixon had to resign the presidency of the United States. The dominant elites in Iran during the Shah's reign, Brazil, Chile, the Philippines, Indonesia, and South Africa, among others, have often been frustrated with the "slowness" and "cautiousness" of American foreign policy-making. They often complain about the inability of United States decision-makers to "understand" their situation and make "binding commitments" to defend them. After United States bombers and troops killed more than a million Vietnamese and defoliated thousands of acres, the Saigon elites were still complaining about the "cautiousness" and "indecisiveness" of America in conducting the war. The Shah of Iran had purchased more than $20 billion worth of sophisticated weapons and military technology from the United States in ten years, and at the time he was deposed in 1979 he was still complaining about America's inability to respond to his arms request with greater speed. Of course, there is a contradiction between democracy and imperialism, but often this contradiction has been dealt with at the expense of democracy.

Another source of tension related to America's "democratic indecisiveness" is the conflict between United States imperialist strategy and regional rivalries. The Middle East is a clear example of such conflict. The historic rivalry between Iran and Saudi Arabia was both exploited and intensified by United States arms sales to Iran. The Israeli military might, for the most part an American gift to the Jewish state, frightens America's Arab allies; and arms sales to Saudi Arabia and Egypt irritate Israel. There is a logic to United States strategy in the region, but the strategy does not always coincide with the American allies' perceptions of their own interests.

Beside the actual or potential revolutionary threat to the structure of power within the subordinated societies, there are three other sources of challenge to the transnational system of privilege. First, the Soviet Union, as the second most active power in world politics, is challenging the system of Western privilege wherever the opportunity presents itself. Given Soviet imperialism in Eastern Europe and the repressiveness of its domestic rule, it is clear that Russian policy makers are not challenging the existing system of privilege in the interest of justice or freedom. However, absence of honorable intentions on the part of the Soviet leaders should not confuse the fact that in many countries throughout the world the Soviet Union has aided the liberation movements against the forces of reaction. Cuba, Chile, Vietnam, Angola, and Mozambique are the outstanding examples. This is not to claim that the Soviet Union will continue to aid the revolutionary or progressive regimes without imperialistic design of its own.

The nature of Soviet imperialism is different from that of the United States or any other world power in the past. Soviet imperialism is historically unique and thus it is difficult to speculate about its future development. The important point for this paper is that when Soviet policies toward the underdeveloped countries are judged by their consequences, they constitute a source of challenge to the existing system of privilege in the world.

The second source of challenge to the system of transnational privilege from without is in the example and ideological pronouncements of the established revolutionary regimes such as China, Vietnam, and Cuba. These countries profoundly inspire the revolutionary elements throughout the world. Cuba is the only one actively participating in the national liberation movements of Africa. Ideologically, China is the most compassionate opponent of the structure of privilege in the world. But given its present categorical opposition to whatever the Soviet Union is for, China has taken an ideologically incomprehensible position with respect to a number of struggles against the structure of privilege in the underdeveloped countries.

The third source of challenge to the system of transnational privilege is located in the radical nationalist regimes seeking a more equitable definition of the international economic order. Nations like Algeria, Syria, Iraq, and Peru can be placed in this category.These countries have not experienced structural social change, but they do seek a more populistic distribution of income. The multinational corporations do not have a free hand in these countries, for the satisfaction of basic human needs has been given priority over the development of markets for consumer goods. The government of the United States attempts to have an open relationship with some of the less radical nations of this category, but it generally regards their foreign and domestic policies as antagonistic to American interests.

During the cold war, "national security" was the favorite slogan of the United States foreign policy makers. The requirements of national security were supposed to explain and justify subversion, militarism, and war. The national security arguments were greatly enhanced by the scholarly or academic analyses of international politics which viewed threat to national security as a permanent and universal feature of politics among nations. The rhetoric of national security and the so-called realist analyses of international politics epitomized a particular way of reacting to the events in the world.

The issues that appeared to concern the national security managers of the cold war era were mostly related to alleged Soviet military aggressiveness as well as revolution and radicalization of nationalism in the Third World. The seeming absence of international economic concerns in the rhetoric of the policy makers and the scholars during this period was due to the fact that there was already a dictatorship of world commerce headed by the United States of America.

Now the rhetoric of national security has been replaced by the rhetoric of interdependence. Former Secretary of State Henry Kissinger officially began the new rhetoric in his address before the sixth special session of the United Nations General Assembly: "We are all engaged in a common enterprise. No nation or group of nations can gain by pushing beyond the limits that sustain world economic growth. No one benefits from basing progress on tests of strength."(13)

There is some truth to the rhetoric of interdependence so far as it relates to the interests of the advanced industrial states. The issues involved in this interdependency are unrelated to the topic of this essay simply because they do not involve an imperialistic relationship. The industrial capitalist states are competing partners within their common privileged position. When there is a confluence of interests between two advanced industrial states, it can lead to reciprocal gains by the societies concerned. But the principle of reciprocal gains for the society at large does not apply to those underdeveloped countries in which the rigid class structure and absence of consensus politics make the interests of the state representing the privileged few antagonistic to those of the populace.

The new rhetoric of interdependence with respect to the subordinated countries in the transnational system of privilege is not different from the national security symbolism of the cold war era – it is intended to serve the interests of the United States and justify the defense of the status quo in the class-ridden underdeveloped nations.

It is certain that imperialism as a transnational system of privilege has produced an unprecedented amount of resentment among the populace in the subordinated societies. This resentment, which is a response to exploitation, coercion, and consumption-oriented manipulation, has intensified and expanded the revolutionary challenge from below. Thus, installation of repressive technology in the dominated society and militarization of its state have become necessary in order to maintain the status quo. And yet it is a mistake to think of the export of manipulation, repression, and militarism to the underdeveloped countries as a reaction to the resentment of the wretched. Since the resentment itself is a product of imperialism, the response to it is also a product of imperialism. Manipulation, repression, and militarism are the organic commodities of imperialism in search of global markets.

NOTES

(1) James Caposaso, "Methodological Issues in the Measurement of Inequality, Dependence, and Exploitation," in Testing Theories of Economic Imperialism, Steven J. Rosen and James R. Kurth Lexington, (Mass.: D.C. Heath and Co., 1974), pp. 87-91.

(2) George Lichtheim, Imperialism (New York: Frederick A. Praeger, 1971), Ch. 1.

(3) Ibid., Ch. 8.

(4) Hans J. Morganthau, Politics among Nations (New York: Alfred A. Knopf, 1967).

(5) Rupert Emerson, From Empire to Nation

(6) Karl Marx and Frederick Engels, The German Ideology (New York: International Publishers, 1970), p. 64.

(7) Richard Barnet and Ronald Muller, Global Reach (New York: Simon and Schuster, 1974).

(8) Richard Sklar, "Postimperialism: A Class Analysis of Multinational Corporate Expansion," Comparative Politics (October 1976), pp. 77-8.

(9) Walt W. Rostow, The Stages of Economic Growth (Cambridge: The University Press, 1969).

(10) Michael T. Khare, Supplying Repression (New York: The Field Foundation, 1977), pp. 31-40.

(11) Ibid., p. 9.

(12) Robert O. Keohane and Joseph S. Nye, Power and Interdependence: World Politics in Transition (Boston: Little, Brown and Co., 1977, p. 26.

(13) Henry Kissinger, "A New National Partnership," Department of State Bulletin, (February 17, 1975).

9 Nationalizing British Firms in Shanghai: The Politics of Hostage Capitalism in People's China, 1949-1957*

Thomas N. Thompson

For more than a hundred years Western nations and Japan in the persons of their various officials, troops, businessmen, and missionaries asserted and enforced their right to do what they pleased in semicolonized China. In all aspects the impact of the West and Japan was blunted by the retention of Chinese sovereignty, the continued capabilities of the indigenous economic system, and a general resistance to and suspicion of foreign-induced change beyond the treaty ports. Yet foreigners controlled large areas of the Chinese urban economy – certain northeastern and southwestern railroads, the principal mines and heavy industry, a part of the textile industry, the principal urban services, and the major share of steam navigation.(1) This control was all the more solid because foreign capitalism in China, unlike Chinese capitalism, was highly integrated. An English firm such as Jardine Matheson or a Japanese firm such as Mitsui simultaneously managed a wide variety of businesses: import-export, textiles, insurance, breweries, steam naviga- tion, and printing, for example.

The vigor with which the treaty ports were rejected demonstrates their profound impact on Chinese society. In reaction to the de facto power and influence of foreign enterprise, the Chinese Communists

---

*The method of research for this article was dictated by the subject matter. The only way to piece together China's nationalization policy was through interviews of witnesses to that policy, mainly British businessmen; and through access to various confidential documents of individual British firms and various business organizations in Hong Kong and London. Some of these sources required nonattribution. Since China has said so little about its nationalization policy, a degree of nonattribution is the price which the author shares with the reader in order to tell the story at all, a common problem among analysts of nationalization throughout the world. See Jessica Pernitz Einhorn, Expropriation Politics (Toronto: Lexington Books, 1974).

were committed to eliminate foreign capitalist ownership of industrial and commercial enterprise in China. Yet this goal could only be achieved after political power was won and consolidated, followed by land reforms, cooperatives for the production and distribution of goods, and eventually collectivization and nationalization. Political commitments do not become political realities in a short time, especially in a China that was a "semi-colonial and semi-feudal society."

It was in this context that the Chinese Communists' main revolutionary thrust just after taking political power was to overthrow the forces of external imperialism and internal feudalism, not to eliminate capitalism and abolish private property.(2) What Mao termed the new democratic revolution was to establish the conditions for both a bourgeois revolution and a socialist one. As a result, there was little that was specifically socialist in the policies pursued by the Communists in early years of the People's Republic of China (PRC).

As a matter of moving from one revolution to the other Mao understood the necessity of slow-motion nationalization of direct foreign investment. In 1947 he criticized as "ultra-left" the Party policies of 1930 to 1934 which included the proposal by the provisional soviet government of Kiangsi Province to expel directly and confiscate foreign economic and political power.(3) By contrast, Mao stressed that while it was necessary "to do away with the special privileges of imperialism in China, the revolution should distinguish between political and economic annihilation."(4) Criticizing the short sightedness of past thinking on nationalization, Mao stressed that it would be necessary to permit the existence of a capitalist sector in the economy for an uncertain period after the victory of revolution. As Mao spelled it out:

> In the interest of the whole economy and in the present and future interest of the working class and the laboring people, we must not restrict the private capitalist economy too much or too rigidly, but must leave room for it to exist and develop within the framework of the economic policy and planning of the People's Republic.(5)

This balanced and cautious policy made good sense, because as the Chinese Communists decisively shifted their attention to urban areas with war-related problems of administrative decay and structural dislocation, China's new leaders had neither the experience nor the training necessary to cope with the demands of an urban, industrial economy. Initially, much of the economy had to be run using existing conventional methods, often with the assistance of incumbent, non-Communist personnel, including the foreigners who had come to dominate China's urban economy.(6) The Chinese Communists intended to direct the transition as fast as possible to a state-owned and state-controlled economy.(7) As part of the transformation process, Mao wrote: "We must learn to do economic work from all who know how, no matter who they are. We must esteem them as teachers, learning from them respectfully and conscientiously."(8)

LINGERING IMPERIALISM IN A REVOLUTIONARY ERA

When the Chinese Communists gained control of China's major coastal cities, British firms in China were virtually defenseless. It was not always this way. Before 1949, if a British firm were having labor troubles, a gunboat from Britain's China fleet would be sent to the area as a "precautionary measure" to make it "easier for consul and others concerned to deal with a difficult situation." Even when business went well, "British Chambers of Commerce recorded their appreciation of the fact that the sight of gunboats comforted British merchants by smoothing the channels of trade."(9) After 1949 British businessmen did not quickly realize the nature of their new business environment. British firms had become hostages both to a past once marked by great political and economic power and to a present devoid of that power. There was no easy withdrawal.

As Chinese Communist forces moved swiftly down the Yangtze Valley in April and May 1949, British business interests concerned themselves with the protection of various fixed, immovable investments, which the British Chamber of Commerce, Shanghai, estimated to be worth $US 2.8 billion.(10) Although it is impossible to precisely calculate all of these assets in monetary terms, it is not disputed that they were large amounts.

Preparing for open battle between Chinese Communist and Chinese Nationalist troops and the likely damage to British investment, the British Chamber of Commerce, Shanghai, responded instinctively in terms of its imperialist past. The chamber advocated the "internationalization of Shanghai" from Chinese armies in the civil war.(11) "Whether or not there will be fighting is impossible to say," reads a Chamber of Commerce memorandum to British China firms, "but the declared intention of the Nationalists is that they will defend to the bitter end." Even if they did not fight, it was thought that the Nationalists remained in Shanghai just for that purpose.

Since its broader "internationalization" proposal to place a military cordon around all of Shanghai was impractical, the Chamber of Commerce proposed a more restricted approach which was still beyond Western capabilities. The chamber proposed a joint armed intervention by the British, American, and French governments to cordon off the Bund, as the Western financial enclave along Shanghai's Whampoa River was called. The chamber reasoned that this was practical since the protective forces needed for such an operation need not be large; and since once the imminent conflict had subsided, the protective intervention of Western troops could then be discontinued.

Although there was little fighting in, or stripping of, Shanghai, as the Chinese Communist troops moved into the city in late May, British firms simultaneously had to deal with several severe problems. First, and most immediate, the continuing Nationalist blockade of Shanghai caused the closing of the port, and, as part of a more general industrial paralysis throughout Shanghai, the slow stifling of all enterprises in which British capital was invested ensued. Initially affected were shipping wharves, warehouses, and banking and merchant houses.

Subsequently, manufacturers were affected due to the exhaustion of supplies of imported raw material and fuel and the corresponding reduction in utility services.(12)

British firms did not give up with the internationalization proposal. Even after the Communist takeover of Shanghai they persisted in requesting official British support to intervene directly, hoping to break the Nationalist blockade of China. In a July 1949 letter to British Minister of State Hector McNeil, representatives of various firms suggested that "unless some relief is found, it would have to be recognized that the British commercial stake in Shanghai might be lost."(13) Owing in part to policy differences between the United States and Britain over China, McNeil's response was a flat refusal of any assistance. The United States leaned toward withdrawal from, and isolation of, China. Britain was anxious at all levels to work out a modus vivendi with China, but Britain's post-World War II policy had become subordinated to that of the United States government which feared that American and British private enterprise, if left alone, would cooperate and do business with the Communists.(14)

To meet the challenge of the difficulties, the British chamber even entertained the possibility of a private "buccaneer" action in an effort to break the blockade and to reopen the vital transport link between Hong Kong and Shanghai. As a last resort to salvage the old days of "business as usual," the chamber proposed putting Taiwan under international jurisdiction. Whatever the outcome of the civil war, it was argued, China would need finance. An international jurisdiction in Taiwan would provide a firm foundation for raising money and sustaining profits.(15)

British firms' problems had many sources. A major problem was that in 1949 the Chinese Communists were not overly sympathetic to foreign firms' problems. New Chinese regulations, for example, prohibited labor cutbacks or economic retrenchment on the part of either Chinese or foreign firms. With little profit being made in Shanghai, many foreign firms were compelled to rely for their continued financing on resources held abroad as reserves.

The Chinese Communists, of course, had pressing problems of their own, and their resolution required actions antagonistic to foreign interests. The new Chinese authorities sought, for example, to reduce the effects of inherited inflation by linking workers' wages to the price of rice. From March to July 1949, there was a three-fold increase in the price of rice in China, and the firms were required to pay the partial cost of it.

British firms' initial problems and fears concerning the new business environment were part of longer-term problems and fears relating to the future of foreign business under Communist rule. As early as July 1949, China Association records indicate fears among foreign firms, particularly small ones, of liquidation.(16) These fears were not groundless. In Tientsin in February 1949, foreign banks were closed and their funds frozen. In practical terms this meant that firms with no local earnings, a common situation in war time, had difficulty even paying their staffs. Some firms, like British-American Tobacco and the oil companies, had stocks to sell, but at various times others had to borrow from outside China. Bringing in funds from outside China was made necessary in July when the Chinese authorities in Tientsin exacted a $US 2.2 million levy from various groups of capitalist firms, including foreign ones.(17)

From the vantage point of Shanghai in summer 1949, nobody knew if the July Tientsin levy or other provisions promulgated by the new regime should be taken as precedents in planning for an uncertain future. Some British merchants felt that Chinese policy would be to try to elbow out foreign traders in favor of Chinese rivals as soon as possible. Yet few taipans, as the heads of foreign firms were called, believed that completely closing down their China-based operations was inevitable. An important reason for this continued hope was that all of the propaganda put forward by the Chinese Communists urged foreign (as well as Chinese) merchants, industrialists, and bankers to remain in areas likely to come under Communist control as their "assistance would be needed in developing the country's trade." After Tientsin was occupied by Communist forces in mid-January 1949, for example, public announcements from General Chu Teh made this point.   A similar propaganda effort followed in Shanghai.(18)

Although British businessmen in China hoped for the best under Communist rule, many taipans of the larger firms recognized that a number of preexisting conditions for doing business in China had been transformed. How to deal with these changes would become an insurmountable problem. As John Keswick of Jardine Matheson put it:

> Our treaties of privilege were gone and we knew that we would never see extraterritoriality again. This meant that we expected to live and trade in China under Chinese law, subject to Chinese habits and customs, and with only such protection as our officials would be able to give us (this will be the same as in the period previous to 1842), and subject to the whims of politics which were bound to change during the formative years of the current Chinese revolution. . . .(19)

REVOLUTIONARY REALITIES

The People's Government was determined that development within China would primarily serve the interests of China and its people. On this basis, with the urban economy in a state of shambles after almost twenty years of continuous warfare, China's new leaders, who were unbeholden to British firms, expressed few sympathies for their profit and loss accounts. At issue to the various firms was whether foreign enterprise would be permitted the minimal security, opportunity, freedom of movement, and freedom from excessive taxation required in their view to stay in China. But these issues could not be separated from the Chinese Communist revolution or the historic downturn in England's imperialist fortunes. The decline of Britain's influence in Asia had important repercussions for the security of British firms since in the past the preventive and punitive roles of British military power had assured protection for these firms in China and helped to maintain imperialist privileges.

British merchants realized very early after the Communists took power that the Chinese Communist Party was "here to stay," although some British merchants felt that few Chinese were really Communists and that it would take many years to convert them. In the new environment, where British merchants no longer could depend on warships to solve their problems, the various firms' only hope of remaining in China was to reach a mutually acceptable modus vivendi with the People's Government.

Because of the "natural anti-communism," which many British firms viewed as a permanent Chinese characteristic, "the best and only way of checking the spread of communism," notes a China Association memorandum, "was for democratic powers to maintain and develop friendly relations with the Chinese people and the Chinese government."(20) In pursuit of this policy, the China Association exerted its influence in favoring formal diplomatic relations between England and China as a precondition for settling grievances in the short term, and implementing a Treaty of Commerce from which British firms would no doubt profit, in the long term.

These proposals were only proposals. British merchants in China had become hostages not only to the immovable assets built up in China over the years, but hostages as well to the determination of the People's Government to strictly control the new economic environment in the interests of its own people. The firms were hostages in this sense because the People's Government demanded that they continue to operate in China irrespective of their losses. While operating with immediate losses, a major effort of the firms was to assess exactly what China's long-term policy toward foreign capitalism would be. Some firms, under the cumulative effect of several incidents mainly involving labor and tax disputes between British firms and Chinese workers, concluded that their future in China was a limited one. In representing these firms, Michael Lindsay, the former British Embassy press attaché, personally delivered a memorandum to Cho En-lai noting the impression that "it is the deliberate policy of the new government to subject foreign business to obstruction and annoyance as part of a plan to drive them out of China."(21)

The cause of Sino-British troubles in late 1949, according to Lindsay, lay in differences between Chinese and British approaches to problem-solving. Lindsay's impression of the Chinese perspective was, for example, to decide on a basic policy of principle to be worked out in practice. Lindsay interpreted the normal British approach, on the other hand, to be based on solving immediate practical problems and, on this basis, to develop a "working policy of principle." If both sides would only understand and appreciate these differences, Lindsay hoped that British firms and the People's Government might be able to live together on good terms.

But Lindsay misperceived. The issue was not whether the People's Government and the British firms could live together on some abstract "good terms," but on whose terms they would live together, if at all. The answer to that question became increasingly clear. In one of the rare public statements of its position, the Chinese approach was summed up by China's Liberation Daily in a note on August 6, 1950:

> Although foreign interests are owned by foreigners under the jurisdiction of the People's Government, these enterprises have been deprived of their special privileges which they enjoyed in the past . . . . If they can dutifully obey all ordinances and rulings of the People's Government and engage in business which is beneficial to the livelihood of the people and the livelihood of our country, they will be permitted to exist and will be protected.

Since explicit policy statements were rare, China's policy toward foreign firms has to be extrapolated from these few statements and from China's practice. It appears to be the following. The Chinese, in the long run, wanted to completely take control of their economy. This required, in the Chinese view, driving foreign capitalists out of the country. The method to achieve this goal, as the Liberation Daily statement suggests, was through ordinances and rulings by the People's Government. The ensuing indirect approach necessitated that foreign capitalism operate under terms profitable for China; however, such operations would become relatively unprofitable for the firms. Requiring the continued payment of taxes and wages by firms was in the People's Government's interest; outright confiscation was not. The opportunity of British firms for profit-making was thus limited by a variety of factors.

First and foremost, the People's Government was primarily concerned with the employment of Chinese workers and with production, not with profits. Cities were swollen by refugees, industrial production and most other economic activities were far below prewar peaks, unemployment was high, and inflation and food shortages were increasing. The People's Government tried immediately to deal with this difficult situation which involved regulating the conditions for the sale of China's labor power and completely undercutting the ability of foreign capitalism to maintain an environment congenial to their profit-making. Closure of businesses was not permitted in China after 1949 without explicit permission from the People's Government. In practice the Government refused to seriously consider requests for firms to close down and withdraw staff until the liabilities of the firms, mainly back taxes and fines for overdue wage payments, had been built up to be nearly equal to or in excess of their assets. The length of time during which liabilities accumulated was determined by the People's Government in the exercise of its sovereign prerogatives, and not by foreign firms who were not subject to the conditions set forth by the new government. Conditions included approval for closure only on the condition of labor's agreement to the necessity for closing and an acceptable severance pay agreement for former employees of the firms.

The firms were caught. On the one hand, hostage capitalism meant the refusal on the part of the People's Government to permit by any means the closure of industry or business of value to the nation's economy. On the other hand, firms were not in control of their labor policy. Like most laws, China's were framed in such a way as to permit several interpretations. For example, "Unions shall not usurp or interfere with the administrative rights of management," but "unions shall have the right of suggestion and protest of any matter which in the opinion of the union affects the worker's present or future livelihood." In applying such potentially conflicting principles, the arbitration seldom found sympathy with foreign firms. Glaring examples of the lack of freedom to "do business as usual" occurred during both the Nationalist blockade and the UN embargo when wharves in Shanghai and other areas were almost completely closed but workers nonetheless had to be paid by the firms.

A future dimension of the squeeze further complicated the reality of hostage capitalism. If efforts at closure ultimately were dependent upon the good will of the People's Government, that good will was important to the firms for more reasons than one. There still remained the hope for future profits in trade. For fear of jeopardizing the potential longer-term profitable trade relationship between the People's Government and newly consolidated British firms operating outside of China, the firms were generally uncertain about how energetically they should pursue closure. Thus short-term uncertainty and hard times had to be weighed against longer-term hopes and expectations.

For many British firms, remittances from reserves abroad were necessary to keep the firms operating in times of depressed business. And they had to keep operating unless they received permission to close. In order to operate they had to retain their property, which in turn meant paying taxes. To insure that such obligations would be met, the Chinese required the continuing presence of a senior European firm executive in China. Thus hostage capitalism was reinforced with hostage capitalists. At least one of the senior executives, who was required to have power of attorney, was typically held personally responsible for performance of his firm's obligations and payment of taxes, refusal of which (even with good reason) did in fact on occasion result in short-term imprisonment.(22)

When a manager of a large firm desired to leave he was required to produce a letter or telegram from the head office appointing his successor and notifying the successor of this appointment and request-ing his acceptance; a letter from the named successor to the existing manager accepting the post and accepting full responsibility attached to the position; the successor's power of attorney, or the incumbent's power of attorney with a deed of substitution in favor of the successor; and a fairly detailed history of the successor's education, working life, and qualifications. For fear of jeopardizing the safety of their European staffs, while this requirement was in effect British firms never used the frequently discussed tactic of unilaterally stopping remittances to China to force liquidation negotiations.

The poor bargaining position of British firms in China starkly determined their defensive policy. Differences in the degree of optimism for the firms' future prospects in China among senior executives, and their differences in outlook (which in normal times might have been significant) were made insignificant by that harsh reality. No matter what the differences were in attitude, the immediate policy was to reduce overhead, reduce commitments by refusing all offers of new business, trade only to profitable fields, and prepare for closure when the opportunity arose.

If the closure of the firms' China operations was inevitable, hopes for a long-term relationship based solely on trade were often difficult to sustain. The short-term trade prospects varied with more general international conditions. British firms benefited by the beginning of the Korean War, which resulted in a 23-fold increase in Hong Kong exports to China from the 1950 level of $US 14,600 to $US 335,080 for the six-month period prior to June 1951.(23) On the other hand, six months later British firms in China suddenly and swiftly had become victims of the UN embargo of China, which Britain agreed to observe. Under these conditions any British trade with China became difficult. In response to the embargo, most Western nations, including Britain, restricted their trade with China to items such as cotton, fertilizer, textile machinery, dyes, and drugs.

In this context, China feared the complete halt of imports from abroad.(24) Because of the conditions imposed by the Korean War and the UN embargo, China abandoned normal methods of commercial trading and financing in favor of various types of barter deals in which exports were permitted only against virtually assured imports. Any imbalances which accumulated were kept small and short-term. China shifted to barter trade as a direct result of China's unfortunate experience when in December 1950, the United States government froze Chinese assets located in the United States. After that Peking wanted to avoid maintaining or building up other assets abroad that might be frozen without warning or redress should America's more forward policy be followed by its allies in the West.

For their part, the Chinese tried to circumvent the effect of the embargo in another way, by switching the main flow of China's trade from the West to the Soviet and East European bloc. They also sought to make it as uncomfortable as possible for those who maintained the embargo. What this meant, as Chen Ming, China's vice-minister of the foreign trade ministry for the East China region, explained to a British business executive, was that China was only prepared to trade provided there was "full security for China." Evidently this is why in late 1951 the Chinese promulgated new regulations denying permission for Chinese export goods to be shipped until the purchase money was deposited in China by telegraphic transfer. Thus foreign importers and exporters had to finance the cost of their imports to China until time when they could recover their outlay from the sale of exports from China. Foreign firms were reluctant to remit money to China on the terms demanded; there was no guarantee in the event of a nonexecuted contract that the goods would be shipped or that the deposit would be refunded.

As part of the Chinese policy of obtaining "full security for China," the Chinese required that all foreign contracts be guaranteed against noncompliance. Because British banks charged an insurance fee of one-eighth of 1 percent of the value of the contract, and put a time limit on their guarantees unacceptable to China, British firms established a policy of guaranteeing each other's contracts. This meant that in the event a firm such as Butterfield and Swire failed to meet the provisions of a contract with the People's Government, the guaranteeing firm, for example, Shell, would be liable. In this situation many firms decided that the benefits of trading with China were outweighed by the risks.

British China firms were in a bind. Faced with a Chinese government hostile to foreign capitalism and the British Government's compliance with the United States-directed UN embargo of China, British business-men concluded that even "from a purely trading angle there is little justification for continuing trade with China," as a late 1951 China Association memorandum noted. The only hope for a profitable future was the potential for exporting and importing not as direct investors but as traders, which, it was hoped, would still allow a basis for preserving profitable relations.

SANFAN WUFAN – "BRITISH CHINA TRADE HAS HAD IT"

Chinese firms and foreign firms were organically linked. They did business with each other. Any change in business conditions affecting Chinese firms would automatically affect foreign firms. This was the case with China's Sanfan Wufan campaigns in late 1951 and early 1952.

Prior to 1949 the Chinese Communists had developed a high degree of organizational skill in an agrarian environment. It remained to be seen after the Communist victory in 1949 whether they could handle the task of governing and developing a city like Shanghai. Shanghai was not simply a war-torn, refugee-swollen city which would become the industrial heart of the People's Republic. Shanghai had also been a base for the defeated Chinese Nationalists and the center of foreign imperialism in China. To the Chinese Communists, Shanghai represented "the struggle against the cynicism of bureaucratic capitalist speculation and the dead weight of imperialism."(25)

The struggle proved to be protracted. Although from the outset the Chinese Communists' governing of Shanghai included a system of price controls to force private Chinese firms out of business, Chinese capitalist elements retained a dominant position in Shanghai during the first eighteen months under Communist rule. Rapid recruitment of new members into the Communist party to organize Shanghai could not and did not prove adequate to prevent continuing speculation, corruption, and otherwise illegal business dealings in the lingering atmosphere of permissiveness for which Shanghai had been well known under National-ist rule. The Communist party in part reflected the society within which it had developed. Many Party members were willing to enrich themselves by engaging in bribery, the use of public funds for private ventures, and the sale of public property to private individuals.(26)

China's continuing struggle against these undesirable elements in its society and within the Party took the form of a series of mass movement campaigns during late 1951 and early 1952. The Sanfan (or Three-Anti) campaign against "corruption, waste, and bureaucracy" in government offices in the winter of 1951 to 1952 reviewed the conduct of and disciplined Party and non-Party officials who failed to meet Chinese Communist party standards. The subsequent Wufan (or Five-Anti) campaign, which grew out of the immediately preceeding Sanfan campaign, was specifically directed at Chinese businessmen who allegedly engaged in bribery, tax evasion, theft of state property, cheating on government contracts, and stealing state economic secrets. The effect of these two campaigns was to weaken drastically the position of urban capitalists in China. Sanfan and Wufan reduced the wealth and assets of urban capitalists, ostracized many as being potentially dangerous and subversive, and eliminated any possibility of their maintaining or achieving significant political influence during the period when China's leaders wanted to socialize the country's economy. The campaigns took the form of wide-scale denunciations and confessions encouraged by the Chinese Communist party. Many of the charges had less to do with Chinese laws than with the general judgment that private profit-making was exploitative, the equivalent of "stealing from the people." As a result of the campaigns, People's Daily reported in October 1952 that 76 percent of all merchants and capitalist industrialists in seven cities were found guilty of one or more offenses and punished by fines exacted by the newly established People's Tribunals.(27) At the same time, while the tribunals required payment of various fines, Chinese firms were prohibited by law from hiring or firing workers, altering their wages, borrowing private capital, or ceasing to operate.

The combination of economic hardship and psychological demoralization so weakened China's capitalist sector that the Chinese Communist leadership was able to organize and reinforce a variety of control mechanisms – rejuvenated labor unions, for example – in an effort to prevent a resurgence of capitalist influence. Most Chinese firms, weakened by the mass campaigns that forced them to accept loans from the People's Bank, were simply managers of production under state control and direction. The campaigns "pushed private industry and commerce a big step towards state capitalism," Cho En-lai later remarked.(28)

The Sanfan Wufan campaigns were conducted with such intensity and effectiveness against Chinese firms that foreign firms were affected as well. "Everything per force has come to a virtual standstill," wrote a British businessman from Shanghai. Many Chinese government offices and Chinese firms barely opened for normal business two hours a day. This situation hardly enabled them to deal with day-to-day routine business and made all new business of any consequence out of the question.   Chinese firms which normally would have had business dealings with British firms were tied up with Sanfan Wufan activities. Meanwhile liabilities for foreign firms mounted.

British firms also came under direct fire in the campaigns over matters concerning irregular practices, wages, and corruption. To illustrate, British firms usually paid higher wages than most Chinese firms; jobs with these firms were enthusiastically sought by Chinese workers. However, since most British employers relied on a gang-boss system, whereby the number one foreman recommended the workers to be employed, foremen acquired immense power over workers seeking jobs. In exchange for work, foremen usually exacted tolls from the wages of both men and women workers; and with attractive women they exacted other favors as well. Sustained criticism of these practices during Sanfan Wufan disrupted business for British firms.(29)

British firms were directly involved in the campaigns on yet another level. Under the impact of the mass campaigns in China the courts ruled that it was illegal for any Chinese worker not to receive his wages or for his livelihood to be jeopardized in any way. Although this was a monumentally reasonable decision from the worker's point of view, it was a very difficult one for foreign firms to accept. From the firm's point of view past practices should be a guide for the present. As a result, in the spring of 1952 several "responsible persons" in charge of British firms were summarily locked up for short periods of time for their failure to meet monthly wage bills.

"THIS IS TOO MUCH"

Until winter 1952, the larger British firms had adopted an attitude of continuing to operate their various enterprises in China. "We have never said we plan to quit," wrote a businessman from London. Unlike a year before when British businessmen were less certain that their firms would have an unprofitable future in China, it was now universally agreed that "we plan to quit." How to do this inexpensively, of course, was a great issue when the Chinese government, and not British firms, decided all business conditions. Indications were that the bill was mounting.

Consequently, in March 1952, China Association member firms agreed that business conditions were so irreversibly dismal that the British government should be asked to use whatever offices it might have to expedite closure for British firms in China. An immediate concern, noted in a China Association memorandum, was how firms could be protected from being required by the conditions of hostage capitalism to remit funds from outside China to British firms in China.

An often proposed, but never implemented, defense was enactment of British government enforced licensing restrictions on the transfer of sterling to China. China firms in the spring of 1952 energetically discussed this defense, but were afriad that such a licensing system might only bring swift retaliation by the Chinese.

Some British firms, Jardine Matheson for example, advocated a collective approach among China firms working closely with the British government. A central component of this approach entailed announcing a date for cutting off all remittances from abroad in order to force negotiations for closure to begin. Even if all of the firms could agree that it was time to withdraw, there was hardly sufficient agreement about a cutoff date for remittance of sterling to China. The British banks did not like the idea of a deadline date because they had commitments to the Chinese government for the return of U.S. dollars which the United States government had frozen. Individually, firms were engaged in their own efforts to close down. British-American Tobacco, for example, was engaged in its own negotiations for closure with the Chinese, which (in the view of the firm's directors) were coming to a close. Shell, having been expropriated outright a year earlier, was only interested in getting its five remaining staff members out of China and opposed any deadline. At China Association meetings Butterfield and Swire waffled and seemed more interested in their Tientsen freight. In short, all of the firms still perceived themselves as being in their own canoes, still hoping to find a paddle or two that would allow individual profits so they could paddle according to their own specific circumstances. Without unanimity among the firms, the British government would not consider arranging the restrictive licensing procedures discussed.

Despite the lack of agreement on a cutoff date, various British firms and the British government were able to agree to a plan of action they hoped would expedite closure. A "two-shot" approach was agreed upon. First, a statement was to be sent to the Chinese by Leo Lamb, the British charge d'affaires in Peking, simply noting the various disabilities of the firms in hopes of affecting some modification in business conditions.(30) This note would "lift the official veil of secrecy" of British discontent by suggesting that the continuation of various disabling policies affecting British firms could only result in the elimination of British business interests in China. This first note, hopefully, would pave the way for a second note asking for negotiations to begin for the liquidation of British firms in China.

Though in a poor bargaining position, British firms and the British government hoped to be able to deliver the notes in such a way that would not provoke the People's Government into sudden and violent reaction, especially at the local level. Knowing that the involvement of the British government in negotiating with the Chinese government was not likely to significantly reduce the pressures of hostage capitalism, the various firms' executives continued to pursue their own efforts towards closure. It was a difficult no-win situation. On the one hand, a collective approach required the gamble that individual concerns of various firms might be sacrificed to a greater degree than in an individual effort. On the other hand, British firms feared that negotiating withdrawal individually would increase the likelihood that "not only would one firm be played off against the other, but outstanding contracts made prior to the embargo of China might have to be executed to the letter," as a British businessman suggested.

British firms had no option but to sit tight in anticipation of the British diplomatic notes, the first of which was communicated by Leo Lamb to the People's Government on April 12, 1952. As previously planned, this note outlined the firms' difficulties and added: "If this situation continues it can only result, sooner or later, in the elimination of British business interests in China to the detriment of friendly relations between China and the United Kingdom." A second British note was communicated to the Chinese on May 19, even before China had replied to the first note. This stated the obvious: "Nearly all, if not all, of the British companies in China have come to the conclusion that the change in Sino-British business conditions brought on by the Chinese Communist Revolution necessitates a corresponding change in the nature of their obligations and in the scope of their activities." Closure, as the British charge d'affaires put it, was in order, although the firms still hoped to engage in a newly developed import-export business, the proper machinery for which, as the note went on to suggest, should be established.

All of Britain's diplomatic notes, including a third one in November 1952, sought a quick resolution of the difficulties facing British firms. The British, however, would offer nothing in return, such as relaxation of the trade embargo. In fact, other than agreeing to relations of mutual equality, there was little that Britain could do to facilitate a rapid withdrawal. Other options varied from publicity through "planted" articles in Western newspapers, to cutting off remittances, closing Chinese banks in London or Singapore, halting the purchase of Chinese exports, or even withdrawing the British chargé d'affaires. The steps Britain might have taken probably would have produced only a "mounting spiral of reciprocal brutality," a "game" which Humphrey Trevelyan, British chargé d'affaires to the People's Government from 1953 to 1955, pointed out later "we were unlikely to win."(31) The British notes turned out to be little more than pleas for mercy.

The People's Government replied to the British notes in July. As expected by the firms, the reply did not help them. Chang Han-fu, responding on behalf of the People's Government, asserted that "the predicament of the British firms in China is the bitter fruit of the policy of trade control and embargo of the British Government. By following the US Government in carrying out the trade control and embargo, the British Government had not only contravened but also jeopardized the interests of the British people."

Because of what the Chinese viewed as the British government's official hostility to China, the People's Government refused to establish full diplomatic relations with Britain. And Peking was not prepared to discuss closure for British firms with the British government. Rather than dealing with the matter of British interests in China with the British government, the Chinese preferred to respond directly to approaches from the British firms involved.

China did not object in principle to taking over British industrial assets. But in 1952 China feared increasing diplomatic isolation from the West. The United States Navy was pressing for a blockade of the entire Chinese coast. As a matter of prudence, the Chinese tried to prevent further isolation by holding hostage the various British firms, which while being restrained from closing, would be certain to exercise their influence on the British government against such a blockade.

When the Chinese Government was prepared to allow the firms to leave, the terms were expected to be difficult for the firms. Nobody doubted this. If nothing else, the firms hoped that when closure eventually did take place, trade relationships with China from abroad, rather than inside China, would permit continued profit-making. To realize expectations of future trade relationships with China, the various British firms felt that they had to first allay Chinese fears that closure and withdrawal were part of a plan to further retaliate against China for its involvement in Korea. This is why Leo Lamb, in his diplomatic note of May 19, stated that "while existing machinery is not appropriate to present day needs, the firms feel that they can still perform a useful service in the interests of Sino-British trade."

Establishment of a trade association to stay on in China after all closures was a continuing topic of discussion among British businessmen in the fall and winter of 1952. Two alternative proposals were discussed.(32) One was for a loose association of representatives who, with Peking's approval, would act as contact men in Peking to keep British manufacturers abreast of Chinese trade developments. The association would not accept responsibilities for the behavior of individual manufacturers in Hong Kong or London. The other proposal was for a trading company which would act as an agent for British importers and exporters. For two reasons the prevailing view throughout 1952 favored the former.

First, because individual firms and their human agents were in difficult straits (in part because of taxes and tax fines) no British China firm wanted to assign to an agent in China any business that might attract Chinese tax liabilities. The firms wanted to close down and avoid such troublesome responsibilities in the future. A trade company in China was contradictory to the single most important goal of the various British firms, getting out of China.

Second, a loose association was favored because of the different preferences for closure and future trade among individual firms. The easiest way to make a consensus proposal to the People's Government was to let the association start with the most flexible terms of reference and try to solve its problems as they arose. The firms agreed, however, that merely raising the issue of future Sino-British trade with Chinese authorities might help their negotiations for closure. A possible bargaining chip which was never played with the Chinese was to propose establishment of a trade association on the precondition that a Peking-approved closure of direct investments preceded its operation.

No one knew in mid-June 1952 what the Chinese reaction to a trade association proposal would be. "We are dependent on guesswork," noted Leo Lamb. When an outline of the proposal was finally presented to the Shanghai foreign affairs bureau in late summer 1952, the Chinese quickly announced their position. Such a trade mission should be established prior to the various firms' withdrawal from China. An official suggestion by Leo Lamb that British business interests discuss a future trade association with Chinese officials in Peking was ignored by the Chinese.

The Chinese were in no hurry to ease closure for the firms. Nor did they accept responsibility as the exclusive or prime source for the firms' difficulties. The Chinese blamed strategic trade regulations enforced by the British government for much of the difficulties of the British firms. The People's Government felt that the British government's position was one of hostility toward them. The Chinese argued, in addition, that many of the traditional British firms were psychologically incapable of accepting the Chinese Communist revolution and were still seeking excess profits "as if China were still the old corrupt foreign colony."(33)

Because of these problems associated with the old China firms, China saw the possibility of doing business with other more sympathetic British firms. When China sent delegates to the Moscow economic conference in April 1952, they ignored the British firms with long experience in China by signing agreements with a delegation of assorted British businessmen and left-wing politicians for $US 28 million. None of the traditional British firms were represented. As a result, the old firms feared their complete exclusion from future Sino-British trade. China's establishment of major trade offices in East Berlin and rumors that China planned to circumvent Hong Kong for trade with the West exacerbated these fears.

As the world split into two giant blocs, British firms continued throughout 1952 to find themselves caught in a difficult confrontation and transition. As business in China grew less and less profitable during China's Sanfan Wufan campaigns, the British firms – which before had been able to do much as they pleased – now wanted to cease operations and withdraw from China. China, however, was not willing to simply approve their applications for closure. In these difficult times the firms hoped, at least in the future, to play an important role in Sino-British trade from their home bases of Hong Kong or London. But even that prospect appeared increasingly dim as China showed signs of excluding the old British China firms from future China trade. China was still calling all the shots, which to British firms signaled not only their present difficulties but possible future problems as well. The British government, once the military backbone of imperialism in China, was (like the old China firms it had once fought for) now a lingering remnant of an era the Chinese Communists were helping to put to rest.

Even at the expense of totally abandoning assets in China, British firms in the spring of 1953 only hoped to be able to negotiate a withdrawal from China. Due to the policies associated with hostage capitalism, one of the major firms had already remitted $US 2,000,000 to China with no prospect of improved business conditions. In order to meet continuing overhead, firms tried wherever possible to raise local funds from the sale of the unnecessary – silk, tea, tobacco, equipment, a few trucks, and accounting machines. But these sales had to be approved by the People's Government, which preferred that the firms remit foreign currency. The firms were desperate to close, if only to cut off remittances to China.

The continuing need to remit currency from Hong Kong led the firms to propose a formula of offsetting assets against liabilities as a base for permission to withdraw from China. Using the 1942 British Shanghai

Realty Guide to calculate their assets, British firms attempted to move through China's transitional state in the least painful manner.

While British enterprise used the guide's terms of the past to carry the firm into the present transitional era, the Chinese rejected what they saw as a continuing attempt by foreigners to assert imperialist prerogatives. "From our point of view," a Chinese foreign affairs bureau official noted to a British businessman, "the value of your properties does not appear very much to us." The Chinese pointed out that, unlike 1942, there were no potential buyers for what firms listed as their assets. By the firms' capitalist standards these assets had no value. Without a capitalist environment British firms were no longer profit-making concerns.

The unprofitability of the various firms' assets was a primary reason given for China's rejection of the firms' calculations of their assets and liabilities. A second reason for China's rejection of British efforts to cease business operations arose when China challenged the actual ownership of the assets claimed by British firms because of the manner in which they were acquired. The Chinese also pointed to other liabilities unrecognized by the firms.

On the basis of British firms' unprofitability, the People's Government argued that the People's Government would have a difficult time helping British firms find private Chinese firms willing to take over their responsibilities. Chinese Government take-overs were considered an impossibility.

China's firmness in enforcing various measures, such as insisting that contracts be exactly performed, prolonged hostage capitalism and raised the levels of frustration and impatience among British firms. In early February 1953, a British taipan noted "how galling it was to look back to a year ago when I was thinking of putting a stop to the drain on money."

The firms continued to lose money throughout 1953 and many firms' directors consistently described prospects for closure as "disappointing," a "deadlock," or "dreary as a funeral." Once more, in early 1953, British businessmen considered cutting off remittances from Hong Kong. But, fearing a negative effect on the twin goals of quick withdrawal from China and later trade with China from abroad, cutting off remittances was not tried. Months later, in an effort to speed up what the firm's directors thought was an inevitable closure, the British government sent the Chinese foreign affairs bureau another note seeking "renewed assistance in causing instructions to be issued so that facilities may be given to British firms to close at an early date." In the same vein, a British taipan appealed directly to Prime Minister Cho En-lai in a summer 1953 telegram. A follow-up letter from the taipan, which was never answered, suggested the possibility that he might visit Cho En-lai in Peking to settle all outstanding matters for withdrawal.

China appears to have required British firms to suffer the Western discriminatory trade policies associated with the Korean War as China did. Limited settlement of British firms' closure was aided by the easing of tensions between China and Britain as the Korean armistice in July 1953 drew near. It was only after the Korean armistice that China appeared willing to bring to a close negotiations for the closure of various firms. The protracted negotiations for their withdrawal were further eased by the Geneva Conference of April 1954 which resulted in generally improved Sino-British relations. Coincidentally, China was moving quickly in 1953 and 1954 to completely socialize its economy so that too much significance would not be attached to the Korean armistice or to the Geneva Conference as an explanation for the end of hostage capitalism.

Progress towards closure did not always initially include parent firms but often involved only China-based subsidiaries. Parent firms' closure seems to have been handled seriously only after the 1954 Geneva Conference. It was during the Geneva Conference that Anthony Eden, Britain's secretary for foreign affairs, and China's Prime Minister Cho En-lai discussed a number of questions affecting relations between Britain and China, including the difficulties of British firms in China.

As a result of the Geneva talks between Eden and Cho, a Chinese diplomatic mission was established in London under a chargé d'affaires corresponding to the British post in Peking. In a brief period of near cordiality between Britain and China, Prime Minister Cho En-lai agreed personally to look into sources of conflict between China and Britain. This included seeing if something could be done to help British businessmen in China close their businesses and leave the country. As if to emphasize China's interests in improved relations with Britain, a month after the Geneva Conference ended (when a British civil aircraft was shot down by Chinese aircraft resulting in the loss of ten lives) the Chinese Government surprised the world by publishing an immediate apology and paying in full the claim for compensation subsequently put forward by the British government.

How much this brief détente in Sino-British relations helped British firms is difficult to ascertain without access to Chinese sources. Even after Geneva, various firms' directors discovered that the assets for liabilities formula, as it has been envisioned, did not work. "Eventually it will boil down, I suppose to the price – cash payment – the Chinese will want from the firm to be allowed to close the doors," a British taipan exclaimed in late 1953.

He was somewhat correct. The larger British firms began withdrawal from China in the summer of 1954. The negotiations were difficult and cashsettlements from the firms were necessary for the Chinese to arrive at a final agreement. In 1954 to 1955, Jardine Matheson and Butterfield and Swire, whose names had been household words in China for many generations, ceased operations and withdrew from China. Other firms followed; the last one to withdraw was Paton and Baldwins in 1957.

TRADING WITH CHINA

Throughout the years of hostage capitalism, the Chinese insisted that the root cause of Sino-British trade difficulties was Britain's trade restrictions on the export of various goods to China, which increased the difficulties of British firms and affected Britain's import and export trade with China.(34) The Chinese argued that without British trade controls and the embargo, the terms of British firms' withdrawal from China might have been easier. To what degree the terms would have been easier is impossible to know.

One indication that British firms would have had an easier time is the Chinese reaction to restrictive trade policies. China redirected as much of the Sino-British trade as possible away from the traditional China firms into entirely new British channels. Until 1954 China sought to deal directly with manufacturers in Britain, although early efforts do not appear to have been fruitful. Neither the old British China firms nor the British government was happy with this arrangement. If they could no longer invest in China the old British China firms wanted at least to trade with China. Some firms involved in hostage capitalism counted on the possibility of future trade as a kind of compensation for enduring the difficult terms of withdrawal from China.

The British government believed that, in contrast to the new "fellow traveler" firms, the older British China firms would be more likely to follow British government trade policies. In November 1953, the British government declared the British Council for the Promotion of International Trade to be a Communist-front organization and warned British businessmen against taking part in its activities. In November 1955 the British government reminded Parliament that the decision to use the British Council for the Promotion of International Trade was a matter for the "patriotic judgment of each British firm or individual."

In the cordial mood of official Sino-British relations at Geneva in July 1954, British government officials made a strenuous effort to persuade the Chinese government to redirect trade between Britain and China into more traditional channels. The effort was successful and Chinese authorities openly declared their willingness to deal with the old British China firms. As a result, in June 1954, a new semiofficial British China trade organization, the Sino-British Trade Committee (later Council), was formed. This new organization had no imperialist history with which it could be associated, although it represented the China Association, the Federation of British Industries, the National Union of Manufacturers, the London Chamber of Commerce, and the Association of British Chambers of Commerce. On behalf of these member organizations, the Sino-British Trade Committee invited a Chinese mission to Britain in late June and early July 1954. China accepted.

At these meetings, which were a courtship between British commercial interests and China, the former successfully promoted a Sino-British policy which provided that trade with the latter should be channeled through an organization that was acceptable to traditional British China interests. The leading Chinese official at the meetings even expressed his pleasure that the British delegation included a number of old China firms whose experience in the China trade was of such value to China. The Chinese also expressed a new flexibility in dealing with merchants instead of manufacturers. The old China firms enthusiastically welcomed this new development.

China's leaders realized that the old British China firms could play a valuable role in helping to develop Sino-British trade. China desired trade with the West, so the older China firms' reputation within the West as dependable importers-exporters was useful. Without an international sales network of its own, China's leaders must have realized the precarious status of organizations like the British Council for the Promotion of International Trade, with which the Chinese were said to be dissatisfied. Trading with such organizations did not improve official Sino-British relations. It was the older China firms, which China had nationalized domestically, that China had to cooperate with for the sale of China's products abroad. They provided China with free access to sterling deposits, insurance headquarters, and commodity market centers.(35) Because of their size and experience with these matters in the China trade, firms like Jardine Matheson and Butterfield and Swire in Hong Kong were especially suited to China's needs.

Although no specific contracts were negotiated in the summer of 1954, British representatives of the older China firms considered the discussions a great success. A return trip to China by British merchants who were affiliated with the Sino-British Trade Council met with progress on the trying question of payments, which were made difficult by the Korean War. China agreed to payments by irrevocable letters of credit instead of by letters of guarantee, and to make the adjustments to earlier trade requirements.

Major difficulties between Britain and China continued after the brief détente brought on by the 1954 Geneva Conference. Britain did not unilaterally relax controls on China trade until 1957. After the relaxation of the British embargo in 1957 an intensive trade drive was conducted by British exporters. "A large British motor manufacturer," writes Evan Luard, "placed a quarter-page advertisement in People's Daily six times the size of any normal advertisement in that paper."(36) Perhaps in a different era these advertisements would have borne fruit. Since the Chinese Communist revolution, however, China's basic policy of promoting economic self-sufficiency has limited the growth of Sino-British trade.

The firms' relationship with China did not end with hostage capitalism. It only changed. Since the Geneva Conference in 1954, the traditional British China firms have played an active role in developing Sino-British trade relations. From Hong Kong, British firms now trade with China without direct investment and involvement in China's economy which marked the imperialist past.

CONCLUDING REMARKS

Nationalizing foreign assets often includes the risk of retaliation by the foreign parent country if compensation is not agreed to the satisfaction of the firm. In the Chinese case, Britain's weakened position as a world power after World War II lowered the risk of retaliation. China's bargaining position allowed the terms of nationalization to be decided by the Chinese government. With the founding of the People's Republic in 1949, China moved from an era of imperialism to a new era of revolutionary nationalism. As John Swire, of Butterfield and Swire, put it, "we must, I think, face the fact that the old Palmerston methods of protecting British merchant adventurers who decide to make their living outside the Empire have gone for good."(37)

China's nationalization policy, which I have called hostage capitalism, was not simply a policy of revenge for the historic injustices of the imperialist era of Palmerston methods. China's new society had to be built on the inherited foundations of the previous era. Political and economic realities meant that China's leaders had to move step-by-step in the transition to state owned economy. In the short run, maintaining foreign capitalism hostage provided jobs for Chinese workers employed in production at the firms' expense. At the same time that China was training its people to take over these firms, the firms were building up their liabilities. Eventually these liabilities were used to offset the firms' assets upon their withdrawal from China, when the country was ready to socialize its economy. The Korean War-related embargo of China by the United States and the United Nations was not directly related to the policy of hostage capitalism; the embargo seems only to have prolonged hostage capitalism making China's own course of development more difficult.

Beyond limited comments, China has said little explicitly about its own program of nationalization of foreign firms. Even in the decrees which took control of United States assets in late 1950, China avoided all references to "confiscation," "expropriation," or "nationalization."(38) In the only Chinese article on the general subject of nationalization, Li Hao-pei noted in 1958 that nationalization of private property for public purposes is recognized under international law as a proper exercise of a state's sovereignty.(39) In the absence of specific requirements, Li also argued that the payment of compensation is only at the discretion of the nationalizing state, as long as it does not discriminate in the application of its policy which is a right of economic sovereignty. When standards for compensation are referred to among writers on the subject, there is a great deal of variation, ranging from those that permit the payment of little or no compensation to those that require the payment of what may in fact amount to full compensation.(40) Thus, when nationalization of foreign property is involved, it is seldom legal norms but instead the balance of political forces that determines the ramifications of nationalization. Lawyers and legal scholars merely serve as the instruments of the interests involved. In 1949 the balance tilted heavily away from Britain toward China.(41)

NOTES

(1) The analysis here concentrates on British firms because of all the historically large traders and investors in China, only British ones survived World War II. Japanese and German investments were transferred to the Chinese government as a result of World War II

losses. American investment in China was never very great; the general case of U.S. corporation's assets in China remains to be settled. But for an analysis of a single firm's experience, see Warren W. Tozer, "Last Bridge to China: The Shanghai Power Company, The Trueman Administration and the Chinese Communists," Diplomatic History vol. 1, no. 1 (Winter 1977), pp. 64-78.

A list of British China firms would include the following: Imperial Chemical Industries China Ltd.; Jardine Matheson and Co., Ltd.; Sir Elly Kadoorie and Sons, Ltd.; Arnold Trading Co., Ltd.; Harvie Cooke and Co., Ltd.; Chartered Bank of India; E.D. Sasson Banking Co., Ltd.; Mercantile Bank of India, Ltd.; China Engineers, Ltd.; Harvey Main and Co., Ltd.; Butterfield and Swire; Liddel Brothers and Co., Ltd.; Wheelock Marden and Co., Ltd.; Caldbeck, MacGregar and Co., Ltd.; Mackenzie and Co., Ltd.: Asiatic Petroleum Co. S.C. Ltd.; Hong Kong and Shanghai Banking Corporation. These firms made up the inner circle of the London-based China Association, a business lobby whose purpose was to preserve and protect British investment in China.

(2) Maurice Meisner, "The Maoist Legacy and Chinese Socialism," Asian Survey, (January 1978), pp. 1016-27.

(3) See O. Edmund Clubb, Twentieth Century China (New York: Columbia University Press, 1964), pp. 321-2.

(4) Mao Tse-tung, SW, vol. IV (Peking: Foreign Language Press), p. 167.

(5) Ibid., p. 367.

(6) See William Brugger, Democracy and Organization in Chinese Industrial Enterprise, 1948-1953 (Cambridge: Cambridge University Press), pp. 67-76 and Christopher Howe, Employment and Economic Growth in Urban China, 1949-1957 (Cambridge: Cambridge University Press, 1971), pp. 9-11.

(7) For an analysis of China's nationalization of Chinese capitalist firms, see George Ecklund, "Protracted Expropriation of Private Business in China," Pacific Affairs, Fall 1963, pp. 238-49. An early superficial account of China's nationalization of foreign capitalist firms is Lucien Taire, Shanghai Episode Hong Kong: Rainbow Press, 1957. With few exceptions China nationalized foreign assets indirectly. In addition to the policy of hostage capitalism, another indirect though minor way in which foreign property, mainly land and houses of private individuals was nationalized in China was by simple abandonment by owners. Property was treated as ownerless if it was not registered with the local land office. Ownerless land was taken over by the local land administration bureau and the government reserved the right to expropriate such land. At various times notifications were inserted in the Chinese press by the authorities listing properties that would be treated as ownerless unless formal claims were made, in which case taxes were usually owed. Evidently such notices appeared only in

Chinese newspapers there are many in Liberation Daily in the early 1950s. In many cases the properties were not identifiable because of changes in street names or street numbers.

(8) Mao Tse-tung, SW, vol. IV (Peking: Foreign Language Press, 1969), p. 423.

(9) Stephen Endicott, Diplomacy and Enterprise (Vancouver: University of British Columbia Press, 1975), pp. 1-25.

(10) China Association Minutes and Circulars C.A.M.C., John Keswick, Chairman, British Chamber of Commerce, Shanghai, to British Consul-General, Shanghai, (December 11, 1948).

(11) C.A.M.C., British Chamber of Commerce to the British Ambassador to China, (November 30, 1948).

(12) C.A.M.C., British Chamber of Commerce, Shanghai, to China Association, (London, July 4, 1949), No. 49/B/40.

(13) C.A.M.C., Notes of a meeting between China Association representatives and Mr. Hector McNeil, minister of state, (July 28, 1949).

(14) See C.R. Attlee, "Britain and America: Common Aims, Different Opinions," Foreign Affairs, (January 1954).

(15) Ibid.

(16) C.A.M.C., "The Present Position of British Traders in China," (August 17, 1949), no. 49/G/49.

(17) C.A.M.C., British Chamber of Commerce, Shanghai, to China Association, London, (July 14, 1949), no. 41/F/13.

(18) C.A.M.C., "General Bulletin," (January 20, 1949), no. 49/M/1.

(19) Sir John Keswick, London interview, (November 27, 1975).

(20) C.A.M.C., Memorandum, (October 11, 1949).

(21) C.A.M.C., Memorandum, (November 1, 1949), no. 49/E/15.

(22) C.A.M.C., Memorandum, (April 4, 1950), no. 50/G/27.

(23) Evan Luard, Britain and China Baltimore: (Johns Hopkins Press, 1962), p. 68.

(24) Pauline Lewin, The Foreign Trade of Communist China (New York: Praeger, 1964), pp. 30-8.

Hostage Capitalism in People's China 189

(25) Soong Ching Ling, "Shanghai's New Day Has Dawned," in The Struggle for New China (Peking: Foreign Language Press, 1963).

(26) John Gardner, "The Wufan Campaign in Shanghai," in A. Doak Barnett, ed., Chinese Communist Politics in Action (Seattle: University of Washington Press, 1969), pp. 477-539.

(27) People's Daily, October 7, 1952).

(28) See Chou En-lai, Ten Great Years (Peking: Foreign Language Press, 1960), p. 57.

(29) W.C. Gomersall, The China Engineers, Ltd., Quarterly Review, (November 1951).

(30) Great Britain Foreign Office G.B.F.O. 1952, Correspondence between the Government of the United Kingdom of Great Britain and Northern Ireland and the Central People's Republic of China on British Trade in China, Peking, April 12-July 5 cmd. 8639, London: HMSO.

(31) Humphrey Trevelyan, Worlds Apart: China 1953-5, Soviet Union 1962-5 (London: Macmillan Co.), p. 59.

(32) See Thomas N. Thompson, Imperialism and Revolution in Microcosm: China's Indirect Nationalization of Foreign Firms and the Politics of Hostage Capitalism, 1949-1954 Ph.D. diss., (Johns Hopkins University, 1977), p. 120.

(33) South China Morning Post, (May 6, 1952).

(34) For trade developments between China and Great Britain, I have benefited greatly from the previous work of Robert Boardman, Evan Luard, and B.E. Porter.

(35) See Edward Friedman, "The International Political Economy and Chinese Politics," Stanford Journal of International Studies, (Spring 1975), p. 6.

(36) Luard, Britain and China, p. 165.

(37) C.A.M.C., China Association Annual Dinner Speech, (April 28, 1952).

(38) The two major occasions China did confiscate foreign property outright China stated that these actions were taken specifically in retaliation for British actions in Hong Kong. One case, in May 1951, involved the requisitioning of all installations of the Shell Oil Co. in China after the Hong Kong government took possession of an oil tanker whose ownership was in dispute with China. A second case involved a judgment in July 1952 by the Hong Kong authorities that forty aircraft

Chinese government, should be handed over to a U.S. airline company. Following this action the Chinese authorities requisitioned the British registered Shanghai Dockyards Ltd. and Mollere Shipbuilding and Engineering Works. In February 1953 China requisitioned the Canton assets of Butterfield and Swire for reasonsI have been unable to learn. See Jerome A. Cohen and Hungdah Chiu, People's China and International Law (Princeton: Princeton University Press, 1974) and James Chieh Hsiung, Law and Policy in China's Foreign Relations, A Study of Attitudes and Practice (New York: Columbia University Press, 1972).

(39) Li Hao-pei, "Nationalization and International Law," Cheng-fa yen-chiu Studies of Politics and Law, no. 2:10-15.

(40) Richard Lillich, ed. The Valuation of Nationalized Property in International Law, vol. I-III (Charlottesville: The University Press of Virginia, 1972). See especially Norman Girvan's "Expropriating the Expropriators," pp. 149-79.

(41) Although "hostage capitalism" was a key aspect of China's nationalization policy from 1949 to 1957, a number of incidents occurred subsequently, during the Cultural Revolution in particular, which demonstrated that "hostage capitalism" made possible by the presence within China of foreign firm's staff was not exclusively a tactic confined to the early years of the PRC. The detention of such persona as Reuter and Vickers-Zimmer's employees in 1967, and the similar treatment of other nationals represent a continuation of "hostage" policies. See Jerome A. Cohen, "The Personal Security of Businessmen and Trade Representatives," in Victor H. Li, ed. Law and Politics in China's Foreign Trade (Seattle: University of Washington Press, 1977), pp. 287-307.

10 The Role of the German Democratic Republic in the Communist Penetration of Africa

Robert M. Bigler

Soviet block interaction with the African states was minimal prior to Khrushchev's rise to power in 1955. After that date the Stalinist coolness toward African nationalism was replaced with a new emphasis on winning over some of the African nationalist leaders. Moscow recognized that many African nationalists were anti-Western as a result of their colonial experiences and that the neutralism they professed was to the advantage of the communists since it led away from Western control and influence. It was hoped that the African states would limit Western access to their minerals and other vital resources and thereby put a cramp in the capitalist economic system. Cooperation among former colonial areas could be a strong and useful weapon in the struggle against the capitalist world.(1)

Krushchev's "secret speech" at the Twentieth Congress of the Communist Party of the Soviet Union in February 1956 initiated the anti-Stalin campaign, but it was also noteworthy for its revision of Soviet African policy. Stalin was blamed for not realizing that the African nationalist leaders had the support of their people and were basically hostile to the Western powers; they were not puppets of the imperialists. According to the new theme of peaceful coexistence, parliamentary transition to socialism and the nonevitability of war were considered relevant to Africa, and a "Peace Zone" concept, in which the communists and Afro-Asian states were considered aligned against imperialism, was introduced.(2) However, in contrast to the great efforts taken by the Soviets in Asia and the Middle East, Africa seemed to have much less importance in the communist scheme of things. Especially after the failure of Khrushchev's adventure in the Congo in the early 1960s, Moscow appeared to share the American view that Africa should be kept out of the cold war competition, not because of détente, but because it was just not that important to either superpower.(3)

INCREASED COMMUNIST ACTIVITY AFTER 1975

The past few years have seen a decided change. Relatively quiescent in Asia and the Middle East, the communist leaders have entered a new phase of activity in black Africa. The chaos resulting from the withdrawal of Portuguese troops from Angola provided the communists with an opportunity to intervene directly in African affairs in 1975, and to increase their influence dramatically in that part of the world. Paralyzed by the aftermath of Vietnam and Watergate, the United States failed to behave like a superpower – not because its administration did not wish to do so, but because it was inhibited by its own public opinion as expressed in Congress. With the United States staying out and China quietly disengaging herself from her ties with UNITA, one of the factions in the Angolan civil war, the Soviets decided to intervene and assure the victory of the so-called Popular Movement for the Liberation of Angola (MPLA), led by the Marxist Agostinho Neto. For the first time since the onset of Africa's modern independence, an African government was actually helped to establish its power through open communist intervention. The provision of Soviet arms in large quantities and the transportation of over 15,000 Cuban troops to take a direct part in the fighting resulted in the establishment of a Marxist regime in Angola.

With détente constraining direct Soviet armed intervention, the Cubans have in fact acted as surrogates to advance Soviet interests and to extend the Soviet sphere of influence in Africa. The purpose of this study is to focus attention on the less known but no less significant role and activities of communist East Germany, officially known as the German Democratic Republic or GDR, in the communist penetration of Africa, and on the interaction of the Moscow-Havana-East Berlin axis with some African states.

The phenomenal economic achievements of the GDR in the last two decades have been referred to as the "red economic miracle." Success has been evident and documentable. Next to the Soviet Union, the GDR is the most advanced communist industrial country in the world with the highest productivity and a standard of living unequalled in any communist nation. Closely tied to the Soviet Union militarily, economically, and ideologically, the economic power of the GDR has enabled it to exert considerable international influence within the general framework of Soviet foreign policy.(4) Having achieved a high level of economic performance and having arrived on the international scene through membership in the United Nations and diplomatic recognition by practically all nations including the United States, the GDR can now pursue somewhat less spectacular but no less substantive international policy goals.

In foreign policy generally, the GDR has been a firm supporter of Soviet goals and views from China to Africa.(5) Sometimes, as in the communist penetration of black Africa, the GDR has served as a surrogate of the Soviet Union and as an advance detachment for revolutionary Marxism.

Until the withdrawal of Portugal from Africa in 1974 and 1975, the

GDR's influence in that part of the world was not very impressive. Despite its strong anticolonial stand and strenuous efforts to impress the Africans with the GDR model of economic development, German communist success remained very modest.(6) The discontinuation of the Hallstein Doctrine after the basic agreement between the two German states in December 1972 resulted in the establishment of diplomatic relations with most African states and enabled the GDR to increase its influence. But only after 1974 did the GDR begin to enjoy the benefits of its long efforts to "build solid bridges of solidarity" with the guerrilla leaders of the MPLA in Angola, the FRELIMO in Mozambique, and the PAIGC in Guinea-Bissau and the Cape Verde Islands.(7)

After Portugal's military withdrawal from Africa the guerrilla liberation movements in the former colonies became political parties. The leaders of these groups had been exposed to the influence of the GDR for many years. Some of the contacts had developed in the 1950s and were firmly established in the 1960s. Suddenly the GDR found its longtime friends in positions of power in the newly independent states. Such former guerrilla leaders as Agostinho Neto and Samora Machel had long felt themselves inspired by the "genius of Lenin" and had looked to the GDR and other communist countries as their "natural allies" in the "liberated zone of mankind."(8)

East German Influence In Angola

Long before most people in the West knew what the letters MPLA stood for, the GDR had developed close contacts with the Popular Movement for the Liberation of Angola. In 1961, five years after the merging of the Communist Party of Angola and several guerrilla organizations in the MPLA, the GDR journal Deutsche Aussenpolitik published the program of the MPLA.(9)

From the beginning of the guerrilla war between rival factions in Angola the GDR supported the "unambiguous anti-imperialist foreign policy of the MPLA" and denounced the other guerrilla groups as agents of the capitalist West. The MPLA was considered an active participant in the worldwide struggle against the imperialist camp, in close cooperation with the socialist camp led by the Soviet Union.(10) To strengthen the ties between the GDR and the MPLA, many members of the latter were invited to meetings, conferences, and sport events held in the GDR. MPLA leaders participated at the conference "Against Racism and Neocolonialism, for the Liberation of South Africa" in 1968, and they also attended the meetings of the World Peace Conference in the early 1970s, as well as many sports events of GDR youth organizations. Members of a delegation of MPLA youth pioneers spent the summer of 1973 in GDR youth camps, and reported about "the wonderful life of the young German communist pioneers working together with young men and women from various parts of Europe, Asia, Africa, and Latin America."(11)

Agostinho Neto, the Marxist leader of the MPLA and first president of the People's Republic of Angola, visited the GDR in 1971 and 1974. In

1976 he acknowledged the massive contributions of the GDR to the long struggle of the MPLA against "the imperialist forces" in a special statement of gratitude. "During those many years of struggle we could always count on the fighting solidarity of the people of the GDR."(12) This "fighting solidarity" is demonstrated in Angola today. Next to the Soviet Union and Cuba, the GDR is the most active participant in the building of a Marxist state in the People's Republic of Angola. Specialists of the GDR armed forces continue training the members of the Angolan military units, and GDR pilots are flying the Soviet-built MIG-21 jet fighter planes.(13) German medical personnel from the GDR are taking care of the wounded, disabled, and sick in the hospitals. Most of the equipment and medical instruments are also from the GDR.(14)

Practically all tugboats and other vessels used in the ports of Luanda and Lobito were made in the GDR. The massive presence of the GDR is visible everywhere in the new Marxist state.(15) In August 1976, the Angolan cargo ship "Ngola" carried 200 trucks and a number of rescue vehicles from the GDR port Rostock to Luanda. And in November 1976, Radio East Berlin reported that 6 ships and 18 airplanes filled with "cargoes of solidarity" had been sent to Angola. According to reports published in the journal Der Spiegel on August 30, 1976, such "cargoes of solidarity" included weapons and even heavy artillery.(16) According to Die Welt, another West German periodical, hundreds of MPLA soldiers had been transported in Soviet aircraft from Brazzaville to the GDR for training in November 1975. In addition to the obvious activities of GDR military advisors in Angola, there was also evidence indicating the presence of members of the GDR secret police.(17) As far as the actual fighting during the civil war was concerned, there were reports that what we described as MPLA units on the north front consisted mainly of Cubans and East Germans. More specifically, it was reported that the offensive of the MPLA forces in the northern part of Angola was carried out by 7,500 Cuban and 2,500 East German soldiers.(18)

In addition to its massive military involvement in Angola, East Germany continues to provide technical training for black Africans and also educates a considerable number of future reporters and journalists. Seriously wounded soldiers and civilians of the various liberation movements are sent to the GDR where they receive expert medical attention.   Year after year African children are brought to GDR summer camps where they learn about Marxism-Leninism and about the GDR as a "socialist model" state.(19)

There was hardly a month in 1976 when there were no delegations representing the various elements of the GDR model state arriving in Angola. Probably the most impressive was the 4-day visit of a 40-member delegation of GDR party and government representatives in Luanda in July. The German communists were showered with expressions of gratitude and loyalty in the Angolan capital.(20) In addition to all the material help provided by the GDR, the efficient propaganda apparatus of the East German mass media has done everything to present the Marxist dictatorship in Angola as a truly representative and popular leadership of the people. The slogan identifying the MPLA with the Angolan people – O MPLA e o Povo, O Povo e o MPLA – has been repeated by the GDR media in hundreds of broadcasts and TV shows in several languages. Until its involvement in Ethiopia in 1977 to 1978, the GDR concentrated most of its efforts in Angola to influence the shaping of a future communist world order.(21)

East German Influence in Mozambique
and Other Parts of Africa

There have also been close relations between the GDR and the Front for the Liberation of Mozambique or FRELIMO. Samora Machel, the leader and later president of the Mozambique People's Republic, has visited the GDR on several occasions, and has established close personal relations with Erich Honecker and other German communist leaders. He had been to the GDR long before Mozambique became independent and had always expressed the appreciation of the FRELIMO for the help and know-how provided by the German communist regime. Weapons and munitions, medicine, tents, clothing, trucks and other vehicles, medical care in GDR hospitals, field hospitals with medical personnel in Mozambique, German instructors and textbooks at the Mozambique Institute at Dar-es-Salaam, as well as training of FRELIMO leadership cadres at GDR universities and technical schools, have been provided for the African Marxist movement by their German ideological allies.(22) On the occasion of the signing of several treaties concerning GDR economic and technical aid as well as cultural and scientific cooperation in September 1976, President Machel declared the GDR a country "which is also our homeland."(23)

As in the case of Angola, the GDR asserts with pride that the People's Republic of Mozambique constitutes part of a "worldwide revolutionary movement based on the mutual interests of the progressive part of mankind fighting against imperialism, colonialism, neocolonialism, and racism."(24) Amilcar Cabral, the Marxist founder of the African Party for the Independence of Guinea and the Cape Verde Islands (PAIGC), who before his assassination in 1973 was considered the most successful African revolutionary, believed that it was "the historical duty" of the Soviet bloc countries to support the revolutionary movements because "our struggle means also the defense of the socialist countries."(25) This identity of interests has remained the main theme of the ideological propaganda campaign conducted by the GDR media. A number of East German journalists who had reported about the struggles of the various liberation movements in the former Portuguese colonies act today as a journalistic Africa lobby in East Berlin. They cultivate their contacts in the new states, obtain scholarships for the training of African journalism students at "schools of solidarity" in the GDR, and try to exert influence in the newly established communications systems of Angola, Mozambique, and Guinea-Bissau.(26) Practically all the new political leaders of Angola, Mozambique, and Guinea-Bissau had the opportunity to visit the GDR, and some of them had actually been trained there. The MPLA, the FRELIMO, and the PAIGC had originated as nationalist movements, but had become "Marxist revolutionary mass organizations" having close ties with the GDR, the Soviet Union, Cuba, and the other Soviet bloc countries.(27)

The years 1977 and 1978 have seen further significant GDR advances in Africa beyond the influence exerted in the states formerly under Portuguese colonial rule. Leading representatives of the Republic of Benin, Ethiopia, Nigeria, of the Democratic Republic São Tomé and Principe as well as of the African People's Union of Zimbabwe (ZAPU) learned at first hand the impact of the "red miracle" in the GDR. They received assurances of further cooperation with and help from the economically highly developed East Germans, and returned home greatly impressed with the know-how of the "German socialist partners." As a matter of record, the GDR is sending regular shipments of "goods of solidarity," including weapons, to Angola, Mozambique, Guinea-Bissau, Ethiopia, Malagasi, the People's Republic of Congo, and to the liberation movements ANC, SWAPO, and ZAPU.(28)

There is sufficient evidence to indicate that the GDR plays a key role in the operations of the secret police forces to suppress any opposition to the Marxist dictatorships of Neto and Machel in Angola and Mozambique, respectively. Specialists of the GDR secret police advise the DISA (Angolan office of information and security) and the SNASP (the Mozambique office of internal security) and are engaged in the establishment and operation of concentration camps, called Campos de Recuperacão and Campos de Reeducacão. In one of their retaliatory strikes into Mozambique, Rhodesian commando units found and destroyed instruments made in the GDR and operated by East German technicians. The instruments had been used to disturb the broadcasting of the program "Voices of Free Africa" to Mozambique.(29) In his article "The Red Prussians Teach the Black Continent Revolution," Peter Hornung presented convincing evidence of the massive presence and activities of about 430 GDR military officer and noncommissioned officer specialists working together with Soviet and Cuban personnel in Mozambique.(30)

In addition to its involvement in Angola and Mozambique, the GDR has also exerted its influence over the Rhodesian guerrilla forces. Technicians, instructors, weapons, and medicine have been provided for the guerrillas of the People's Army of Zimbabwe. ZAPU leader Joshua Nkomo visited East Berlin in March 1977 and agreed with GDR party Chief Erich Honecker on plans for the continuation of the struggle against Ian Smith's government.(31)

There is no doubt that in addition to the Soviets and the Cubans the GDR plays a leading role in the coordinated efforts of the Soviet bloc to "weaken the bases of imperialism" and to increase the influence of the communists in the so-called "third world." Their efforts have not always been successful. In addition to their setbacks in Egypt and Ghana, the ill-fated invasion of Shaba province of Zaire from Angola proved to be a most painful fiasco. The invasion was widely denounced in the non-Marxist African states as an open intervention by the Soviets, Cubans, and East Germans. It also resulted in the closing of the GDR embassy and the expulsion of East German diplomats from Zaire.(32) Should there be a peaceful transition of power in Rhodesia that excludes the Zimbabwe guerrilla leaders, it would represent another setback for the Moscow-Havana-East Berlin axis.

The East German Role in the
Horn of Africa Conflict

Intelligence reports reaching the West in February 1978 confirmed the massive involvement of the GDR in the conflict between Ethiopia and Somalia. Apparently Moscow decided that Ethiopia, with its 29 million people, would prove to be more valuable an ally in the strategically significant horn of Africa than little Somalia with a population of merely 3 million. Having decided to support Ethiopia in the war between the two leftist governments, Moscow has sent the most imposing arsenal of military equipment that the Soviet Union has assembled outside the communist world — close to one billion dollars worth of tanks, field guns, rockets, radar, artillery, mortars, and missiles. To help in the use of the hardware and otherwise shore up the sagging regime of Lieutenant Colonel Mengistu Haile Mariam, Moscow has also provided Addis Ababa with a polyglot army of soldiers and technicians including about 1,000 Russians, 11,000 Cubans, 1,000 East Germans, 1,000 South Yemenis, and hundreds of Czechs, Hungarians, Poles, and Bulgarians. Zbigniew Brezinski, President Carter's national security advisor, told a White House news briefing on February 24, 1978 that General V.I. Petrov, one of the Soviet Union's top-ranking officers, was in direct command of military operations in the Harar combat area of the Ogaden desert war. Expressing deep concern over the communist involvement, Brezinski also told newsmen of the more than threefold increase to about 11,000 in the number of Cuban troops.(33)

The amazingly efficient and ideologically rigorous "red Prussians" of the GDR have apparently been selected as the most trustworthy allies of the Soviet Union to further the cause of communism in Africa. First sent to Ethiopia in the summer of 1977, GDR military specialists, including senior officers assigned to the Ethiopian Defense Ministry, helped to reorganize the country's armed forces. There is no doubt that the East Germans contributed significantly to the planning of the great offensive to regain the Ogaden region from the Somali forces in February 1978. The success of the offensive could drastically upset a complex balance of forces throughout the whole region. GDR specialists have been advising the Ethiopians on the military and ideological training of the police, militia, regular armed forces, and youth groups. During the preparation for the offensive, the hard-liner GDR Politburo member Werner Lamberz headed a delegation that advised Addis Ababa about reconstructing the country's economy on orthodox Marxist lines.(34)

The army and secret police of the leftist Arab state of South Yemen have also been learning the latest security techniques from some 2,000 GDR specialists who are assisted by about 4,000 Cubans. The GDR is also believed to be running training camps in South Yemen for radical

Palestinian commandos. The German communist state continues to send "Brigades of Friendship," consisting of military, ideological, security, and medical cadres, to Angola. In Mozambique the GDR "diplomatic" mission has become the largest in the country, exceeding even that of the Soviet Union. The increasingly complex operations of the GDR in Africa are now handled by a special secretariat in East Berlin, headed by Deputy Minister of Foreign Trade Alex Schalk.(35)

Some African Reactions To Communist Activities

The activities of the GDR in support of the revolutionary movements in Africa have been conducted as part of the coordinated foreign policy of the Soviet bloc. The Soviet Union has marked out areas of operation and has also assigned particular roles to Cuba and the GDR. The activities of the Moscow-Havana-East Berlin axis have alarmed not only the Western powers but also such African leaders as President Sadat of Egypt, Zambian President Kenneth Kaunda, Emperor Bokassa of the Central African Empire, and King Hassan II of Morocco. In direct reference to the GDR activities in Mozambique, Kaunda stated in April 1977 that "the Prussians are at work again, this time in Africa," and Hassan warned of "a red belt from Angola over Zaire to Mozambique."(36) In view of recent developments in the horn of Africa, the dimensions of a much more ambitious Soviet strategy have become apparent.

SIGNIFICANCE OF THE COMMUNIST COUNTERIMPERIALISM OFFENSIVE

The massive communist involvement in Africa has demonstrated to the world the Soviet Union's turn from "antiimperialism" to "counterimperialism" in the mid 1970s. Apparently Moscow now considers the Middle East, the Indian Ocean, and Africa as regions of the target area in which the "counterimperialist" offensive is being fought.(37) These parts of the world are linked both geographically and in the strategic conceptions of the communist leaders, and there is little doubt that they intend to establish a permanent military presence there. The United States now faces a potentially explosive Soviet strategy aimed at regaining the Soviets' once powerful foothold in the Middle East through the back door — the Horn of Africa. The stakes go far beyond the Ogaden, a sparsely inhabited desert region of Ethiopia that Somalia claims. Involved is ultimate control of the Gulf of Aden and the Red Sea lanes over which Middle East oil goes to Western Europe. Ethiopia can be seen as the centerpiece of a future Soviet wedge that would cut right through the Middle East and Africa.

At one end Moscow's strong link to radical Iraq already gives the Soviets access to the Persian Gulf on the flanks of Iran, Saudi Arabia, and the oil-rich Arab Emirates. Communist influence in Marxist South

Yemen plants Soviet power on the soft underbelly of the Arabian peninsula and along the approaches to the Arabian Sea and the Indian Ocean. The western edge of the Soviet wedge rests on Angola, maintained by the GDR and Cuba. It is there that the Kremlin's shadow falls on the South Atlantic Ocean and its strategic shipping routes, and reaches toward southern Africa and its exploitable racial conflicts. Policy makers in the Carter administration concede that the Soviets are gaining a new window on the Middle East from their Ethiopian venture. There is little doubt that in the Horn of Africa President Carter is facing one of his most crucial foreign policy decisions. Following his report to President Carter on a recent visit to Peking, Senator Henry M. Jackson indicated to newsmen that the Soviet involvement in Africa "deeply disturbs the top leadership" there. Jackson also added that the Chinese leaders viewed Soviet activities as a long-range move on the part of the Soviets toward the Middle East and toward strategic oil reserves which pass through shipping lanes of the Ethiopian and Somalian coasts. "We are going to have to do something," Jackson said. "The Chinese may very well get involved in all this."(38)

Moscow's calculation is that the combination of Soviet weapons, East German know-how, and Cuban as well as African fighting men can succeed in establishing stable zones of influence in Africa. Essential to communist success is the willingness and cooperation of African leaders and their followers who can derive significant benefits from a close cooperation with the Soviet bloc. It seems evident that the repressive dictatorships of Neto, Machel, Mengistu, and of Ali Nasser Mohammed of South Yemen are helped significantly by the massive presence of Soviet bloc personnel and their well-developed terror mechanisms for the supression of opponents. In addition to military help, the communists have provided considerable amounts of economic aid as well as models of Marxist development. As the economically most efficient and productive country of the Soviet bloc, the GDR has become a valuable and highly respected partner of the new Marxist states. The German communist model seems to fascinate the African Marxist leaders who find the "red miracle" very attractive since it transformed the GDR from a country in ashes to a "model of socialism" in two decades.(39)

The enormous costs of its activities in Africa may strain the productive capacity of the GDR, and they also set limits to the East German involvement in that part of the world. But as long as the GDR is willing and able to conduct its coordinated foreign policy with the Soviet Union, the long-term benefits may prove to be very significant to communism. The optimistic Africa-euphoria of the GDR leaders was expressed by East Berlin TV commentator Ulrich Makosch on the occasion of the 60th anniversary of the Bolshevik Revolution when he saw "the ripening of the fruits of our labor after so many years" and stated jubilantly:

The rays of the October Star in black Africa signify one of the most momentous developments of our century, and they will also illuminate that continent during times of the most complicated and certainly difficult developments.(40)

Within the framework of the world revolutionary process in the making, the GDR asserts itself as "the reliable ally of fighting Africa." Dedicated to world revolution and to the goals of Soviet foreign policy, the GDR is willing to offer a helping hand and a Marxist-Leninist model of development for "countries with socialist orientation."(41) The fact is ignored that most African countries lack the socioeconomic conditions for the importation of the German variety of communism that led to the "red miracle." And together with the Cubans the GDR shares a serious handicap; perceptive Africans realize that the GDR and Cuba represent the interest of the Soviet Union and are acting as its agents.

The communists can hardly escape the many reminders of how quickly allegiances can change in Africa. As for the latest involvement in the Horn of Africa, Somalia's Marxist President Mohammed Said Barre was Moscow's most loyal friend in the area until he became so irritated by Soviet help to Ethiopia that he expelled the Soviet and GDR advisers and specialists in November 1977. And the Ethiopian regime's loyalty to Moscow has yet to be tested. Mengistu is a nationalist above all, and there may be some truth in his claim that he turned to the communists because the United States would not sell him weapons. According to the latest reports, the Ethiopian soldiers still wear American-supplied uniforms; many of their weapons, much of their ammunition, and even their slang are mostly United States-issue, too. Only a few have the new caps, supplied by the Soviets, that show a hammer and sickle.(42)

The GDR is in the forefront of Soviet efforts to penetrate Africa in a coordinated strategy of a "counterimperialist" offensive in a new target area. Consequently the East Germans find themselves in a series of complex developments involving other Soviet allies as well as African countries interacting with each other. The GDR and the other Soviet bloc countries will have to be prepared for serious setbacks once Africans realize the long-term goals of Soviet foreign policy aimed at domination, and once the United States and other Western powers face up to the seriousness of the communist challenge.

NOTES

(1) See E.M. Zhukov, "The Bandung Conference of African and Asian Countries and Its Historical Significance," International Affairs, no. 5 1955, pp. 18-32.

(2) "The Twentieth Congress of the C.P.S.U., and the Problems of Studying the Contemporary East," translated and reprinted in Thomas Thornton, ed., The Third World in Soviet Perspective (Princeton: Princeton University Press, 1964), pp. 80-4.

(3) John C. Campbell, "Soviet Policy in Africa and the Middle East," Current History, (October 1977), p. 100.

(4) See Philip J. Bryson, "The Red Miracle in the International Arena:

Economic Foundations of East German Foreign Policy," East Central Europe 3 (1976): 84-96.

(5) Henry Krisch, "The German Democratic Republic in the Mid-1970's," Current History, (March 1976), pp. 119-22.

(6) Nicole Guez, "L'Afrique entre l'Est et l'Ouest," Jeune Afrique, no. 545, (Nov. 6, 1971), p. 26.

(7) Ulrich Makosch, "Sudliches Afrika – Strom der Zeit, Reaktion und Lebensfrage," Deutsche Aussenpolitik 2 (1976): 285.

(8) See Lew Klezki, "Afrika und Lenin," Neue Zeit 27 (June 4, 1969): p. 7.

(9) Deutsche Aussenpolitik 6 (1961): 482-7.

(10) Lothar Killmer, "Erfolge des Kampfes um die Befreiung Angolas," Neues Deutschland, (February 5), 1977.

(11) Vitoria ou Morte, (May-July 1973), p. 16.

(12) Horizont, 1976, no. 14, p. 11.

(13) Vida Mundial, no. 1900, (August 12, 1976), p. 46.

(14) Neues Deutschland, (August 26, 1976), p. 1.

(15) Aussenpolitische Korrespondenz 33 (August 12, 1976): p. 264.

(16) Jornal de Angola, (August 5, 1976), p. 2.

(17) Die Welt, Nov. 21, 1975; and Hans Germani, "Sprungbrett Luanda," Ibid., (December 5, 1975), p. 2.

(18) Allgemeine Zeitung, January 1976, p. 3; Comment and Opinion (January 16, 1976), p. 3.

(19) Diario de Noticias, March 12, 1976, p. 1; Neues Deutschland, (August 24, 1976), p. 1.

(20) See the official communique in Aussenpolitische Korrespondenz 20 July 15, 1976: 230.; and Horizont 9 (1976): 5.

(21) "Die Volksrepublik Angola im antiimperialistischen Kampf," Einheit 31 (1976): 494.

(22) Der Spiegel, August 30, 1976, p. 63; Standard (Dar-es-Salaam, November 29, 1971), p. 1; Daily News (Dar-es-Salaam, May 5, 1972), p. 2.

(23) Neues Deutschland, (October 9/10, 1976), p. 1. See also Washington Post, (February 16, 1977), p. 1.

(24) Neues Deutschland, (June 25, 1975), p. 1.

(25) Tricontinental, no. 8, (November-December 1968), p. 123.

(26) Sonja Brie, "Grosse Aufgaben fur Angolas Massenmedien," Neue Deutsche Presse (1976): p. 13, 25ff.

(27) Azinna Nwator, "Die Befreiung Angolas," Monthly Review 1 1975/76: 9, 7; Le Monde, (October 15, 1976), p. 12; Pravda, May 18, 1976, p. 1.

(28) Neues Deutschland, (April 27, 1977), p. 4.

(29) See Vida Mundial, no. 1910, October 21, 1976, p. 9 and no. 1920, December 30, 1976, p. 57; Suddeutsche Zeitung, November 30, 1976, p. 3; The Economist, (April 23, 1977), p. 76.

(30) Die Welt, (November 10, 1976), p. 1.

(31) Aussenpolitische Korrespondenz, (March 17, 1977), p. 82.

(32) Le Monde, (May 2, 1977), p. 1; Die Welt, (May 2, 1977), p. 3.

(33) Los Angeles Times, March 3, 1978, p. 1., and February 25, 1978, pp. 1, 8, 10; Time, (February 20, 1978), pp. 28f., Newsweek, (January 23, 1978), p. 16.

(34) Time, (February 20, 1978), p. 28; Neues Deutschland, February 10, 1977, p. 1.

(35) "Moscow's Helping Hands," Time, (February 20, 1978, p. 29.

(36) General Anzeiger, (April 7, 1977), p. 1; and Die Welt, (April 20, 1977), p. 2.

(37) See Richard Lowenthal, Model or Ally: The Soviet Union and the Developing Countries (New York: Oxford University Press, 1977), p. 360ff.; and David Rees, "Soviet Strategic Penetration in Africa," Conflict Studies, no. 77, November 1977.

(38) Los Angeles Times, February 25, 1978, p. 1.

(39) Siegfried Kupper, DDR und Dritte Welt (Munich-Vienna: Oldenbourg 1976).

(40) "Die Strahlen des Oktobersterns," Horizont 10 (1977): 2.

(41) Aussenpolitische Korrespondenz 21 (April 21, 1977): 122.

(42) Time, (February 27, 1978), p. 40.

Index

Shah of Iran, 33, 102, 103, 154, 162
Shanks, Michael, 76
Sklar, Richard, 157
Smith, Adam, 26
Smith, Ian, 196
Social change, 149
Social policy
    American, 57, 60
    comparative, 57-58
    in industrialized countries, 57
    international regime, 58
    internationalization of, 59
    multinational management, 59
    multinational regime, 58
    and states rights, 60
    transformation of, 57
    Western European, 57-58, 60,
        63, 64, 65, 67-69,
        70-72, 73, 75, 77
Social rights, 59
Social security policy
    bilateral agreements, 66
    focus of study, 57
    foreign and migrant workers,
        65, 66, 77
    France, 66
    Germany, 66, 67
    global regime for, 58, 59, 63,
        72, 73, 74, 75, 76-77
    influence of multinational
        enterprise, 63
    international cooperation, 69,
        70, 72
    Italy, 62, 66
    programs, 59, 60
    Scandinavia, 62, 67, 70
    standards, 76
    and trade unions, 64, 65, 77
    transformation of, 57
    transnational influences on,
        60-61, 65
    United Kingdom, 61, 67, 68
Social value, 144
Socialist bloc, 23, 24, 25-26, 27,
    28, 31-32, 35, 53, 108, 193
    See also Soviet bloc
Socialist revolutions, 89
Somalia, 27, 197, 198, 200
South Africa, 162, 193

Soviet bloc, 191, 193, 195, 196, 198,
    200
    See also Socialist bloc
Soviet Union, 23, 24, 27, 158
    African policy, 191, 192, 194, 196,
        198, 199, 200
    Asian policy, 191
    and China, 163, 167, 174, 181
    and Cold War, 163
    and Eastern Europe, 153, 162
    foreign aid, 27, 28
    foreign policy, 192, 200
    and imperialism, 163
    industrialization, 103
    and OPEC states, 108
    oil producer, 25
    policy toward TNCs, 51
    political repression, 104
    and Second World, 89
Sri Lanka, 32
Stalin, Joseph, 191
"State-centric" paradigm, 7
States
    developed democratic, 12, 13
    developed nondemocratic, 12-13
    underdeveloped, 12, 13
Strauss, Robert, 31
Subnational actors. See Actors
Subnational elites. See Elites
Suez Canal, 122
Supernational actors. See Actors
Supranational elites. See Elites
Sweden
    control of TNCs, 45, 49
    oil imports, 129
    social security policy, 67, 73
Switzerland, 42, 51, 129
Syria, 122, 123, 164

Taipan, 170, 182, 183
Taiwan. See China, Nationalist
"Taiwan Basin" oil discovery, 26
Thailand, 24, 159
Theory-building. See International
    relations
Third World, 24, 33, 42, 60, 89, 90,
    94, 107, 108, 163
"Three Worlds" schema, 89
Trade Union Advisory Committee
    (TUAC), 47

About the Editor
and Contributors

ROBERT M. BIGLER (Ph.D., University of California, Berkeley) is a Professor of Political Science at the University of Nevada, Las Vegas. He has also taught at the University of Utah and at California State University, Chico. Professor Bigler is the author of The Politics of German Protestantism and coauthor of American Politics in Transition. His articles have appeared in Eastern Europe and other journals. His area of professional specialization is comparative politics (Western European and communist political systems).

P.G. BOCK (Ph.D., New York University) is Associate Professor of Political Science at the University of Illinois in Urbana. He is coauthor of The Politics of American Foreign Policy, American National Security, and Internal Migration and New Towns. His articles have appeared in World Politics, Society, Studies in Comparative International Development, and Political Science Annual. His areas of specialization are international relations, international organization and foreign policy.

JOHN H. ESTERLINE (Ph.D., University of California, Los Angeles) is Professor and Chair of Political Science at California State Polytechnic University. He has also taught at Tulane University and the University of Miami. Professor Esterline served in the diplomatic service of the United States from 1951 to 1970. He is the author of Inside Foreign Policy: The Department of State Political System and Its Subsystems. His articles have appeared in International Studies Notes, the Fukien Times Yearbook, the Financial Journal (Philippines), the New Orleans Times-Picayune and the Los Angeles Herald-Examiner. His areas of professional specialization are international relations (East Asia) and American foreign policy.

MANSOUR FARHANG (Ph.D., Claremont Graduate School) is Associate Professor of Government at California State University,

Sacramento. Professor Farhang is currently working on a book entitled
Iran: The Politics of Absolute Power. He has presented several papers
on Middle Eastern politics and imperialism to professional associations.
His areas of specialization are comparative politics (the Middle East)
and American foreign policy.

FOREST L. GRIEVES (Ph.D., University of Arizona) is Professor of
Political Science at the University of Montana. Professor Grieves is the
author of Supranationalism and International Adjudication and Conflict
and Order. His articles have appeared in several journals, including the
American Journal of International Law, Western Political Quarterly,
Environmental Affairs, Military Review, The Journal of Correctional
Education, and The International Lawyer. His areas of professional
specialization are international relations (law, organization, politics)
and comparative politics (Western Europe and the Soviet Union).

TIMOTHY W. LUKE (ABD, Washington University in St. Louis) is an
instructor in Political Science at Washington University in St. Louis. He
has also taught at the University of Missouri-St. Louis, the University of
Arizona, and Pima College. He is the coauthor, with Victor T. Le Vine,
of The Arab-African Connection: Political and Economic Realities. His
articles have appeared in Leviathan, New German Critique, and Telos.
His areas of professional specialization are comparative politics and
social theory.

CHARLES W. MERRIFIELD (Ph.D., Claremont Graduate School) is
Professor of Political Science at California State University, Hayward.
He has also served with the Washington International Center, the Joint
Council for Economic Education (New York), and the Council of the
National Organization for Adult Education. His areas of professional
specialization are the scientific analysis of social affairs, cross-cultural
education, and leadership theory.

FREDERIC S. PEARSON (Ph.D., University of Michigan) is a
Research Associate at the Center for International Studies and
Associate Professor of Political Science at the University of Missouri-
St. Louis. His articles on foreign military intervention and conflict have
appeared in Journal of Conflict Resolution, International Studies
Quarterly, Journal of Political and Military Sociology, International
Interactions, and other scholarly journals. His primary research in-
terests are in the field of international politics and particularly the
relationships of major and minor powers regarding intervention policies,
dependency, and small state options.

J. MARTIN ROCHESTER (Ph.D., Syracuse University) is Assistant
Professor of Political Science and Research Associate at the Center for
International Studies at the University of Missouri-St. Louis. He is the
author of a number of articles that have appeared in such scholarly
journals as The American Political Science Review, Western Political
Quarterly, Review of Politics, and International Studies Quarterly. His

primary teaching and research interests are in the fields of international law and organization.

RICHARD L. SIEGEL (Ph.D., Columbia University) is Professor of Political Science at the University of Nevada, Reno. Professor Siegel is the author of Evaluating the Results of Foreign Policy and coauthor (with Leonard Weinberg) of Comparing Public Policies: United States, Soviet Union and Europe. His articles have appeared in India Quarterly and Journal of Social Issues. His areas of professional specialization are Soviet politics and comparative public policy.

THOMAS N. THOMPSON (Ph.D., Johns Hopkins University) is Assistant Professor of Political Science at the University of Oregon. He is also director of Analytics, an independent foreign policy research organization. He is the editor and a contributor to Transnational Firms: The Debate over Threats and Promises. His areas of specialization include international political economy and China.

Pergamon Policy Studies